IN

RUN BABY RUN

Nicky Cruz tells his thrilling life story. The story of a young man's rise from gang warfare, drugs, and degeneracy in the streets of a large city. Written in a clear—frank—shocking manner, RUN BABY RUN contains the answers to the questions facing the "now" generation.

Recommended for all age levels, Nicky Cruz's story is especially beneficial to young people, parents, psychologists, and community agencies.

SEVEN BIG PRINTINGS IN HARDCOVER

OVER TWO-MILLION COPIES SOLD!

AND DON'T MISS NICKY CRUZ'S

THE LONELY NOW

NOW AVAILABLE IN PAPERBACK

RUN BABY RUN

Nicky Cruz

with Jamie Buckingham

A JOVE BOOK

RUN BABY RUN

Distributed by Bridge
Published by Jove Publications, Inc.

Thirty-eighth printing   August 1984

This book or parts thereof may not be reproduced in any form without the
written permission of the publishers.

Copyright © 1968 by Nicky Cruz and Jamie Buckingham

All Rights Reserved

Library of Congress Catalog Card Number: 68-23446

Printed in the United States of America

Jove Publications, Inc.
200 Madison Avenue, New York, N.Y. 10016

a Gloria

El corazón de su marido está en ella confiado.

PROVERBIOS 31:11

Contents

Preface

When I undertook this project Catherine Marshall remarked that writing a book of this nature was like having a baby. I was going to have to live with it until it was born.

In this case, not only did I have to live with it, but so did my family and the congregation of the Tabernacle Baptist Church where I was pastoring. They suffered through every bout of morning sickness, every labor pain, and even a couple of false deliveries. But family and church both realized this book was conceived of the Holy Spirit, written with prayer and tears, and was to be published to the glory of God. The church virtually released me from all obligations until it was finished and several pitched in and helped share the typing duties.

However, it was John and Tibby Sherrill and the editors of *Guideposts* magazine who were the god-parents of the book. It was John's recommendation and confidence that initiated the project and in the end it was the Sherrills' criticism that gave us the final insight into the stark but beautiful story of the life of Nicky Cruz.

But the credit for the actual movement of the story goes to Patsy Higgins, who volunteered her services to the glory of God. She lived and breathed the manuscript as critic, editor and typist—displaying a talent for cutting and rewriting that could have come only from God.

The book itself defies one of the basic literary laws. It closes with an open end. No nice, neat wrap-up here. Every time I'd interview Nicky he'd relate some fantastic new experience taking place in his life. But this is material for a sequel—perhaps several. Therefore, "Run Baby Run" is the story, told as accurately as possible, of the first 29 years of the life of a young man whose greatest days are yet ahead.

Jamie Buckingham
Eau Gallie, Florida

Introduction

RUN BABY RUN, the story of Nicky Cruz is remarkable. It has all the elements of tragedy, violence, and intrigue—plus the greatest of all ingredients: the power of the Gospel of Jesus Christ.

The first chapters form a dark, foreboding background for the thrilling denouement of this unusual story. So, don't despair of the somewhat gory atmosphere delineated in the first half of the story.

Nicky is a young man, and today he is making an impact upon great segments of our youth in these United States. The adult population can no longer ignore the youth with their staggering, twentieth century problems. They search for meaning. They are not enamored with our time-worn social taboos. They press for sincerity in religion, for honesty in politics, and for fairness for the underprivileged. The encouraging thing about these millions of "new folk" (who will by 1970 outnumber the adult population), they are desperately searching for answers. In my contact with hundreds of students on our university campuses, I am tremendously impressed with their quest for truth, for reality, and for honest answers. Some of the young people in our ghettos are restless for a fair deal from society, and justly so. Some of them are influenced by advocates of violence and mob rule, and are easily sucked into the vortex of rioting, burning and looting. Nicky Cruz is a glowing example that restless youth can find meaning and purpose in Christ.

In our crusades nearly half of our audiences are under the age of twenty-five. They do not come to scoff, but in a sincere search for truth and purpose, and hundreds of them respond to the call of Christ.

Run Baby Run, is a thrilling story! My hope is that it

shall have a wide reading, and that those who read shall come to know the Christ who changed the empty, restless heart of Nicky Cruz and has made him a Christian legend in his time.

Billy Graham

Foreword

Nicky's story is possibly the most dramatic in the history of the Pentecostal movement, but it is not unique. Nicky is only a very colorful representative of a vast number of people who, in the past few decades, have been delivered from crime, alcoholism, drug addiction, prostitution, homosexuality, and almost every type of perversion and degeneration known to man. Psychiatric care, medical treatment, and spiritual counseling had failed to affect these people, when with astounding abruptness they were set free from their bonds by the power of the Holy Spirit and led to a life of useful service and sometimes of profound prayer.

It is natural to suspect the genuineness of changes that are so radical and abrupt. But there is no theological reason to discount them. God's grace can take hold of a man in an instant and transform a sinner into a saint. "I say to you that God is able out of these stones to raise up children to Abraham" (Luke 3:8). Human effort cannot produce such changes, either in oneself or in others, because nature needs time to develop gradually; but God can do in an instant what takes man years and years.

Such conversions have occurred in the history of Christianity ever since the beginning. Zachaeus, Mary Magdalene (i.e. the penitent of Luke 7:37), the 'Good Thief,' St. Paul, and even St. Matthew are the beginning of a long list. However, the great number of such conversions that are taking place today in connection with what is called the "Pentecostal Movement" is, I believe, without precedent. What is the meaning of this amazing fact?

I have often wondered about this, and what comes to my mind over and over is the parable of the marriage feast (Matthew 22:1-14). When the invited guests did not show, the master told his servants, "Go out quickly into the streets and lanes of the city, and bring in here the poor, and the crippled, and the blind, and the lame" (Luke 14:21). When even that did not suffice, the servants were sent out once more, this time to the highways and hedges, with the order, "Make them come in, so that my house may be filled."

I believe that this is what we are seeing take place today. The 'invited guests' at the table of the Lord, that is the "born Christians," the righteous, the law-abiding members of society, have too often proved themselves unworthy. They have "gone to Church," but they have not really partaken of the banquet provided by the King. This is why the Church, instead of being a living Body and a challenging witness, so often appears as an ineffectual pious custom.

But while the pundits discuss what new vocabulary will bring God back to life (because all they know about Him is words), and what new symbols will make the liturgy meaningful (because all they see in religion is man's part), God Himself is quietly gathering new guests for His Banquet. And He is gladly taking in those who, by human standards, are spiritually and morally poor, crippled, blind, and lame. And by the power of His Spirit, He is indeed 'making' them come in, snatching them off the streets of degradation and the by-laws of perversion.

Nicky Cruz and the thousands like him are not just moving examples of the Good Shepherd's faithful love, they are also signs of the times which we had better not fail to read. They are an encouraging sign that God is acting with new power in our time, so that we should not be afraid to declare the Gospel boldly to anyone. They are also a sign of warning to anyone who feels that, because of his habits of piety, or his sacred ministry, or for any other reason whatsoever, he has an established title to a place at the banquet table. "I tell you that none of those who were invited shall taste of my supper" (Luke 14:24). For "the marriage feast indeed is ready, but those who were invited were not worthy" (Matthew 22:8).

Prof. Edward D. O'Connor, C.S.C.
University of Notre Dame

1

No One Cares

"Stop that crazy kid!" someone shouted.

The door of the Pan Am Constellation had just swung open and I darted down the steps toward the terminal at New York's Idlewild Airport. It was January 4, 1955, and the cold wind stung my cheeks and ears.

Just hours before my father had put me aboard the plane in San Juan, a rebellious, bitter 15-year-old Puerto Rican kid. I had been assigned to the pilot's custody and told to remain in the plane until turned over to my brother, Frank. But when the door opened I was the first one out, running wildly across the concrete apron.

Three line attendants converged on me, pinning me against the rough chain link fence beside the gate. The bitter wind whipped through my thin, tropical clothing as I tried to pull free. A gate policeman grabbed me by the arm and the attendants scurried back to their jobs. It was a game to me and I looked up at the cop and grinned.

"You crazy Puerto Rican! What the hell do you think you're doing?" he said.

My grin faded as I sensed the hatred in his voice. His fat cheeks were flushed in the biting cold and his eyes watered from the wind. He had a stub of an unlit cigar chomped in his flabby lips. Hate! I felt it surge through my body. The same hate I had felt toward my father and mother, my teachers, the cops in Puerto Rico. Hate! I tried to twist free but he held my arm in an iron-vise grip.

"Com'on, kid, let's go back to the plane." I looked up at him and spat.

"Pig!" he snarled. "Filthy Spic!" He loosened his hold on my arm and tried to grab me by the back of the neck.

Ducking under his arm, I slithered through the open gate that led inside the terminal.

Behind me was shouting and pounding feet. I raced down the long concourse swerving in and out of the mobs making their way to planes. Suddenly, I emerged in a large terminal room. Spotting an outside door, I darted across the floor and out into the street.

A large bus was sitting at the curb, door open, engine throbbing. People were boarding and I elbowed my way into line. The driver grabbed me by the shoulder and asked for my fare. I shrugged my shoulders and answered him in Spanish. He gruffly shoved me out of line, too busy to fool with a silly kid who could barely understand English. As he turned his attention to a woman who was fumbling with her purse, I ducked my head and squeezed behind her through the door and into the crowded bus. Glancing over my shoulder to make sure he hadn't seen me, I jostled my way to the rear and sat down next to a window.

As the bus pulled from the curb, I saw the fat gate guard and two others puff out the side door of the terminal looking in all directions. I couldn't resist knocking on the window, waving and grinning through the glass. I had made it.

Slumping down in the seat, I put my knees against the back of the seat in front of me and pressed my face against the cold dirty glass of the window.

The bus ground its way through the heavy New York traffic toward the middle of the city. Outside, there was snow and slush along the streets and sidewalks. I had always pictured snow as clean and beautiful, stretched out over acres of fairyland. But this was dingy, like dirty mush. My breath made fog on the window and I leaned back and ran my finger through it. It was a different world entirely from the one I had just left.

My mind flashed back to yesterday when I stood on the hillside in front of my home. I remembered the green grass under my feet, spotted with pastel dots of tiny wild flowers. The field sloped gently away toward the village below. I remembered the soft breeze against my cheek and the warmth of the sun against my bare bronzed back.

Puerto Rico is a beautiful land of sunshine and barefoot children. It is a land where men wear no shirts and women walk lazily in the sun. The sounds of the steel drums and strumming guitars are heard day and night. It's a land of singing, flowers, laughing children, and sparkling azure water.

But it is also a land of witchcraft and voodoo, of religious superstition and great ignorance. At night the sounds of the voodoo drums roll down from the palm-covered mountains as the witch doctors practice their trade—offering sacrifices and dancing with snakes in the light of flickering fires.

My parents were spiritualists. They made their living casting out demons and supposedly contacting dead spirits. Papa was one of the most feared men on the island. Well over six feet, his huge stooped shoulders had led the islanders to refer to him as "The Great One." He had been wounded during World War II and received a government pension. But there were 17 boys and one girl in the family and after the war he turned to spiritualism to make a living.

Mama worked with Papa as a medium. Our house was the headquarters for all sorts of voodoo, seances, and sorcery. Hundreds of people came from all over the island to participate in seances and meditation sessions.

Our big house on top of the hill had a winding path that led to the sleepy little village of Las Piedras snuggled in the valley below. Villagers would climb the path at all hours of the day and night to come to the "Witch's House." They would try to talk to departed spirits, participate in sorcery, and ask Papa to deliver them from demons.

Papa was the director, but there were many other Puerto Rican mediums who would come and use our home for headquarters. Some would stay for weeks at a time conjuring up evil spirits and chasing out devils.

There was a long seance table in the front room around which the people sat while trying to communicate with dead spirits. Papa was well read on the subject and had a library of magic and sorcery books that was unequaled in that part of the island.

Early one morning two men brought an afflicted woman to the house. My brother, Gene, and I slipped out of bed and peeked through the door as they stretched her on the long table. Her body was twitching and loud moans came from her lips as the men stood at each end of the table holding her down. Mama stood at her feet with her eyes raised toward the ceiling chanting strange words. Papa went to the kitchen and returned with a small black urn which was filled with burning incense. He also had a large green frog which he placed on the woman's quivering stomach. Then, suspending the urn over her head with a small chain, he sprinkled powder on her twitching body.

We stood shaking with fear as he commanded the evil spirits to leave the woman and enter the frog. Suddenly, the woman threw her head back and emitted a piercing scream. The frog jumped off her stomach and smashed itself against the doorsill. Suddenly she began to kick, and twisting free from the grip of the men, rolled off the table and fell heavily to the floor. She was slobbering and gnawing her lips and tongue while blood mixed with froth drooled from her mouth.

Eventually, she quieted down and lay very still. Papa pronounced her cured and the men gave him money. They picked up her unconscious form and backed out the door, thanking Papa over and over and calling him, "The Great Miracle Worker."

My early childhood was filled with fear and resentment. The large family meant there was very little individual attention given to each child. I resented Papa and Mama and was afraid of the sorcery that took place each night.

The summer before I started to school Papa locked me in the pigeon house. It was late in the evening and he had caught me stealing money out of Mama's purse. I tried to run but he reached out and grabbed me by the back of the neck, "You can't run, baby. You're going to have to pay the price for stealing."

"I hate you," I shouted.

He grabbed me off the ground, shaking me in front of him. "I'll teach you to talk to your Papa like that," he bit out. Putting me under his arm like a sack of grain he strode across the dark yard to the pigeon house. I heard him fumbling with the lock as he opened the door. "Inside," he snarled. "You can stay in there with the birds until you learn your lesson."

He shoved me through the door and slammed it behind me, leaving me in total blackness. I heard the lock snap into place and Papa's muffled voice came through the cracks in the walls. "And no supper." I heard his footsteps fade into the distance back toward the house.

I was petrified with fear. Hammering my fists against the door, I kicked it frantically, shouting and screaming. Suddenly the shack was filled with the sound of wildly flapping wings as the frightened birds slammed against my body. I threw my hands over my face and screamed hysterically as the birds smashed against the walls and ferociously pecked at my face and neck. I collapsed to the filthy floor burying my head in my arms trying to protect my eyes and shut out the sound of the flapping wings overhead.

It seemed like an eternity before the door opened and Papa yanked me to my feet and dragged me into the yard. "Next time you'll remember not to steal and sass back when you're caught," he said harshly. "Now wash up and go to bed."

I cried myself to sleep that night, dreaming of the fluttering birds that slammed against my body.

My resentment against Papa and Mama carried over the next year when I started school. I hated all authority. Then, when I was 8 years old, I turned against my parents completely. It was a hot summer afternoon and Mama and several other mediums were sitting at the big table in the living room drinking coffee. I had grown tired of playing with my brother and entered the room bouncing a small ball on the floor and catching it in my hand. One of the mediums said to Mama, "Your Nicky's a cute boy. He looks just like you. I know you must be very proud of him."

Mama looked hard at me and began to sway in her chair, rocking back and forth. Her eyes rolled back into her head until only the whites showed. She held her arms straight out in front of her across the top of the table. Her fingers stiffened and quivered as she slowly raised her arms above her head and began to speak in a sing-song tone of voice . . . "This . . . not . . . my . . . son. No, not Nicky. He never been mine. He child of greatest of all witches. Lucifer. No, not mine . . . no, not mine . . . Son of Satan, child of Devil."

I dropped the ball and it bounced across the room. I slowly backed up against the wall while Mama continued in her trance, her voice rising and falling as she chanted.

"No, not mine, not mine . . . hand of Lucifer upon his life
. . . finger of Satan touch his life . . . finger of Satan touch
his soul . . . mark of beast on his heart . . . No, not mine
. . . no, not mine."

I watched as the tears coursed down her cheeks. Sud-
denly, she turned at me with eyes wide and in a shrieking
voice cried: "Get out, DEVIL! Get away from me. Leave
me, DEVIL. Away! Away! Away!"

I was petrified with fear. I ran to my room and threw
myself on my bed. The thoughts flowed through my mind
like rivers churning down a narrow canyon. "Not her child
. . . child of Satan . . . not love me . . . No one cares. No
one cares."

Then the tears came and I began to scream and wail.
The pain in my chest was unbearable and I pounded my
fists against the bed until I was exhausted.

The old hate welled up inside me. Suddenly it con-
sumed my soul, like a tidal wave over a coral reef. I hated
my mother. God, how I hated her! I wanted to hurt
her—to torture her—to get even. I threw open the door
and ran screaming into the living room. The mediums were
still there with Mama. I smashed my hands against the top
of the table and screamed. I was so frustrated with hate I
was stuttering and the words would not come plainly. "I-I-
I . . . h-h-hate you." I pointed a quivering finger at Mama
and shouted, "I-I-I . . . g-g-gonna make you pay. I gonna
make you pay."

Two of my younger brothers stood curiously in the door
as I pushed by them and ran out the back. Plunging down
the steps, I turned and crept under the porch in the cool
dark place where I had often gone to escape before.
Crouching under the steps in the dry powdery dirt, I could
hear the women laughing and above all the others I heard
my mother's voice as it penetrated the floorboards. "See, I
told you he Satan's child."

How I hated her! I wanted to destroy her but didn't
know how. Pounding my fists into the dust I cried in frus-
tration, my body shaking in convulsive sobs. "I hate you! I
hate you! I hate you!" I cried. But no one heard—no one
cared. In my frustration, I grabbed great handfuls of the
soft dirt and furiously flung it in all directions. It settled on
my face and turned to rivulets of mud as it mixed with the
tears.

Eventually, the frenzy wore off and I sat silently. In the side yard, I could hear the other children playing. One of the younger boys was singing about birds and butterflies. But I felt isolated, alone. Tortured with hate and persecution, obsessed with fear. I heard the door of the pigeon house close and the heavy crunch of Papa's feet as he rounded the back corner of the house and started up the steps. Pausing, he peered into the shadows through the cracks in the wooden steps. "What you doing under there, boy?" I remained silent, hoping he wouldn't recognize me. He shrugged and went on up the steps, letting the screen door slam behind him.

No one cares, I thought.

Inside the house I could hear more laughter as my father's deep bass voice joined with the women. I knew they were still laughing at me.

The waves of hate flooded over me again. The tears coursed down my face and once more I began to scream. "I hate you, Mama! I hate you. I hate you. I hate you." My voice echoed against the emptiness under the house.

Reaching a stage of complete emotional climax I collapsed on my back in the dirt and rolled over and over, the dust covering my body. Exhausted, I closed my eyes and wept until I fell into a tortured sleep.

The sun had already sunk in the western sea when I awoke and crept out from under the porch. Sand still gritted between my teeth and my body was caked with grime. The frogs and crickets were chirping and the dew felt damp and cool against my bare feet.

Papa opened the back door and a shaft of yellow light fell on me as I stood at the foot of the steps. "Pig!" he shouted. "What you been doing under that house so long? Look at you. We don't want no pigs around here. Go clean up and come to supper."

I obeyed. But as I washed my body under the pump, I knew I would hate forever. I knew I would never love again . . . anyone. And I knew I would never cry again . . . never. Fear, dirt, and hate for the Son of Satan. I had started to run.

It is the practice of many Puerto Rican families to send their children to New York when they are old enough to take care of themselves. Six of my older brothers already had left the island and moved to New York. All were married and trying to make a new life for themselves.

But I was too young to go. However, during the next five years, my parents realized I couldn't stay in Puerto Rico either. I had become a rebel at school. I was picking fights, especially with the smaller children. One day I hit a small girl in the head with a rock. I stood and stared with a warm feeling as the blood oozed through her hair. The child was screaming and crying while I stood laughing.

That night my father slapped my face until my mouth bled. "Blood for blood," he shouted.

I bought a B.B. gun so I could kill birds. It wasn't enough to kill them. I loved to mutilate their bodies. My brothers would shy away from me because of my unusual craving for blood.

In the 8th grade I had a fight with my shop teacher. He was a tall, skinny man who liked to whistle at the ladies. One day in class I called him "nigger." The room became quiet and the other kids backed off among the shop machines, sensing tension in the air.

The teacher walked back through the class to where I was standing beside a lathe. "You know what, kid? You're a phony."

I sassed him back, "Sorry, nigger. I don't mean to be a phony."

Before I could move, he lashed out with his long skinny arm and I felt the flesh of my lips mash against my teeth under the savage blow. I tasted blood flowing into my mouth and down over my chin.

I started toward him flailing both arms. He was a grown man and I weighed less than 100 pounds, but I was filled with hate and the blood set off the fuse. He put his hand against my forehead and held me away with his arm while I helplessly beat the air with my fists.

Realizing the hopelessness of the situation, I backed off. "You've had it now, nigger," I shouted. "I'm going to the police. Just wait and see." I ran out of the classroom.

He ran after me calling, "Wait. I'm sorry." But I was gone.

I didn't go to the police. Instead, I went to Papa and told him the teacher tried to kill me. He was infuriated. He marched in the house and came out with his huge pistol stuck in his belt. "Let's go, boy. I'm gonna kill myself a bully."

We headed back toward the school. I was having difficulty keeping up with Papa's long strides, half running behind him. My heart skipped as I thought of the thrill of seeing that tall teacher cringe beneath the fury of my Papa.

But the teacher wasnt in the classroom. "Wait here, boy," said Papa. "I'll talk to the principal and get to the bottom of this." I cringed, but waited.

Papa was in the principal's office a long time. When he came out, he walked rapidly toward me and yanked me up by the arm. "Alright, boy, you've got some explaining to do. Let's go home."

Once again we marched through the little village and back up the path to the house. He was pulling me behind him by my arm. "You filthy liar," he said to me in front of the house. He raised his hand to slap me but I ducked out of his reach and ran back down the path. "That's right. Run baby run!" he shouted. "You'll come home. And when you do I'm gonna lash you."

I did come home. But it was three days later. The police picked me up walking alongside a road heading back toward the inland mountains. I begged them to let me go but they returned me to my father. And he was true to his promise.

I knew I would leave again. And again. And I would run and run until I was so far away no one could ever bring me back. During the next two years, I ran away five times. Each time, the police found me and brought me home. Finally, in desperation, Papa and Mama wrote my brother, Frank, asking him if he would let me come and live with him. Frank agreed and plans were made for me to go.

The morning I left, the children lined up on the front porch. Mama hugged me close to her bosom. There were tears in her eyes when she tried to speak, but no words came. I had no feeling for her one way or the other. Picking up my little suitcase, I sullenly turned my back and walked to the old pickup truck where Papa waited. I never looked back.

It was a 45-minute drive to the San Juan airport where Papa gave me my ticket and stuck a folded $10 bill in my hand. "Call Frank as soon as you reach New York," he said. "The pilot will take care of you until he comes."

He stood and looked at me for a long moment, towering over me, his shock of gray wavy hair blowing in the warm breeze. I must have seemed small and pathetic to him as I stood by the gate with my little bag in my hand. His lower lip quivered as he stuck out his hand to shake mine. Then, suddenly, he wrapped his long arms around my frail body and pulled me close to him. I heard him sob just once. "Hijo mio," (my son).

Releasing me, he said quickly, "Be a good boy, little bird." I turned and ran up the steps of the huge plane and took my seat beside a window.

Outside I could see the gaunt solitary figure of my father, "The Great One," as he stood beside the fence. He raised his hand once as if to wave but was self-conscious and turned and walked quickly back toward the old pick-up.

What was it he had called me? "Little bird." I remembered that rare moment so many years before when sitting on the steps of the big porch Papa had called me that.

He sat in a rocking chair on the veranda smoking his pipe and told me about a bird that had become a legend in Puerto Rico. It had no legs and was continually on the wing. Papa looked down sadly at me, "That's you, Nicky. You're restless. Like a little bird, you'll ever be on the run." He slowly shook his head and looked up at the sky, blowing smoke toward the vines that tumbled off the porch roof.

"The bird is tiny and very light. He weighs no more than a feather and he picks the moving air currents and sleeps on the wind. He's always running. Running from hawks. Eagles. Owls. Birds of prey. He hides by keeping himself between them and the sun. If they ever get above him they can see him against the dark earth. But his little wings are transparent, like the clear water in the lagoon. As long as he stays high they can't see him. He never rests."

Papa sat back and blew a stream of blue smoke into the fresh air. "But how does he eat?" I asked.

"He eats on the wing," Papa replied. He talked slowly, like he had seen the tiny creature. "He catches insects and butterflies. He has no legs—no feet—he is forever moving."

I was fascinated by the story. "But what about in gray weather?" I had asked him. "What happens when the sun doesn't shine? How does he escape his enemies then?"

"In gray weather, Nicky," Papa said, "he flies so high no one can see him. The only time he ever stops flying—the only time he ever stops running—the only time he comes to earth—is when he dies. For once he touches the earth, he can never run again."

Papa patted me on the bottom and shooed me away from the house. "Go now, little bird. Run and fly. Your Papa will call you when it is time to run no more."

I skipped through the grassy field flapping my arms like a bird trying to take off. But for some reason I could never seem to gain enough speed to be airborne.

The motors of the plane coughed, belched black smoke, and roared to life. At last, I was going to fly. I was on my way. . . .

The bus jerked to a stop. Outside, the bright lights and multicolored signs blinked and gleamed in the cold darkness. The man across the aisle got up to leave. I followed him out the back door. The doors swished shut behind me and the bus pulled away from the curb. I was left alone in the middle of 8 million people.

I picked up a handful of dirty snow and brushed the crust off the top. There it was, sparkling white and pure. I wanted to put it to my mouth and eat it but as I watched, small dark spots began to appear on the surface. I suddenly realized the air was filled with soot from the chimneys above and the snow was taking on the appearance of cottage cheese sprinkled with black pepper.

I threw it to one side. It made little difference. I was free.

For two days I wandered through the city. I found an old coat thrown across a garbage can in a back alley. The sleeves drooped over my hands and the hem scraped the sidewalk. The buttons had been ripped off and the pockets torn open, but it kept me warm. That night I slept on the subway, curled up on one of the seats.

By the end of the second day, the excitement had worn

off. I was hungry . . . and cold. On two occasions, I tried to talk to people and ask for help. The first man simply ignored me. He walked by like I wasn't there. The second man pushed me back against the wall, "Beat it, Spic. Don't put your greasy hands on me." I was afraid. I kept trying to keep the panic from bubbling up from my stomach into my throat.

That evening I walked the streets again. The long overcoat dragging the sidewalk, my little suitcase clutched in my hand. People would move around me and look back but no one seemed to care. They just looked and walked on.

That night I spent the $10 Papa had given me. I stopped in a little restaurant and ordered a hot dog by pointing at a picture of one that hung over the greasy counter. I gobbled it up and pointed that I wanted another. The man at the counter shook his head and held out his hand. I reached in my pocket and pulled out the wadded up bill. Wiping his hands on a towel, he opened it up, stretched it a couple of times, and then slipped it in the pocket of his dirty apron. He then brought me another hot dog and a bowl of chili. When I finished, I looked for him but he had disappeared into the kitchen. I picked up my bag and went back into the cold street. I'd had my first experience with American enterprise. And how was I to know that American hot dogs didn't cost $5 each?

Moving on down the street I stopped in front of a church. A heavy iron gate had been pulled across the front doors and it was fastened with a chain and padlock. I stood in front of the gray stone building, looking up at the steeple which pointed toward the heavens. The cold stone walls and dark stained glass windows huddled for protection behind the iron fence. The statue of a man with a kind face and sad eyes peered through the locked gate. His arms were outstretched and covered with snow. But he was locked in. And I was locked out.

I shuffled on down the street . . . moving . . . moving.

The panic was creeping back. It was almost midnight and I was shaking not only from the cold but from fear. I kept hoping someone would stop and ask if they could help me. I don't know what I would have said if someone had offered to help. But I was lonely. And afraid. And lost.

The hurrying crowd moved on and left me. I never

knew a person could be lonely in the midst of a million people. To me, loneliness was being lost in the woods or on a desert island. But this was the worst of all loneliness. I saw fancy-dressed people coming home from the theater . . . old men selling newspapers and fruit from little all-night stands . . . policemen patrolling in pairs . . . sidewalks full of busy people. But as I looked in their faces they, too, seemed full of loneliness. No one was laughing. No one was smiling. All were in a hurry.

I sat down on the curb and opened my little suitcase. There, tucked inside, was a folded piece of paper with Frank's phone number in Mama's handwriting. Suddenly I felt something poking me from behind. It was an old shaggy dog, nosing at the huge overcoat draped around my thin frame. I put my arm around his neck and pulled him close to me. He licked my cheeks as I buried my head in his mangy hair.

I don't know how long I sat there trembling and stroking the dog. But when I looked up I saw the feet and legs of two uniformed policemen. Their rubber overshoes were wet and dirty. The mangy cur sensed danger and darted away into an alley.

One of the cops poked me in the shoulder with his night stick. "What'cha doing sittin' here in the middle of the night?" he demanded. His face seemed a hundred miles above me. Laboriously I tried to explain in my broken English that I was lost.

One of them muttered something to the other and walked off. The one who remained knelt beside me on the dirty sidewalk. "Can I help you, kid?"

I nodded and shoved the slip of paper with Frank's name and phone number at him. "Brother," I said.

He shook his head as he looked at the scrawled writing. "Is this where you live, kid?"

I didn't know how to answer and just said, "Brother." He nodded and pulled me to my feet and we made our way to a phone booth behind a newsstand. Fishing in his pocket he found a coin and dialed the number. When Frank's sleepy voice answered he handed the phone to me. In less than an hour I was safe in Frank's apartment.

The hot soup at Frank's tasted good and the clean bed was nice. The next morning Frank told me I was to stay with him and they would take care of me and get me in school. But something inside me told me I'd never stay. I had begun to run, and nothing would stop me now.

2

Blackboard Jungle

I stayed with Frank two months learning how to handle the English language. But I wasn't happy and the tensions from within were driving me away.

Frank enrolled me in the 10th grade the first week. The school was almost entirely Negro and Puerto Rican. It was run more like a reformatory than a public school. The teachers and administrators spent more of their time trying to maintain discipline than they did teaching. It was a wild place of fights, immorality, and a constant battle against those who had authority.

Every high school in Brooklyn had at least two or three gangs represented. These gangs were made up of boys and girls who lived in certain neighborhoods. Sometimes the gangs were enemies which invariably caused fights when they were thrown together in school classrooms.

This was a new experience for me. Every day in school there would be a fight in the halls or in one of the classrooms. I would cower against the wall, afraid some of the bigger kids would pick on me. After school, there would always be a fight in the school yard, and someone would be left bleeding.

Frank used to caution me not to walk the streets at night. "The gangs, Nicky! The gangs will murder you. They run like packs of wolves at night. They'll kill anyone who is a stranger on the streets."

He warned me to come straight home from school each afternoon and stay in the apartment away from the gangs.

I soon learned that the gangs weren't the only ones I should fear. There were also the "little people." These were the 9 and 10 year olds who roamed the streets during the afternoons and early evenings or played in front of their slum apartments.

I got my first experience with the little people walking home from school that first week. A gang of about 10 kids, ranging in age from 8 to 10, came charging out of a side door and ran into me on the sidewalk.

"Hey, you kids. Watch what you're doing."

One of the kids whirled and said, "Go to hell!"

Another crept up behind me and knelt down and before I knew it, I was sprawled on the sidewalk on my back. I tried to get up but one of the kids grabbed hold of my foot and began to pull. They were shouting and laughing all the time.

I lost my temper and swung at the nearest one, knocking him to the sidewalk. Just then, I heard a woman screaming. I looked up and she was leaning out a window about two floors up. "Get away from my boy, you stinking Spic, or I'll kill you."

At the moment there was nothing I wanted more than to get away from her boy. But now the others were coming at me. One threw a coke bottle at me. It hit the sidewalk beside my shoulder and the glass showered over my face.

The woman was screaming louder, "Leave my kids alone! Help! Help! He's killing my baby."

Suddenly, another woman appeared out of a doorway with a broom in her hand. She was a fat woman, waddling as she ran, and had the meanest look on her face I'd ever seen. She waded into the gang of boys with the broom held high over her head. I tried to roll away from her but she smashed the broom against my back. I turned over and she hit me again on top of the head. She was screaming and I was suddenly aware that several other women were leaning out of their windows screaming and calling for the police. The fat woman hit me a third time before I could get to my feet and start to run. Behind me I heard her call out, "If you ever come around here again picking on our boys, we'll kill you."

The next afternoon I came home from school a different way.

A week later I had my first run-in with a "gang." I had taken my time coming home from school and was loitering around in a park looking at a man who had a talking parrot. I was dancing around him, laughing and talking to the bird when the man suddenly lost interest, held his parrot against his chest and turned to leave. I looked up and about 15 boys were standing behind me in a semi-circle. These weren't "little people." They were "big people." Most of them bigger than me.

They quickly formed a circle around me and one of the boys said, "Hey, kid, what you laughing at?"

I pointed to the man with the parrot who was now hurrying out of the park. "Man, I was laughing at that crazy bird."

"Yeah, you live around here?" the mean looking boy asked in return.

I sensed that something was wrong and began to stammer a little. "I-I live with my brother down the street."

"You mean just because you live down the street you think you can come into our park and laugh like a hyena? Huh? That what you think? Don't you know this is Bishop turf? Man, we don't allow no strangers in our turf. And especially be-boppers who laugh like hyenas."

I glanced around and saw they meant business. Before I could answer, the mean looking kid pulled a knife out of his pocket and with a flick of a button it opened, revealing a gleaming 7 inch blade.

"You know what I'm gonna do?" he said. "I'm gonna cut your throat and let you bleed like the animal you sound like."

"Hey, m-m-man," I stammered. "What's wrong with you? How come you want to cut me?"

"Because I don't like your looks, that's why," he said. He jabbed the knife toward my stomach and started to move in on me.

Another member of the gang, a tall, colored boy, spoke up. "Aw, come on, Big Daddy. Leave him be. This kid just got in from Puerto Rico. He doesn't even know what's going on."

The mean boy backed off, still sneering. "Okay, but one of these days he'll find out what's going on. And he better keep off Bishop turf."

They turned and walked away. I hurried to the apartment and spent the rest of the afternoon thinking.

The next day at school some of the kids had heard about the incident in the park. I found out that the mean kid with the knife was named Roberto. That afternoon during physical ed class we were playing baseball. Roberto deliberately knocked me down. The other kids all began to shout, "Fight him, Nicky. Jump him. Show him he's not so tough if he doesn't have a knife. Come on, Nicky, we'll back you up. Hit him!"

I got up and brushed myself off. "Okay," I said, "let's see how good you are with your fists."

We squared off and the other kids all formed a big circle around us. I could hear shouts of "Fight! Fight!" and knew the crowd was growing bigger.

Roberto grinned because I had taken a traditional boxing stance, with my hands up in front of my face. He slumped down and awkwardly put his hands up too. It was obvious he was unaccustomed to fighting this way. I danced toward him and before he could move, hit him with a left jab. Blood squirted from his nose and he backed up, looking surprised. I moved toward him.

Suddenly, he put his head down and charged into me, knocking me backwards to the ground. I tried to get up but he kicked me with his pointed shoes. I rolled over and he jumped on my back and pulled my head back, deliberately jamming his fingers into my eyes.

I kept thinking the other kids would join in and help me out, but they just stood there and yelled.

I didn't know how to fight this way. All my fights had been following boxing rules. But I sensed that this boy would kill me if I didn't do something. So, I reached up and pulled his hand down out of my eyes, grabbing his finger with my teeth. He howled with pain and rolled off my back.

I jumped to my feet and took my boxing stance again. He slowly got off the ground holding his injured hand. I danced toward him and hit him with two left jabs on the side of the face. It hurt him and I moved in to hit him again when he reached out and grabbed me by the waist, pinning my arms to my side. Using his head like a battering ram, he hit me time and time again in the face with his forehead. It felt like he was hitting me with a sledge hammer. My nose was bleeding and I couldn't see from the pain. He finally turned me loose and hit me twice with his fists until I collapsed in the dirt of the school playground. I felt him kick me once before a teacher arrived and pulled him away from me.

That night I went home and Frank screamed at me. "They're going to kill you, Nicky. I told you to keep away from the gangs. They'll kill you." My face was badly hurt and it felt like my nose was broken. But I knew from now on, no one would take advantage of me any more. I could fight just as dirty as they could—and even more. And the next time, I'd be ready.

The next time came several weeks later. School was out and I was walking down the hallway toward the door. I was aware that some kids were following me. I glanced over my shoulder. Behind me were 5 Negro boys and a girl. I knew there had been some pretty mean fights between the Puerto Rican kids and the Negro kids. I began walking faster but sensed they had speeded up also.

Going through the outside door, I started down a concrete passageway that led to the street. The colored kids caught up with me and one of them, a big boy, slammed me up against the wall. I dropped my books and another of the kids kicked them down the concrete sidewalk and into a little gutter filled with dirty water.

I looked around but there was no one I could call for help. "What you doing in this turf, baby?" the big boy asked. "Don't you know this is our turf?"

"Man, this high school turf. This turf don't belong to no gangs," I said.

"Don't get smart with me, kid, I don't like you." He put his hand against my chest and pinned me back against the wall. Just then I heard a "click" and realized it was the sound of the switchblade knife.

Nearly all the teenage boys carried knives. They preferred to carry the "switchblade." The knife is operated on a spring. When a small switch button on the side of the knife is pressed, a strong spring is released and the blade flips open and locks in place.

The big boy held the knife against my chest, picking at the buttons of my shirt with the needle sharp point.

"Tell you what I'm gonna do, smart boy," he said. "You're new in this school and we make all new kids buy protection from us. It's a pretty good deal. You pay us twenty-five cents a day and we make sure no one hurts you."

One of the other boys gave a crazy snicker and said, "Yeah, man, like we makes sure we don't hurt you either."

The other kids all laughed.

I said. "Yeah? And what's to prove that even if I give you twenty-five cents a day you won't take advantage of me anyway?"

"No proof, wise guy. You just give it to us anyway. If you don't, you get killed," he answered.

"Okay, man. You better kill me now, then. Because if you don't, I'll be back later and kill every one of you." I could tell the others were a little scared. The big boy with the knife against my chest thought I was right handed. Therefore, he didn't expect me to grab him with my left hand. I twisted his hand away from my chest and spun him around and bent the hand behind his back.

He dropped the knife and I scooped it up off the ground. It felt good in my hand. I put it against the side of his throat, pressing it just hard enough to indent the skin without puncturing it.

I pushed his face against the wall with the knife at the side of his neck just under his ear. The girl began to scream, afraid I was going to kill him.

I turned to her and said, "Hey, baby. I know you. I know where you live. Tonight I'm gonna come to your place and kill you. How you like that?"

She screamed louder and grabbed hold of one of the other boys and began to pull him away. "Run! Run!" she screamed. "This guy's crazy. Run!"

They ran, including the big boy who had been pinned against the wall. I let him go, knowing they could have killed me if they had tried.

I walked on down the sidewalk to where my books were lying in the water. I picked them up and shook them off. I still had the knife in my hand. I stood still for a long time, opening and shutting the blade. It was the first switchblade I'd ever held. I liked the feel of it. I slipped it in the pocket of my jacket and started home. From now on, I thought, they better think twice before they try to tangle with Nicky.

The word soon got out that I was to be feared. That made me fair bait for anyone who wanted to fight. I soon realized it was just a matter of time until something drastic happened. But I was prepared—regardless of what it was.

The final explosion came after I had been in school two months. The teacher had just called the class to order and was calling the roll. A Negro boy was late to class. He came swinging in, wiggling his hips and laughing. There was a pretty little Puerto Rican girl sitting on the back row. He bent over and kissed her on the side of the neck.

She jerked away from him and sat back upright in her desk. He reached around and kissed her on the mouth, at the same time putting his hand on her breast. She jumped up from her seat and began to scream.

The other boys in the class were laughing and shouting, "Go, man, go."

I glanced at the teacher. She started down the aisle but a big boy stood up in front of her and said, "Now, Teach, you wouldn't wanna spoil a little fun would you?" The teacher glanced up at the boy who was taller than she. She retreated back toward her desk while the class howled in delight.

By this time, the boy had the girl pinned against the wall and was running his hands all over her body while he tried to kiss her mouth. She was screaming and pushing him away from her.

Finally, he gave up and flopped down in his seat. "No sense in fighting for it," he announced to the class, "I'll get her tonight and she'll be glad to give it to me when I finish."

I heard the teacher clear her throat and begin again with the roll call.

Something snapped inside of me. I got up from my desk and walked around to the back of the room. The girl had taken her seat and was sitting there sobbing while the teacher called the roll.

I walked up behind the boy who was now sitting at his desk picking his fingernails. I reached over and picked up a heavy wooden chair that was sitting at the rear of the aisle. "Hey, look baby, I have something for you."

As he turned to look back, I brought the heavy chair down on top of his head. He collapsed in his seat, blood pouring from a deep cut in his head.

The teacher ran out of the room and returned in a moment with the principal. He grabbed me by the arm and pulled me down the hall to his office. I sat there while he called an ambulance and made arrangements for someone to take care of the hurt boy.

Then he turned to me. After telling me that all he had heard for the last two months was the trouble I had been in, he asked me for an explanation of what went on in the classroom. I told him exactly what happened. I told him the boy was taking advantage of the Puerto Rican girl and that the teacher hadn't done anything to stop it, so I stood up for her.

As I talked, I could see his face beginning to flush. Finally, he stood up and said, "Well, I've had all I'm going to take of these fights. You kids come in here and think you can act the same way you act out on the streets. I think it's about time I made an example and maybe we can have some respect for authority around here. I'm not going to sit here day after day and listen to you kids try to lie your way out of killing each other. I'm going to call the police."

I was on my feet. "Mister, those police will put me in jail."

"I hope so," said the principal. "At least the rest of these monsters around here will learn to respect some authority for a change if they do."

"You call the police," I said, backing up against the door shaking with fear and rage, "and when I get out of jail, I'll be back. And one day, I'll catch you alone and I'll kill you."

I was gritting my teeth as I talked.

The principal blanched. His face turned white and he thought for a moment. "All right, Cruz. I'll let you off this time. But I don't ever want to see you around this school again. I don't care where you go, go to hell as far as I care, but don't you ever let me see your face around here again. I want you to leave here running and don't stop until you're out of my sight. Understand?"

I understood. I left . . . running.

3

On My Own

A life motivated by hate and fear has no room for anyone but self. I hated everyone, including Frank. He represented authority. And when he began to object to my being out of school and staying out late at night, I made up my mind to leave.

"Nicky," he said, "New York is a jungle. The people who live here live by the law of the jungle. Only the tough survive. You really haven't seen what it's like, Nicky. I've been here for five years and I know. This place is crawling with prostitutes, junkies, winos and killers. Those guys out there, they'll kill you. And no one will even know you're dead until some junkie stumbles over your rotting body under a pile of trash."

Frank was right. But I couldn't stay here. He was insisting I go back to school and I knew I'd have to make it on my own.

"Nicky, I can't force you to go back to school. But if you don't you're lost."

"But the principal kicked me out. He said for me never to come back."

"I don't care. You're going back if you live here. You've got to go to school someplace."

"If you think I'm going back," I spit back, "then you're crazy. And if you try to make me, I'll kill you."

"Nicky, you're my brother. That's crazy talk. Mama and Papa told me to look out after you. I'm not going to have you talk like that. Either you go to school or you get out. Go ahead, run if you want. But you'll be back because you don't have no place to go. But if you stay, you're going to school, and that's final."

That was Friday morning before Frank went to work.

That afternoon I left a note on the kitchen table telling
him some friends had invited me to come stay with them
for a week. I had no friends, but I couldn't stay at Frank's
any longer.

That night I wandered into the Bedford-Stuyvesant sec-
tion of Brooklyn to look for a place to stay. I walked up to
a group of young teenagers hanging around a street corner.
"Any you guys know where I can find a room?"

One of the young kids turned and looked at me, puffing
at his cigarette. "Yeah," he said, jerking his thumb over his
shoulder in the direction of Brooklyn Technical High
School. "My old man's the super at those apartments across
the street. Talk to him and he'll find you a place. That's
him sitting there on the steps playing cards with those
other guys. He's the one that's drunk." The other kids all
laughed.

The apartment the boy had reference to was on Ft.
Greene Place, in the heart of one of the world's largest
housing projects. More than thirty thousand people lived
in the towering buildings, most of them Negro and Puerto
Rican. The Ft. Greene Project runs from Park Avenue to
Lafayette Avenue, surrounding Washington Park.

I walked over to the group of men and asked the super-
intendent if he had a room to rent. He looked up from his
cards and grunted, "Yeah. I got one. Why?"

I hesitated and stammered, "Well, because I need
a place to stay."

"You got fifteen bucks?" he said, spitting tobacco juice
at my feet.

"Well, no, not right now, but . . ."

"Then, I ain't got no room," he said, and turned back to
his cards. The other men didn't even look up.

"But I can get the money," I argued.

"Look kid, when you can show me fifteen bucks in ad-
vance the room is yours. I don't care how you get it. Rob
some old lady for all I care. But until you got the money
get your nose out of here, you're buggin' me."

I walked back toward Lafayette past Papa John's, Har-
ry's Meat House, Paradise Bar, Shery's, The Esquire,
Valhal Bar, and Lincoln's Rendezvous. Pausing beside the
last one I stepped into an alley trying to figure out how to
raise the money.

I knew that if I tried to rob someone and got caught, I'd

go to jail. But I was desperate. I'd told Frank I wouldn't be back for a week. A room was going to cost money and I didn't have a penny. It was almost 10 p.m. and the winter wind was freezing cold. I shrank back into the shadows of the alley and saw people passing by on the sidewalk. I pulled the switchblade out of my pocket and pressed the button. The blade snapped open with a soft click. I pressed the tip against the palm of my hand. My hand was shaking as I tried to imagine just how I would perform the robbery. Would it be best to pull them into the alley? Should I go ahead and stab them or just scare them? What if they yelled? . . .

My thoughts were interrupted by two people talking at the entrance of the alley. An old wino had stopped a young man in his late teens who was carrying a huge sack of groceries. The old man was begging him for a dime to buy a cup of coffee. I listened as the young man tried to get away—telling the wino he didn't have any money.

The thought ran through my mind that the old man probably had a pocket full of money he had begged and stolen. He wouldn't dare scream for help if I robbed him. As soon as the boy left I'd pull him into the alley and take it from him.

The young man was putting his grocery sack on the sidewalk. He fished in his pocket until he found a coin. The old man mumbled and shuffled away.

"Damn," I thought to myself. "Now what will I do?"

Just then the boy tipped over his sack of groceries. A couple of apples rolled onto the sidewalk. He bent to pick them up and I pulled him into the alley and smashed him up against the wall. Both of us were scared to death but I had the advantage of surprise. He was petrified with fear as I held my knife in front of his face.

"I don't want to hurt you, but I need money. I'm desperate. Give it to me. Now! Quick! All you got before I kill you."

My hand was shaking so badly I was afraid I'd drop the knife.

"Please. Please. Take it all. Don't kill me," the boy pleaded. He pulled out his billfold and tried to hand it to me. He dropped it and I kicked it down the alley. "Take off," I said. "Run, man, run! And if you stop running for two blocks, you're a dead man."

He looked at me, eyes wide with horror, and started to
run. He tripped over his groceries and sprawled on the
pavement at the mouth of the alley. Scrambling to his
feet, he tripped again as he half crawled, half ran down
the sidewalk. As soon as he turned the corner, I grabbed
the wallet and sprinted down the alley. Emerging in the
darkness on De Kalb, I vaulted the chain link fence sur-
rounding the park and ran through the high grass into the
trees. Squatting behind an embankment, I paused to catch
my breath and let my pounding heart settle down. Open-
ing the wallet I counted out $19. It felt good to hold the
bills in my hand. I tossed the wallet into the high grass and
counted the money again before I folded it and put it in
my pocket.

Not bad, I thought. The gangs are killing hobos for less
than a dollar and I get nineteen on my first try. This isn't
going to be so bad after all.

But my confidence didn't remove all my fear, and I
stayed hidden in the high grass until after midnight. By
then it was too late to get the room and I walked back to
the spot where I had committed the robbery. Someone had
already picked up all the spilled groceries with the excep-
tion of a crushed box of crackers. I picked up the box and
shook it as the crumbs fell out on the pavement. I relived
the experience in my mind and grinned. I should have cut
him, just to find out what it felt like, I thought. Next time I
will.

I walked to the subway entrance by Papa John's and
boarded the first train that came along. I spent the night
on the subway and early the next morning I was back on
Ft. Greene Place to rent the room.

The super walked with me up three flights of stairs. The
room opened out over the street facing Brooklyn Tech. It
was small with cracks in the ceiling. The super told me
there was a public bathroom on the 2nd floor and that I
could adjust the heat by turning the handle on the steel ra-
diator. He handed me the key and told me the rent was
due every Saturday a week in advance. The door closed
behind him and I heard him clomping down the steps.

I turned and looked at the room. There were two single
beds, a chair, a small table, a wash basin on the wall and a
small closet. Walking to the window, I peered into the
street below. The early morning traffic was moving with a

steady hum on Lafayette at the end of the block. Across the street, Brooklyn Tech towered into the sky. It ran the length of the block and shut out any view I might have had. But it made little difference. I was on my own.

Later that morning I made my first tour through the neighborhood. Coming down the steps of the slum apartment I saw a young man stagger out from under the stairwell. His face was blanched white and his eyes sunk deep in their sockets. His filthy, tattered jacket hung half off one shoulder and his pants were unzipped where he had urinated behind the radiator. I couldn't tell whether he was drunk or high on dope. I stood on the landing and watched him as he reeled through the door and onto the outside steps. He bent over the side of the steps and heaved and retched as he threw up on the sidewalk below. A gang of little people burst out a side door on the first floor and ran into the street completely oblivious of his presence. The man finished gagging and slumped on the top step, looking blankly at the street.

I walked past him and down the steps. Overhead I heard a window open and looked up just in time to duck a barrage of garbage thrown from the third floor to the sidewalk below. Next door one of the little people was squatting in the shadows under the steps, using an abandoned basement entrance for a latrine. I shuddered but told myself I could get accustomed to it.

Behind the apartment building was an open lot, waist high with weeds and scraggly bushes. A few scrawny trees poked their naked branches toward the gray sky. Spring had begun but the trees seemed almost reluctant to put forth new buds and face another summer in the ghetto. I kicked an empty beer can—the trashy lot was covered with them. Old cardboard boxes, newspapers, and rotting boards were strewn in the high weeds. A broken down wire fence stretched across the lot to another apartment building that opened on St. Edward Street. Looking back at my building I could see some of the first floor windows boarded shut or closed in with sheets of galvanized tin to keep out the cold wind. Two apartments down, I could see the round faces of little Negro children with their noses pressed against a filthy window pane watching me as I kicked through the rubbish. They reminded me of small

animals in a cage yearning for freedom and yet afraid to
venture out for fear of being hurt or killed. Part of the
window had been broken out and replaced with sheets of
waterstained cardboard. I could count five frightened
faces. There were probably five more in the small three
room apartment.

I walked back around toward the front of the building.
The basement apartment under No. 54 was vacant. The
iron gate hung loose on its hinges. I kicked it open and
started in. The smell of urine, body excretions, wine,
smoke and grease was more than I could stand and I
backed out gagging. At least I had a room on the 3rd floor.

I started down the sidewalk. The whores on the street
were a pathetic sight. The white girls worked the right
side of the street and occupied apartments down the block
from me. The colored girls worked the opposite side of the
street and lived near the subway entrance. All the girls
were addicts. They were standing around in leotards and
dirty coats. Some were yawning because they were sick or
because they needed a "wake up," an early morning shot
of heroin to get them going.

After two months I still wasn't accustomed to New York.
Back in Puerto Rico I had seen pictures of the Statue of
Liberty and the United Nations building. But here, in the
ghetto, as far as the eye could see there was nothing but
apartments, filled with human flesh. Each window symbol-
ized a family, cramped into tiny living quarters, eking out
a miserable existence. I thought of the zoo in San Juan
with the pacing bears and chattering monkeys behind bars.
They wallow in their own filth. They eat stale meat or wilt-
ed lettuce. They fight among themselves and the only time
they get together is when that are attacking an intruder.
Animals aren't meant to live this way, with only a painted
jungle scene on the rear of the cage to remind them of
what they're supposed to be. And neither are people. But
here, in the ghettos, they do.

I paused on the curb at the corner of Myrtle Avenue,
waiting for the light to change. Overhead an elevated train
roared and clattered by, showering those below with a fine
coat of soot and grime. The streets were covered with a
slushy mixture of snow, dirt, and salt which the people
waded through as the light changed.

Behind the apartments the clothes lines hung from one

dingy balcony or fire escape to another. The blue shirts and khaki pants flopped in the freezing wind. Underclothes that used to be white were now a dirty gray from constant exposure to the filth-filled air.

It was Saturday morning and the store keepers were pulling the heavy iron grates away from their store fronts. For blocks and blocks not a single store was without a mesh grate or iron bars to protect it from the roving gangs at night.

But it was the apartments that depressed me most. There were evidences of feeble attempts of the occupants to reach up from the concrete jungle and brick canyons for some essence of identity. But it was a hopeless reach. Like a man sinking in quicksand who gropes with stretching fingers for a weed on the edge of the quagmire, grasping desperately as he is sucked under with the weed in his clenched fist.

A dirty red clay flowerpot sat behind a soot covered window pane. A scraggly geranium drooped limply against the glass.

Occasionally, one of the apartments would have brightly painted steps, or perhaps a window sill would be painted so it stood out in stark relief against the drab stone. In another window a rough flower box, made from the unfinished lumber of a machinery crate, hung from a dirty sill. In it a few pathetic artificial flowers braved the winter wind, covered with soot that floated down from a thousand smokestacks that towered over the city.

I had gotten as far as St. Edward Street and paused in front of the Walt Whitman Library next to P.S. 67. Across the street was a huge apartment building, 12 stories high and a block long. Its 600 windows faced the street, each one representing some miserable state of humanity shivering behind the panes. In one window hung a tattered drape, once bright with color, now faded and torn from the effects of its environment. Most windows were void of shades or drapes, staring like the naked eyes of a frozen corpse out onto the street below.

I turned and retraced my steps back toward Washington Park. What's wrong with these people here in this filthy place? I thought. Why do they live like this? No yards. No grass. No open fields. No trees. I didn't know that once you moved into one of these concrete cages you became its prisoner. There's no leaving the asphalt jungle.

That afternoon I walked back down the street, I had noticed what looked like a carnival with rides and sideshows in the playground behind the St. Michael-St. Edwards Catholic Church at the corner of Auburn and St. Edwards Streets. I arrived at 4 p.m. and the music from the carnival was blaring out into the street. I still had a little money left over from the robbery and the thought of a carnival tingled my blood. At the gate I noticed a group of kids standing around an Italian organ grinder. They were wearing black jackets with a crimson double M stitched on the back. The music from the organ grinder was almost drowned out by the noise the kids were making as they clapped their hands and jitterbugged in the middle of the sidewalk.

In the center of the group was a dark haired, fair skinned boy about my own age. His handsome face was wreathed in a grin as he kicked his feet against the sidewalk in a fast bebop. Hands on hips, he spun around in time to the music. Suddenly, his black eyes met mine. He came to an abrupt halt, and the grin on his face was instantly replaced with a hard cold look.

"Hey, baby, what you doing this territory? This Mau Mau turf. We don't want no squares hanging around here."

I looked back at him and realized that the other boys with the black jackets had formed a quiet little circle around us. The handsome boy with the steel cold eyes walked up to me and pushed me with his chest, smirking. "What click you belong to, man?"

"I don't belong to no click," I replied. "I come down here to ride on the carnival. That a crime or something?"

A boy in the crowd stepped forward. "Hey man, you know what this is?" he said, brandishing an open knife. "This is a blade, baby. It'll cut your gut. How you like to get smart with me? I ain't as tender as Israel."

The boy referred to as Israel motioned the other boy back and continued, "You see, a square can get killed in a hurry. Maybe I kill you. Now, if you wanna live you better beat it."

I was angry, and felt in my pocket for my own switchblade. But I realized that the odds were too great for me. I didn't want to be a chicken, but knew there would be another time for me to show my courage. I nodded my head and turned back down the street toward Washington Park and my apartment. Behind me, I could hear the gang laughing and hooting. "That's tellin 'im, Israel baby. That little S.O.B. learned his lesson this time. It'll be a cold day in hell before he sticks his nose back around here again."

I was mad and frustrated. Going under the elevated tracks on Myrtle, I walked into the park area and sat down on a bench. I didn't notice that a young kid, maybe thirteen years old, had been following me. I turned and looked at him. He grinned and sat down on the bench beside me. "Gave you a rough time, didn't they?" he said.

"Whatcha mean?" I asked. "I coulda took any one of them but didn't see no sense in fighting all of them at once."

"Man, these gangs are tough around here," he said, reaching into his shirt pocket and pulling out a homemade cigarette. "They'll kill you if you don't run with 'em."

He lit the cigarette and noticed I was watching him. "You smoke pot?" he asked. I shook my head although I knew what he was talking about.

"Howja like to try one? I got an extra. Man, it's cool."

"Sure," I said. I'd backed off once this afternoon and didn't want to back off again.

He fished around in his shirt pocket and pulled out a bent, crumpled cigarette. It was twisted shut on both ends and stained along the side where he had licked the paper to make it stick.

"You gotta puff it," the boy said. "If you don't, it goes out."

He lit it for me and I began to puff on it.

"No," the kid laughed, "like this."

He took a long drag on the cigarette and slowly inhaled the smoke into his lungs. "Man, that's good. If all you do is puff, it burns up and you don't get nothing out of it. Inhale, man!"

I inhaled. It had a strange sweet taste and a strong odor.

"What's it do?" I asked, beginning to feel the dizzy effects of the weed.

"Man, it sends you," the boy answered. "It makes you laugh a lot. Makes you feel like you're the best dancer, best lover, best fighter. All those guys back there at the carnival had been smoking pot. Didn't you see how their eyes were red? You can tell if they're high on grass if their eyes shine."

"Where you get this stuff?" I asked.

"Oh, it's easy. We got a hundred pushers here in the neighborhood. Most any of the big guys can get it for you. They get it from bigger connections. Cuba. Mexico. Me? My old man raises it in the back yard. We got a bunch of weeds in our back yard. No one ever goes back there and my old man planted some of the seeds in the weeds and we raise our own. It ain't as good as some of the other stuff, but it don't cost us anything."

"How much does it cost if you buy it from a pusher?" I asked, trying to learn the vocabulary and a little embarrassed that a thirteen year old kid knew more about it than I.

"Some of it sells for a dollar a stick. Sometimes you can get it for seventy-five cents a stick. But it's best to buy a can. You know, like a Prince Albert can. That way you can make your own for about forty cents. You have to be careful, though. Some of the guys cheat you. They'll mix oregano in with the pot and you won't get pure stuff. Always check it out before you pay for it 'cause they'll cheat you for sure."

I had finished the cigarette and stretched my feet out in front of me and put my head on the back of the bench. I didn't seem to notice the cold wind as much and the dizziness had departed, leaving me feeling like I was floating on a dreamy cloud.

I turned my head so I could see the boy. He was sitting on the bench with his head in his hands. "I thought this stuff was supposed to make you happy. How come you're not laughing?"

"Man, what I got to laugh about?" he said. "My old man's a drunk. Only he's not really my old man. He just moved in with my mother last year. I don't even know who my real old man is. And this man, he beats up on my maw all the time. Last week I tried to pull him off her and he hit me in the face with a bottle and broke off two my teeth. I threw a clock at him and hit him in the back. Then my Maw, my own Maw, called me a S.O.B. and told me to get out . . . that I had no reason to hurt her man. Now I'm living in the street just waiting until I can kill him. I don't run with no gangs. I don't run with nobody. I'm just waiting until that bum gets alone and I'm gonna kill him. I don't even love my mother no more. What I got to laugh about."

He never raised his head while he talked. "This the same man who grows the marijuana in the back yard?" I asked.

"Yeah. He's a pusher too. Man, just wait 'til I catch him alone. I'm gonna push him—push a knife through him." He looked up, his face strained and tired, like the face of an old monkey rather than a thirteen-year-old boy. "What about your old man, he a drunk too?"

"Naw, I'm lucky. I don't even have an old man or old woman," I lied. "I'm on my own."

The kid looked up. "Yeah, me too now, I guess." Then, brightening, he said, "Well, see you around. Watch out for them gangs. They'll kill you if they catch you on the street at night."

"Hey, what about these gangs? How many of there are there?"

"Hundreds," he said. "Man, there's so many of 'em you can't begin to count 'em."

"What do they do?"

"Fight, man what else? Either they're going out and fighting some other gang or they're staying home defending their turf against some invading gang. When they ain't fighting each other, they're fighting the police. They use everything they can find to fight with. They carry knives, clubs, pistols, zip guns, brass knucks, rifles, sawed-off shotguns, bayonets, baseball bats, broken bottles, gasoline bombs, bricks, rocks, bicycle chains . . . man you name it, they use it to kill you with. They even file the tips of their umbrellas, put spikes on their shoes, and some of the dago gangs carry straight razors and put razor blades between their fingers in their fist. You hang around here long and you'll find out. That's why I don't join with 'em. I just hang out in the alleys and in the dark streets and keep away from 'em. You'll learn, though, just stick around and you'll learn."

He got up and sauntered back through the park, disappearing in the twilight. I headed back to 54 Ft. Greene Place. It was already dark.

4

Baptized with Blood

Several weeks later I left my apartment about 8 p.m. and I walked down to Papa John's on the corner of Lafayette. A young Puerto Rican named Tico was leaning against the side of the building smoking a cigarette. I had met him once or twice and understood he was a knife expert.

He looked up and said, "Hey Nicky, would you like to go 'gig'? I want you to meet Carlos, President of the gang."

I had heard of gigs but never attended one, so I readily accepted his invitation and followed him down a side street and into a basement entrance under a flight of stairs in an apartment building.

I had trouble adjusting my eyes to the dim light. A single pole lamp burned in the corner. Some light came in from the windows and a little came in around the door from the street lights outside.

As I moved into the room I could see dim figures clinging to each other, swaying to the sound of soft music. Their heads drooped across each other's shoulders, as their feet moved in unison to the slow music. One of the boys clutched a wine bottle behind his girl's back and staggered as he wrapped his arm around her neck and took a long swig out of the bottle.

Several boys were sitting at a small table playing cards and smoking what I later found out were reefers—marijuana. A bottle of wine sat in the middle of the table.

On the far side of the room, away from the lamp, two couples were lying on a mat. One couple was seemingly asleep in each other's arms. The other was engaged in heavy love play. As I watched they got to their feet, arms around each other and mouths glued together in a passionate kiss, and stumbled through a side door.

Tico looked at me and winked. "There's a bed in there. We keep it so they can shack up when they want to."

A stack of pulp paper magazines with pictures of naked and semi-naked women was on the floor at my feet.

"So this is a gig," I thought.

Tico grabbed my arm and pulled me into the room. "Hey, everybody, This is my friend. How about making him feel welcome?"

A blond girl stepped out of the shadows near the door and took me by the arm. She had on a tight black sweater, a crimson skirt, and was barefooted. I put my arm around her waist and said, "Hey, baby, you wanna dance with me?"

"What's your name?" she said. Before I could answer, Tico spoke up, "His name is Nicky. He's my friend and he's a damn good fighter. He may want to join us."

The girl slid around in front of me and snuggled her body up close to mine. "Okay, Nicky, if you're such a good fighter let's see how good a dancer you are." Gliding out into the floor, I could feel her thighs rub against mine as we shuffled in step to the music.

Her motions began to excite me. She was warm and I could feel every movement of her body as she clung tightly to me. I slipped my hand under her sweater along her back and pressed her close to me.

"Ummmmm," I heard her groan. That's all it took for me and I moved my hand around under her arm.

Suddenly, she put both hands against my chest and gave me a violent shove backward. "Cut it out! What do you think you're doing?" she bit out. "Don't get fresh with me. I belong to Jose and he'd cut you to pieces if I told him you tried to feel me."

She could tell from the expression on my face I was confused. Her face broke into a grin and she reached out and pulled me back close to her. She put her lips close to my ear, "After all, this is only the first time. Don't be in such a rush. If I like you, I'll let you have it all."

We danced a while longer and then stopped to watch a couple of boys playing "chicken" with a knife. One of the boys was standing against the wall and the other was throwing a knife at his feet. The object was to get the knife as close as possible without hitting him. If the boy flinched, he was "chicken."

I caught myself hoping he would hit him. The thought of blood excited me. Even as I stood there, I began to laugh at myself hoping he would slip and stab the boy.

The blond with the black sweater pulled me by the arm, "Come with me. I want you to meet someone important."

I followed her into a side room. A tall lanky Puerto Rican was slouched on a chair with his legs propped on a small table in front of him. A girl was sitting astraddle his lap, leaning over him as he blew smoke through her hair and laughed.

"Hey!" he shouted to us. "Ain't you got no manners? Don't you know you're supposed to ask my permission before you come in like that? You might catch me doing something I don't want nobody to see." He laughed and reached around and patted the girl's hips with both hands.

Looking at me he said, "Who's this punk?" The blond said, "This is my friend, Nicky. Tico brought him. Tico says he's a good fighter."

The tall lanky boy shoved the girl off his lap and looked hard at me. Then he grinned and stuck out his hand. "Slip me some skin, Nicky. Me, I'm Carlos. President of the Mau Maus."

I gently laid my hand against his and pulled it back, sliding my palm along his in the gang's fashion of handshaking.

I had heard of the Mau Maus. They had named themselves for the blood thirsty savages in Africa. I had seen them in the streets with their black leather jackets with the crimson double M stitched on the back. They wore fancy alpine hats many of which were decorated with wooden matches. Most of them carried canes and they wore sharp pointed shoes that could kick a man to death in a matter of seconds.

Carlos nodded toward the corner of the room and I recognized the boy I had seen at the carnival. "That's Israel. He's Vice President of the Mau Maus." Israel's face was expressionless as he stared at me. His deep black eyes boring holes into my soul and making me feel uncomfortable.

I found out later that the president and the vice president are nearly always together. They protect each other in case one is attacked.

"How old are you, Nicky?" Carlos asked.

"Sixteen," I answered.

"You know about fighting?"

"Sure," I said.

"You willing to fight anyone, even police?"

"Sure," I replied again.

"Hey, you ever stab anyone?"

"No," I replied truthfully, but regretfully.

"Anyone ever tried to stab you?"

"Yes," I answered.

"Yeah?" Carlos said, showing renewed interest. "What you do to the guy?"

"Nothing," I replied. "But I will. I'm just waiting to catch him again and when I do, I'll kill him."

Israel interrupted. "Listen, man, you want to join our gang you do as we do. We're the toughest. Even the police scared of us. But we don't want no chickens. You want to join and you no chicken, fine. But if you chicken, we cut you open and kill you."

I knew Israel was telling the truth. I already had heard stories of young boys who had been killed by their own gangs because they ratted on a fellow gang member.

Carlos spoke up, "Two things, man. If you join the Mau Maus, it's forever. No one ever quits. Second, if you're caught by the cops and squeal, we'll get you. Either we get you when you get out of jail, or we go in the jail and get you. But we'll get you."

Israel showed a faint grin on his handsome face. "How about it, baby, you still think you want to join?"

"Give me three days," I said. "If I join your gang, I want to go all the way."

"Okay, baby," Carlos said. "You have three days to think it over. And at the end of that time, you come back here. Let me know what you decide." He was still sitting in the same slouched position with his legs stretched out in front of him. He had pulled his girl back over to him and had his left hand under her skirt and around her hips.

I turned to leave and Carlos said, "Hey, Nicky, I forgot to tell you. If you tell anyone . . . anyone . . . where we are, I'll kill you before you have a chance to turn around. Got it?"

"Got it," I said. And I knew he meant it.

Outside on the street, I quizzed Tico. "What do you think, Tico? You think I ought to join the Mau Maus?"

Tico just shrugged his shoulders. "It's a good deal, man.

If you join 'em, they take care of you. If you don't join 'em they're liable to kill you for not joining. You ain't got much choice now. Besides, you're gonna have to join one of the gangs to stay alive around here."

"What about Carlos?" I asked. "What kind of guy is he?"

"He's okay. He don't say much but when he does, everyone listens. He's in charge and they all know it."

"Is it true that the president gets his choice of the girls?" I asked.

"That's right," said Tico. "We have about 75 girls in our gang and the president gets his pick. A different one each day if he wants it that way. Man, they like it. You know, it's big stuff to go with the president. They fight to see who gets to play up to him. And that's not all. The gang takes care of the president. He gets the first take out of what we steal—usually enough to pay his room and buy his food and clothes. It's a pretty good deal, being president."

"Hey, Tico. If you're so good with a knife, how come you're not president?"

"Not me, man. The president don't get to fight too much. He has to stay back and plan things. Me, I like to fight. I don't want to be president."

That's what I like too, I thought. I like to fight.

Tico headed back to Papa John's and I turned toward 54 Ft. Greene Place. I could feel the blood tingling in my veins as I imagined what was ahead. The gigs, the girls. But most of all, the fights. I wouldn't have to fight by myself any more. I could hurt as much as I wanted to and not have to be hurt back. My heart began to beat faster. Maybe I'll get a chance to really stab someone. I could almost visualize the blood flowing across my hands and dripping down on the street. I made swinging motions with my hands as I walked, pretending I had a knife and jabbing and slashing at imaginary figures in the dark. I had told Carlos I'd let him know in three days. But I had already made up my mind. All I wanted was for someone to give me a switchblade and a gun.

Two nights later, I was back at the gig. I walked in and Carlos met me at the door. "Hey, Nicky, you're just in time. We got another boy who wants to join the Mau Maus. You want to watch the initiation?"

I had no idea what an initiation was but wanted to

watch. Carlos continued, "But maybe you came to tell us you don't want to join, eh?"

"No," I countered. "I came to tell you I'm ready to join. I want to fight. I think I'm just as tough as anyone else and a better fighter than most of these other guys."

"Good," said Carlos. "You can watch and then it'll be your turn. We have two ways to find out if you're chicken. Either you stand still while five of our toughest guys beat you up, or you stand against the wall waiting for the knife. If you run from either, we don't let you join the gang. This kid says he's tough. Let's see how tough he really is. Then we'll see if you're that tough."

I looked across the room and saw the other boy. He was about 13 years old with pimples on his face and a long shock of black hair that fell down over his eyes. He was small and skinny and his arms hung stiffly by his sides. He was wearing a white, long-sleeved shirt that was soiled on the front and pulled out around his belt. I thought I had seen this little pimply faced kid at school, but wasn't sure since he was younger than I.

There were about 40 boys and girls eagerly awaiting the show. Carlos was in charge. He told everyone to clear the floor and they all lined up around the walls. The young boy was told to stand with his back against a bare wall. Carlos stood in front of him with an open switchblade in his hand. The silver blade glistened in the dim light.

"I'm gonna turn and walk twenty steps toward that other wall," he said. "You stand right where you are. You say you're a tough kid. Well, we're gonna find out just how tough. When I get to twenty, I'm gonna turn and throw this knife. If you flinch or duck, you're chicken. If you don't, even if the knife sticks you, you're a tough kid and you can join the Mau Maus. Got it?"

The small boy nodded.

"Now, one other thing," said Carlos, holding the knife in the face of the youngster. "If you turn chicken while I'm walking away counting, all you got to do is holler. But you better not ever stick your nose around here any more. If you do, we'll cut those big ears off and make you eat 'em and then dig your belly button out with a beer opener and let you bleed to death."

The boys and girls started to laugh and clap. "Go, man, go!" they shouted at Carlos.

Carlos turned his back to the boy and started slowly across the room. He held the long glimmering knife by the point of the blade, his arm in front of him bent at the elbow, the knife in front of his face.

"One . . . two . . . three . . ." The crowd began to shout and jeer. "Get him, Carlos! Stick it through his eye! Make him bleed, baby, make him bleed!"

The young boy was cowering against the wall, much like a mouse trapped by a tiger. He was trying desperately to be brave His arms were rigid at his sides his hands balled into tiny fists with his knuckles showing white against the skin. His face was drained of color and his eyes were wide with fright.

"Eleven . . . twelve . . . thirteen. . . ." Carlos counted loudly as he paced off the distance. The tension mounted as the boys and girls jeered and cried out for blood.

"Nineteen . . . twenty." Slowly Carlos turned and pulled his right hand back toward his ear, holding the knife by the tip of its needle sharp blade. The crowd of kids was wild in their frenzy calling for blood. Just as he snapped the knife forward, the little boy bent over, throwing his arms around his head screaming, "No! No!" The knife thudded into the wall just inches from where his head had been.

"Chicken! . . . chicken! . . . chicken!" the crowd roared.

Carlos was angry. The corners of his mouth grew tight and his eyes narrowed. "Grab him," he hissed. Two boys moved from each side of the room and grabbed the cowering child by his arms and slammed him back against the wall.

Carlos moved across the room and stood in front of the shaking form. "Chicken!" he spat out. "Chicken! I knew you were a coward from the first time I saw you. I oughta kill you."

Again the kids in the room picked up the theme. "Kill him! Kill the dirty chicken!"

"You know what we do to chickens?" said Carlos. The boy looked up at him trying to move his mouth but no sound was coming out.

"I'll tell you what we do to chickens," said Carlos. "We clip their wings so they can't fly no more."

He snatched the knife out of the wall. "Stretch him out!" ne said.

Before the boy could move, the two boys yanked his
arms straight out from his body, spread eagle. Moving so
fast you could hardly follow his hand, Carlos brought the
knife up in a fast vicious thrust and jabbed it almost to the
hilt into the child's armpit. The boy jerked and screamed in
pain. The blood gushed out and quickly flooded his white
shirt with a crimson red.

Pulling the knife out of the boy's flesh, he flipped it into
his other hand. "See man," he leered, viciously thrusting
the knife upward again into the other armpit, "I'm left
handed too."

The two boys turned loose and the child collapsed to the
floor, his arms across his chest, his hands clutching pitifully
at his punctured flesh. He was screaming and gagging,
rolling on the floor. His shirt was almost completely cov-
ered with bright red blood.

"Get him out of here," snapped Carlos. Two boys came
forward and yanked him to his feet. The boy threw back
his head and screamed out in agony as they jerked his
arms. Carlos clapped his hand across his mouth and the
screaming stopped. The boy's eyes, wide with horror,
peered across the top of the hand.

"Go home, chicken! If I hear you scream one more time
or if you squeal on us, I'll cut your tongue out too. Got
it?" As he spoke, he held up the switchblade, the silver
blade dripping blood down over the white mother-of-pearl
handle. "Got it?" he repeated.

The child nodded.

The boys pulled him across the floor and out onto the
sidewalk. The gang of kids in the room shouted as he left,
"Go home, chicken!"

Carlos turned. "Who's next?" he said. . . . looking
straight at me. The crowd grew quiet.

I suddenly realized I wasn't afraid. Matter of fact, I had
become so wrapped up in the stabbing and pain that I was
enjoying it. The sight of all that blood gave me a wild, sav-
age, exhilarating feeling. I was envious of Carlos. But now
it was my turn.

I remembered Carlos' statement that I had a choice of
initiations. Common sense told me that Carlos was still
mad. If I let him throw his knife at me, he would try to
stab me on purpose. It seemed the wiser of the two moves
to choose the other method.

"We got another chicken?" Carlos teased.

I stepped out into the middle of the room and looked around. One of the girls, a tall slim girl with tight black slacks shouted, "What's wrong, baby, you scared or something? We got some blood left over if you don't have any." The crowd hooted and shouted in laughter. And she was right. The floor beside the wall where the other boy had been was covered with a sticky puddle of blood.

I said, "Not me. I ain't scared. Try me out, baby. Where's your boys who want to slug me?"

I was trying to put up a good front, but deep inside I was scared. I knew I was going to get hurt. I realized that these people played for keeps. But I would rather die than be chicken. So I said, "I'm ready."

Carlos barked out five names. "Johnny!" And a short, stocky boy stepped out of the crowd and stood in front of me. He was twice my size with a deeply lined forehead and almost no neck at all. His head seemed to rest right in between his shoulders. He walked to the center of the room and cracked his knuckles with a loud popping sound.

I tried to picture my 120 pounds against his 200 pounds. He just looked blankly at me, like an ape. Waiting for the command to attack.

"Mattie!" Another boy stepped out. This one was nearer my size but his arms were long, much longer than mine. He danced into the center of the room flicking his hands out and back like a boxer. He held his chin close to his chest looking out of the tops of his eyes. He circled the room, fists flicking forward with lightning speed. The girls whistled and sighed as he kept up his shadow boxing, blowing and snorting through his nose as he swung and did short jabs.

"Jose!" A third boy joined the group. He had a deep scar on his left cheek running from below his eye to the tip of his chin. He began taking his shirt off and flexing his muscles. He was built like a weight lifter. He circled me—looking at me from all angles.

"Owl!" A roar went up from the other kids in the room. Owl was obviously a favorite. I learned later they called him Owl because he could see as well at night as in the daytime. They used him on the front line in the rumbles so he could spot the enemy gangs as they approached. He had big wide eyes and a hooked nose that obviously had been broken time and time again. One ear was half gone where he had been hit with a board that had a long nail in it. It had happened during a rumble in a school yard and the nail had snagged his ear and ripped more than half of it away. Owl was a short fat kid with the meanest look I had ever seen.

"Paco!" I never did see Paco. I heard him call out behind me, "Hey, Nicky." I turned to look and he hit me in the back just above the belt line with his fist. The pain was excruciating. I felt like he had ruptured my kidney. I tried to gasp for breath but he hit me again. As I straightened up and put my hands behind my back to grasp the hurt, one of the other boys hit me in the stomach so hard I lost my breath. I could sense myself beginning to pass out from the pain when someone hit me in the face and I heard the bone of my nose crumble under the blow.

I never had a chance to hit back. I felt myself falling. I sensed someone grabbing hold of my long hair. My body collapsed to the floor but my head was being held up by my hair. Someone kicked me in the face with a grimy shoe and I could feel the sand grind into my cheek and lips. I was being kicked all over and whoever was holding my hair was hitting me on the side of the head.

Then the lights went out and I remembered nothing else.

Sometime later, I was aware that someone was shoving me around and slapping my face. I heard someone say, "Hey, wake up."

I tried to focus my eyes but could see nothing but the ceiling. I wiped my hand across my face and could feel blood on my skin. I was covered with it. I looked up and saw the face of the one they called Owl. The blood made me go crazy. I lashed out and hit him in the mouth. Suddenly, all my energy came back. I was lying on my back in that big puddle of sticky blood, spinning round and round kicking everyone in sight, cursing, screaming, striking out with my hands and feet.

Someone grabbed my feet and pinned me to the floor until the fury wore off. Israel bent over me laughing.

"You're our kind, Nick. Man, we can use you. You may

be a lot of things, but you're not chicken. That's for sure. Here." He pressed something into my hand.

It was a .32 revolver. "You're a Mau Mau, Nicky. A Mau Mau."

5

Rumble in the Streets

Israel and I became almost inseparable from the beginning. Three nights later he came by the apartment to tell me there was going to be a "rumble" with the Bishops. At last, I thought, a chance to use my revolver—a chance to fight. I could feel the hair rising on the back of my neck as Israel described the plan.

The Mau Maus were to gather in Washington Park near De Kalb. We were to be there by 9:00 p.m. Our War Councilor had already met with the War Councilor from the Bishops, a Negro gang, and arranged the time and place. 10:00 p.m. in the playground behind P.S. 67.

Israel said, "Bring your revolver. All the other guys have their weapons. Some of the guys have made their own zip guns and Hector has a sawed off shotgun. We'll teach those Bishops a lesson. If we have to kill, we kill. But if we go down, we go down fighting. We're the Mau Maus. The people. Them African Mau Maus drink blood, man, and we're just like 'em."

The gang was already gathering at 8:30 when I arrived in the park. They had hidden their weapons in the trees and tall grass fearing the police might come by. But tonight there were no police and Israel and Carlos were giving orders. By 10:00 p.m. there were more than 100 boys milling around the park. Some of them had guns. Most had knives. A few had baseball bats, sticks with nails in the ends, or handmade clubs. Others had bicycle chains which made a vicious weapon when swung at a boy's head. Carlos had a two foot bayonet and Hector had his sawed off shotgun. Some of the boys were to go down two blocks and cut in behind the school ground on Park Avenue to cut

59

off the Bishops' escape. They were to wait until they heard
the fight in progress and then attack from the rear flank.
The rest of us were to come in from the St. Edward Street
side of the school and try to force the Bishops to retreat
where our rear guard would cut them off.

We moved out silently, picking up our weapons from
their hiding places as we went. Tico was beside me grin-
ning. "What about it Nicky, you scared?"

"Man, no! This is what I've been waiting for," I said,
pulling open my jacket so he could see my revolver.

"How many bullets you got in that thing?" he asked.

"It's full, baby. Five of 'em."

"Boy," said Tico, giving a low whistle, "not bad. You
oughta get one of those black bastards tonight for sure.
Me? I'll stick to my blade."

We broke into small groups in order to sneak past the
Housing Police Station on the corner of Auburn and St.
Edward Streets. We reformed in front of the school and
Carlos gave us the attack signal.

We charged around the building into the playground.
The Bishops were waiting for us. "Yeah! Yeah! Kill 'em!
Get 'em" we shouted as we swarmed into the school
ground and ran across the open space that separated the
two gangs.

I broke into the front of the group, pulling my gun out
of my belt. Israel swerved to one side, swinging his base-
ball bat. Kids were milling all around me, screaming and
cursing and slashing out at each other. There must have
been 200 kids in the playground but it was dark and diffi-
cult to tell the gangs apart. I saw Hector running across a
basketball court and someone ran straight into him with a
garbage lid. Hector fell backward, his shotgun going off at
the same time with a loud roar.

A negro boy near him fell forward, blood running from a
wound in his head. I ran by him and kicked at his body.
He felt like a sack of grain.

Suddenly, I was shoved from behind and went sprawl-
ing on the hard asphalt of the basketball court. I put my
hands out to break the fall and felt the skin grind off the
heel of my hand. I turned to see who pushed me and
ducked just as a baseball bat smashed into the pavement
beside my head. I heard the bat splinter as it hit. A direct
blow would have killed me.

A great cry went up from the Mau Maus as the rest of our gang attacked from the rear flank. "Burn 'em, baby, burn 'em!" I stumbled to my feet as the Bishops, now in confusion, started to run toward the alleys that exited on St. Edward. Israel was beside me shouting, "Shoot that one there, Nicky, shoot him."

He was pointing at a small boy who was trying to get away but had been hurt and was half running, half limping as he fell behind the fleeing Bishops. I pointed my gun at the staggering figure and pulled the trigger. The gun went off but he kept running. I grabbed the gun with both hands and pulled the trigger once more.

"You got 'im, man, you got 'im." The small boy was falling forward from the impact of the bullet in his hip. He was still crawling when Israel grabbed my arm and shouted, "Let's blow, baby, here come the cops." We could hear the police whistles and shouts in front of the school as the cops began rounding up the Bishops who were pouring out the alley trying to get away. We ran in the opposite direction, scattering across the back of the school ground. I glanced back as I clambered over a chain link fence. In the dim light, I could see three boys lying still on the ground and several others sitting up holding wounds. The whole battle hadn't lasted longer than ten minutes.

We ran for about six or seven blocks until we were so winded we had to stop. Carlos and two other boys caught up with us and we jumped into a drainage ditch behind a service station.

Israel was out of breath but was laughing so hard he almost gagged. "Did you see that crazy Nicky?" he panted out between laughs. "Man, he thought it was a cowboy movie and he was shooting his gun in the air."

The others were gasping for breath and laughing too. I joined in. We lay on our backs in the ditch laughing until we thought our sides would split. Israel caught his breath and pointing his index fingers up choked out, "Bang! Bang! Bang!" and broke into gales of laughter again. The rest of us held our stomachs and rolled over in the ditch giggling and laughing.

I felt good. I had seen blood run. I had shot someone, maybe killed him. And we had gotten away. I had never sensed this feeling of belonging that I felt in the ditch with those boys. It was almost as if we were a family and for the first time in my life I felt like I was wanted.

Israel reached over and put his arm around my shoulders. "You're alright Nicky. I've been looking for someone like you for a long time. We're the same kind— both of us are nuts."

We broke into laughter again but deep inside I felt it was better to be nuts and be wanted, than to be normal and always on your own.

"Hey, how about something to drink?" Carlos said, still fired up from the excitement. "Who's got the money?"

We were all broke.

I spoke up, "I'll get us some money."

"Whatcha gonna do, rob someone?" Israel asked.

"That's right, baby. Wanna come along?"

Israel punched my arm with his fist, "You're okay Nicky baby. Man, you ain't got no heart, no feelings at all. All you want to do is fight. Let's go, man, we're with you."

I glanced at Carlos who was supposed to be the leader. He was on his feet ready to follow. This was my first indication that the other boys would follow the one who was the meanest, the most bloodthirsty, the most courageous.

We got up from the ditch and ran across the street to the shadows of an alley. On the corner the lights burned in an all night eating joint. I led the way into the store.

There were three people in the luncheonette. Two of them, a man and a woman, were behind the counter. An old man had just gotten up from his stool at the counter and was paying for his meal. I walked up to him and pushed him back against the counter. He turned in surprise and fear, his mouth trembling, as I clicked open the blade of my knife and jabbed it gently into his stomach.

"Com'on, old man. Give it here," I said, motioning with my head toward the bills he had in his hand.

The man behind the counter started toward the pay phone on the wall. Israel flicked open his switchblade and grabbed the man by his upper apron. Pulling him hard across the counter he said, "Hey, man, you wanna die? Huh?" I heard the woman gasp and put her hand over her mouth to muffle a scream. Israel pushed the man backward into the donut case and snatched the phone off the hook. "You wanna call the fuzz, big man?" he sneered. "Okay, here!" he smirked as he ripped the receiver off the wall and tossed it at the man. "Call 'em!" The befuddled man caught it and stood holding it by the dangling cord.

"Hurry up, old man. I can't wait all night," I snarled. He brought his shaking hand up in front of me and I snatched the bills from his fingers. "That all?" I asked. He tried to answer but no sound came from his shaking lips. His eyes began to roll backward in their sockets and saliva drooled from the side of his mouth as he made funny little groans.

"Let's get out of here," one of the other boys said. Carlos hit the key on the cash register and scooped out all the bills as we backed out the door. The old man slumped to the floor, holding his chest with both hands and making funny clucking noises with his mouth.

"Hey, wait," Israel said, as he grabbed a handful of change from the cash register. Nickel's and dimes bounced off the hard floor. Israel was laughing. "Never leave a joint without leaving a tip," he snickered. We all laughed. The man and woman were still huddled at the far end of the counter and the old man was kneeling on the floor, bending over from the waist.

I picked up a heavy sugar container and smashed it through the plate glass window.

"Man, you're crazy," Carlos shouted as we started to run down the street. "That'll bring every cop in Brooklyn. Let's get out of here." The old man fell forward on his face and we ran down the dark street toward home, laughing and shouting.

Two months later Carlos was busted by the police and got 6 months. We had a big gang meeting that night in the auditorium at P.S. 67. Nobody's supposed to go in the school after hours, but we made a deal with Firpo, the Chaplains' vice president, whose old man was the caretaker at the school. He let us use the school auditorium at night for gang meetings because he was afraid of his son. That night we promoted Israel to president and I was the unanimous choice for vice president.

After the gang meeting, we had a gig in the basement of the school. A lot of the debs were there and one of the boys introduced me to his sister, Lydia, who lived across the street from the school. We stayed a long time at the school that night, smoking pot, drinking cheap wine, and sitting on the inside stairwell necking while some of the

others danced to a phonograph. The stairwell was encased
with a heavy iron mesh wire and couples would go up into
the darkness for sex activity.

I pulled Lydia by the hand, "Let's get out of here." As
we walked out the door she snuggled up against me, "I'm
yours forever, Nicky. Anytime you want me, I'm yours."

We walked down to Washington Park but there was no
place we could have any privacy. Finally, I boosted Lydia
over the chain link fence and she fell, laughing, in the
weeds on the other side. I followed her over and we lay in
the tall weeds in each other's arms. She was giggling as I
fondled her but I suddenly had the impression that some-
one was watching us. I glanced up at the building right
across the street and could see the faces of a dozen girls in
the nurses' home as they peered down upon us. It was as
though we were making love on the stage in an opera
house.

I started to get up and Lydia said, "What's wrong?"

"Look up there," I whispered. "The whole damn city is
watching us."

"Who cares?" Lydia giggled and pulled me down.

We returned to the park many times after that, com-
pletely oblivious to the curious faces in the window or to
the other couples who might be lying in the weeds near by.

The next four months were filled with fights, robberies,
and gang activities. I was picked up by the police 4 times
but they never could prove anything against me. Each
time I got off with a warning.

The gang members liked and respected me. I was afraid
of nothing and would just as soon fight in broad daylight
as under the cover of darkness.

One afternoon one of the Mau Maus told me that Lydia
had squealed on me to an Apache. My temper flared and I
said I was going to kill Lydia. I went back to my apart-
ment to get my gun. One of the boys told Lydia's brother
and he ran to warn her. When I got to her apartment, I
talked to Luis, her older brother. He told me one of the
Apaches had caught Lydia on the street the night before
and slapped her around, trying to find out where I lived so
he could come to kill me.

I left the apartment and went to Israel's apartment. We
went looking for the Apache Luis had told us about. We

found him down at the corner of Lafayette and Ft. Greene in front of Harry's Meat House. Six other Mau Maus gathered around in a small circle. I knocked the boy to the ground and hit him with a metal pipe. He was begging me not to kill him. The gang was laughing and I took my time and hit him again and again until he was covered with blood. The bystanders ran as the beating continued. Finally, he could hold his arms up no longer to ward off the blows and I viciously smashed the pipe across his shoulders and kept hitting him until he lay unconscious in a pool of blood.

"You greasy chump! That'll teach you to slap my girl around." We broke and ran. I was anxious to tell Lydia what I had done to defend her honor, even though an hour before I had been ready to kill her.

As the summer wore on the street fights got worse. The heat in the apartments was unbearable and we would stay out on the streets most of the night. Scarcely a night went by without some kind of gang activity.

None of our gang had cars. If we wanted to go someplace, we rode the subway or stole a car. I couldn't drive but one night Mannie Durango came by and said, "Let's steal a car and go for a ride."

"You got one in mind?" I asked.

"Yeah man, right around the block. It's a beaut and some jerk's left the keys in it."

I went with him and there it was, sitting in front of an apartment building. Mannie was right, it was a beaut. It was a Chevrolet convertible with the top down. We jumped in and Mannie got behind the wheel. I slumped down in the seat and smoked a cigarette, flipping the ashes over the door like a sophisticated rich man. Mannie was turning the wheel back and forth and making noises with his mouth like tires squealing and a racing car engine.

"Rrruummmmmm! RruuUUmmmmmm! Rrooowrrrrr!" I began to laugh.

"Hey Mannie, can you really drive this car?"

"Sure, man, just watch this."

He turned the key that was hanging in the ignition and the car roared to life. He pulled the gear into reverse and slammed his foot on the accelerator smashing into a parked delivery truck. We could hear the tinkle of broken glass.

"Hey, man," I laughed, "you real good driver. Boy you really know how to handle this thing. Let's see you go forward."

Mannie slammed the lever into drive and I braced myself as he gunned the car forward into the back of another car. Again, there was a loud crash and we could hear the tinkle of broken glass.

We were both laughing so hard we didn't notice a man running out of the apartment shouting at us.

"Get the hell out of my car you dirty Spics," he shouted, trying to pull me out of the seat. Mannie threw the car in reverse and knocked the man off balance dragging him backward. I picked up a coke bottle off the front seat and smashed it across his hand as he clung desperately to the door. He screamed out in pain. Mannie threw the car in forward and we hurtled out into the street. I was still slouched in the seat laughing. I tossed the coke bottle on the sidewalk and heard it break as we sped away.

Mannie couldn't drive. He squealed around the corner and headed up the wrong side of Park Avenue. We narrowly missed two cars and another car pulled up on the sidewalk, horn blowing, trying to miss a head on collison. Both of us were laughing and hollering. Mannie ran through a service station and turned down a side street.

"Let's burn this car," Mannie said.

"No man! This is a beautiful car. Let's keep it. Com'on, let's show it off to the girls."

But Mannie couldn't turn it around and finally smashed it into the back of a truck at a stop light. We jumped out and ran down the sidewalk leaving the badly dented car crumpled under the back of the truck.

Mannie was my kind of guy. Little did I know what horror lay in store for him.

Each day was full of frenzied criminal activity. The nights were even worse. One night Tony and four other guys grabbed a woman on her way home and dragged her into the park where all five of them went with her twice. Tony tried to choke her to death with his belt. She later identified him and he was sent to prison for 12 years.

Two weeks later, sixteen of us caught an Italian boy walking through Mau Mau turf. We surrounded him and knocked him to the ground. I stood over him teasing him with my knife, flicking at his adam's apple and poking at the buttons on his shirt. Cursing me, he slapped the knife out of my hand and before I could move Tico grabbed it and slashed him across the face. The boy screamed as Tico ripped his shirt off and slashed a huge "M" on his back. "Man, that'll teach you not to come into Mau Mau turf," he said. We ran, leaving him bleeding on the sidewalk.

Every day the newspapers carried stories of killings in the front yards, on the subways, in the back streets, in the halls of the apartment buildings, in the alleys. Every night there was a rumble.

The school officials at Brooklyn Tech put heavy gauge wire screens over all the doors and windows at the school. Every window, even those 5 stories above the street, were covered with wire mesh.

Many of the shop owners were buying police dogs and chaining them inside their stores at night.

The gangs were becoming more organized and new gangs were being formed. Three new gangs sprung up in our area. The Scorpions, the Viceroys, and the Quentos.

We soon found out that New York City law prohibited a policeman from searching a girl. Therefore, we let the girls carry our guns and knives until we needed them. If a cop stopped to search us, the girls would stand back and shout, "Hey, you dirty cop. Leave him alone. He have nothing. He clean. Why not come squeeze me and then I have you put in your own jail. Hey, cop, you wanna put your hands on me? Com'on."

We learned how to make zip guns that would fire a .22 caliber bullet by using a car radio antenna and the workings from a door latch. Occasionally, these guns would explode in a boy's hand or backfire and blind him. But we were turning them out in great quantity and selling them to other gang members—knowing they would use them against us if they ever had a chance.

On July 4th that summer, all the gangs got together at Coney Island. The newspapers estimated that more than 8,000 teenage gang members barged into Coney Island. None of them paid. They just pushed past the gate and no one dared say anything. The same was true with riding the subways.

The first of August, Israel was picked up by the police. When he got out of jail, he told us things were real hot for

him and he wanted to take a back seat until things cooled
off. We agreed and the gang elected me president and told
Israel he would serve as vice president until the heat was
off. I had been in the gang six months when I took over.

It didn't take me long to realize that the Mau Maus
were highly feared and that I had gained quite a reputa-
tion as a bloodthirsty hood. I gloried in the recognition.

One night we all went to a big dance that was sponsored
by the St. Edward-St. Michael church center. The church
was making an attempt to get the kids off the streets and
had opened a canteen down the street from the police sta-
tion for weekend dances. Every Friday night they would
have a big band and all the gang members would come to
the center to dance. They stood around outside and drank
beer and cheap wine. The week before we had gotten
drunk and when the priests tried to get us to quiet down,
we beat them up and spit on them. The police had come
and chased us all away. Seldom a Friday night went by
that the canteen dance didn't turn into a riot.

On this particular night, I went with Mannie and Paco.
We were all drinking heavily and smoking marijuana. I
spotted a cute blond girl and danced several times with
her. She told me her brother was in trouble with the Phan-
tom Lords. They were going to kill him.

"Where's your brother?" I asked. "Nobody gonna hurt
him if I say not. Let me talk to him."

She took me to one side of the room and introduced me
to her brother. He told me that the Phantom Lords over on
Bedford Avenue wanted to kill him for dating one of their
debs. The boy was staggering drunk and scared.

"I tell you what," I said. "Your sister's nice chick. I think
I'd like to take her out some. And since I like her, I'll take
care of you too."

I had already made a date with the girl to take her to
the movies. I told her that she would have to do anything
I wanted her to since I was the President of the Mau
Maus. She was scared and said she would go with me but
she didn't want any of the other guys to handle her. We
kissed and I told her that as long as she went with me I'd
take care of her.

We looked up just as three Phantom Lords came
through the door. They were dressed in loud coats and

checkered pants with long key chains. One of the boys, swinging his key chain, sauntered over and winked at the blond. She backed off and I put my arm around her. "Hey baby," he sneered, "how about going out with me? My brother's got a car outside and we can have the back seat all to ourselves."

"You wanna get killed," I snarled.

"Big man," the Phantom Lord laughed, "we already making plans to kill your drunk friend and we might just kill you too, you punk."

Mannie gave the boy a Bronx cheer—a razz. The boy jerked his head around. "Who did that?"

Mannie began to laugh but I sensed trouble and said, "Nobody." I started to back away, but the boy swung at Mannie and knocked him down. Besides Israel, Mannie was my closest friend. No one was going to hit him and get away with it. I swung and hit the boy a vicious blow in the back, just over his kidneys. He grasped his back with both hands and screamed in agony.

Mannie scrambled to his feet and drew his knife. I fumbled for mine as the other boys in the room formed a semicircle and moved toward us. There were too many for us to fight and we backed toward the door. When we got to the stairs, a big boy lunged at me with his knife. He missed but the knife sliced through my jacket. As he stumbled past I hit him in the back of the head and kicked him down the concrete steps. Two others jumped at me. Mannie pulled my coat and we started to run. "Let's go," I shouted. "I'm going after the Mau Maus and we're gonna burn this place."

The boys glanced at each other. They didn't know I was a Mau Mau since I was dressed in a suit and tie that night. They began to back into the room and Mannie and I turned and left.

The next day I called Mannie and Paco. We were going after Santo, the Phantom Lord who had threatened the blond's brother. Mannie and I had been drinking and were almost drunk. We walked to the Candy Store on 3rd Street and I spotted some Phantom Lords. "Which one of you guys is Santo?" I asked. One of the boys glanced in the direction of a tall kinky headed guy. I said, "Hey baby, what's your name? Santo Claus?"

Mannie laughed and the boy looked up and called me a S.O.B.

"Hey, baby," I said, "you just goofed. You know who the Mau Maus are?"

"Yeah, I've heard of 'em. They know better than to hang around here, though."

"Today they hang around, baby. These are the Mau Maus. My name is Nicky. I'm their president. You're always gonna remember that name baby."

The owner of the store reached for the telephone. I put my hand in my pocket and pressed my finger against the lining like I had a gun hidden inside. "You!" I shouted "Put that down!"

The others were scared and backed off. I walked up to Santo and slapped him twice in the face. I still had my other hand in my pocket. "Maybe you remember me now, baby."

He flinched and I hit him in the stomach. "Com'on," I said to Paco. "Let's get out of here. These kids are scared." We turned and started out and I spat over my shoulder. "Next time tell your mommy to put your diaper on before she lets you out. You're still a baby." We laughed at each other and walked out.

When we got on the street, Mannie put his hand in his jacket pocket and pointed his finger through the cloth. "Bang! Bang! You're dead!" he said. We laughed and sauntered down the street.

That night Israel came by and said the Phantom Lords were getting ready for a big rumble because of the fight at the Candy Store.

Israel and I stopped by for Mannie and headed into Phantom Lord turf to surprise them ahead of time. When we got near the Brooklyn Bridge, we split up. Israel and Mannie went around the block and I walked straight down the street. Moments later, I heard Israel yell and I went dashing around the building. They had surprised one of the Phantom Lords by himself and had him on the sidewalk begging for mercy.

"Take his pants off," I commanded. The boys unbuckled his belt and pulled off his pants. They threw them in the gutter and then ripped his shorts off.

"On your feet, freak, and start running." We watched

him as he ran terrified down the street. We were laughing and calling him names.

"Com'on," said Israel, "none of them bums are around here. Let's go back home." We started back when suddenly we were surrounded by a gang of twelve or fifteen Phantom Lords. It was an ambush. I recognized some members of a Jewish gang with them. A guy came at me with a knife and I hit him with a pipe. Another slashed at me and I spun and hit him in the side of the head with the pipe.

Then I felt an explosion in the back of my head and I was on the sidewalk. My head felt like it was going to roll off. I tried to look up but someone kicked me in the face with a shoe that had cleats on it. Someone else kicked me in the small of the back. I tried to get up and was slugged above the eye with a pipe. I knew they would kill me if I couldn't get away but I couldn't get up. I fell back on the sidewalk on my stomach and felt the boy with the cleats jump on the back of my legs and then stomp on my hips. His cleats were razor sharp. I could feel the sharp steel ripping through my thin trousers and gouging out the flesh on my hips and buttocks. I fainted from the pain.

The next thing I remember was Israel and Mannie dragging me along a back alley. I knew I was hurt bad because I couldn't use my legs. "Com'on. Hurry up," they kept saying. "Those bastards will be back any minute. We gotta get away."

I passed out from the pain again and when I awoke, I was on the floor in my apartment. They had dragged me all the way home and up the three flights of steps to my room. They helped me crawl into bed and I passed out again. The hot sun was streaming through my window when I awoke and crawled out of bed. I was so stiff I could hardly move. The lower part of my body was covered with dried blood. I tried to take my pants off but the cloth stuck to my skin and I felt I was tearing the skin off. I staggered down a flight of steps to the public bath and stood under the shower with my clothes on until the blood softened and I could peel them off. My back and hips were a mass of deep cuts and horrible bruises. I staggered back up the steps naked, remembering the boy running down the street with his pants off.

Boy, I thought, if he could see me now.

I crept into my room and spent the rest of the day nursing my cuts. Being President of the Mau Maus was okay but at times it could be murder. This time it almost was.

6

Hell Burners

That fall my brother Louis, who lived in the Bronx, came to my apartment to plead with me to come live with him. He had read about my trouble with the police in the New York papers. "Nicky, you're playing with life and it's a dangerous game. You're going to get killed." He said he and his wife had talked it over and they wanted me to come to their apartment. I just laughed at him.

"How come you want me come live with you?" I asked. "Nobody else wants me, how come you decided you want me."

"That's not so, Nicky," Louis answered. "We all want you. Frank, Gene, all of us want you. But you've got to be willing to settle down."

"Listen," I said, "nobody wants me. You're just a fake. Not you, not Frank, not Gene, not Papa or Mama. . . ."

"Now hold on," Louis interrupted, "Papa and Mama they love you."

"Yeah? Then how come they sent me away from home? How you answer that smart boy?"

"They sent you away because they couldn't handle you. You're like a wild man . . . like you're running from something all the time."

"Yeah? Well maybe I'm running from you punks. Listen, you know how many times Papa ever sat down and talked to me? Once. Only one time did he ever sit down and talk to me. And then he told me a story about a stupid bird. Once! That's all. Man, don't tell me he love me. He didn't have time for no one but himself."

Louis got up and paced the floor. "Nicky, can't you listen to reason?"

"Why should I go to your place? You'd make me go

back to school just like Frank. Here I've got it made. I've
got 200 boys who do what I tell them and 75 girls who go
with me anytime I ask them. They give me all the money I
need. They help pay my rent. Even the police are scared
of me. Why should I come home with you? The gang's my
family. That's all I need."

Louis sat on the side of the bed long into the night try-
ing to tell me that one day all this would change. He said
that if I didn't get killed or put in prison, one day I was
going to have to get a job and would need an education. I
told him to forget it. I had a good thing going and wasn't
about to back out.

Alone in my room the next afternoon the fear, which I
had so expertly hidden swallowed me up. I lay back on the
bed and drank wine until I was so drugged and dizzy I
couldn't sit up. That night I slept in my clothes but I was
not prepared for what I experienced. Nightmares! Horri-
ble, blood curdling nightmares! I dreamed of Papa. I
dreamed he was chained in a cave. He had teeth like a
wolf and his body was covered with mangy hair. He was
barking pitifully and I wanted to get close to him and pat
him but was afraid he would snap at me.

Then there were the birds. Louis' face kept coming and
going in front of me as he rode off on the back of a bird,
soaring free into the heavens. Then I would be engulfed
by millions of swirling birds, ripping at my flesh and pick-
ing at my eyes. Every time I'd break free from them I'd see
Louis flying like a speck in the sky on the back of a bird,
winging his way to some unknown freedom.

I woke up screaming, "I'm not afraid. I'm not afraid."
But when I dozed back to sleep I'd see Papa chained in
the blackness and the birds would swarm in and attack me.

The effect continued. For more than 2 years I was afraid
to go to sleep. Every time I would doze off the horrible
dreams would reappear. I remembered Papa and wished
he would come to New York and cast the demons out of
me. I was possessed with guilt and fear, and at night
would lie in my bed fighting sleep and saying over and
over, "No good. No good. No way out. No way out." Only
the gang activity kept me from going completely insane.

The Mau Maus had become a part of my life. Even
though we were strong enough to stand alone, occasionally,

we would form an alliance with another gang. In the winter of 1955 the Hell Burners, from Williamsburg, approached us to form an alliance.

It was almost dark and several of us had gathered in the playground at P.S. 67 to discuss an upcoming rumble with the Bishops. I looked up and saw three boys appear out of the shadows and walk toward us. Immediately we were on guard. One of the Mau Maus slipped into the shadows and started around the three who were almost to us.

I shouted out, "Hey, what you guys want?"

One of them spoke up. "We're looking for Nicky, leader of the Mau Maus."

I knew this could be a trick. "Yeah, what you want with Nicky?"

"Man, listen, this ain't no trick. We're in trouble and we need to talk to Nicky."

I was still suspicious. "What kind of trouble?" I asked.

"My name's Willie the Butch," the boy said, close enough now that I could see him. "I'm leader of the Hell Burners. We need help."

I was pretty sure of him now. "What kind of help?"

"You hear what the Phantom Lords did to Ike?" He gestured with his head at the boy on his right.

I had heard. It had been in all the papers. Ike was 14 years old and lived on Keap Street. He had been playing with two other kids when a gang of Phantom Lords attacked them. The other kids got away, but they pinned Ike against a fence. When he tried to fight back, they overpowered him and dragged him into a basement across the street. There, according to the newspaper account, they tied his hands together in front of him and slapped and kicked him until he was unconscious. Then they poured lighter fluid over his hands and set him afire. He staggered out on the street where he collapsed and was found by a passing patrol car.

I took a quick look at the boy Willie the Butch introduced as Ike. His hands and arms were in bandages and his face was badly bruised.

Willie continued, "You're the only guys who can help us. We want to be brother clubs. Everyone's afraid of the Mau Maus, and we need your help to rumble against the Phantom Lords. If we don't avenge Ike, we'll be chicken."

The other gangs knew of my reputation and the reputation of the Mau Mau gang. This wasn't the first time some-one had come to us for help. And we were glad to give it because it gave us an excuse to fight.

"What if I don't help you?"

"Then we'll lose our turf to the Phantom Lords. Last night they came into our turf and burned our candy store."

"They burned your candy store? Well, baby, I'm gonna burn them. All of 'em. Tomorrow night I'll be in Hell Burner turf and we'll make plans on killing those dudes."

The next night I left my apartment after dark and walked into Williamsburg. On the way, I picked up ten members of my gang. As we walked into their turf we could sense the tension in the air. The Hell Burners were scared and had taken to the roof tops. Suddenly we were bombarded with stones and bottles. Fortunately, their aim was bad and we quickly ducked into the door of an apart-ment building to escape the barrage of rocks and glass hur-tling down from the upper levels.

I told the other boys to stay put and I went up through the apartments to the top floor. There I found a ladder leading to the ceiling with a trap door to the roof.

Easing the door open, I could see the boys on the front side of the roof leaning over the edge looking toward the street below. I quietly slipped through the trap door and hid behind an air ventilator pipe.

Sneaking up behind two of them I tapped them on the shoulder. "Aughhhhhhhh!" they screamed. Both of them almost fell off the roof. They looked back at me with eyes wide, hands gripping the side of the parapet and mouths pen in fear.

"W-w-w-whoooooo you?" they stuttered.

I couldn't help but grin. "Hey, baby, I'm Nicky. Who you? An owl or something?"

"W-w-w-hoooo Nicky?" one of them stammered out.

"Come on, baby, I'm the leader of the Mau Maus. We've come to help you guys unless you kill us first. Where's your leader? Where's Willie the Butch?"

Willie was on another roof. They took me to him. About 15 of the Hell Burners crowded around as the rest of the Mau Maus came up and joined us.

Willie told me how they were trying to ward off the in-vasion of the Phantom Lords, but so far had been unsuc-cessful. Everything was quiet tonight, but they never knew when the gang would appear in the street and rip them to pieces. The police knew there was a gang war going on but there wasn't anything they could do to stop it.

Willie had a revolver in his hand, but from what I could understand, none of the other boys had guns.

I listened and then began to map the strategy for the rumble. The gang grew quiet as I talked. "The reason you're losing is you're on the defensive. You're letting them come here and you're having to defend your own turf. Man, the way to rumble is to go to them."

I paused for effect, then continued. "And no guns."

There was a stir in the crowd. "No guns? How can you handle a rumble without guns?"

"We'll use silent weapons." I reached into my coat and pulled out a 2-foot bayonet, complete with scabbard. I slipped it out of the scabbard and slashed it through the air. I could hear low whistles from the crowd of boys standing around.

I had won their respect and approval. They were listening to me now, anxious to see how I was going to lead them.

I turned back to Willie. "I want five of your toughest boys. We'll take five of ours. And tomorrow night we'll go into Phantom Lord territory and talk to their leaders. They don't want the Mau Maus after them. I'll tell them we're brother clubs and if they don't let you alone, they'll have to fight us, too. If they disagree, we'll burn their candy store just to let them know we mean business. Whataya say."

"Yea, yea, baby," the gang began to clamor. "Let's burn those bastards. Let's rip 'em good. Yeah, let's show 'em baby."

The next afternoon I came with five of our boys and we met at the candy store on White Street in Hell Burner territory. The store had been fixed up since the gang fight several nights before. Five of the Hell Burners, including Willie the Butch, met us there. I talked to the manager and told him we were sorry the Phantom Lords had torn up his store and we were going to make sure it never happened again. Then I asked him to hold my bayonet until we returned.

It was about 5 p.m. and a light rain was falling in the cool twilight. We left the store and walked across town to-

ward 3rd Street into Phantom Lord turf. There were 5 of
them in the candy store. They saw us coming but couldn't
escape because we had the door blocked.

We were all standing with our hands in our coat pockets
like we had guns. I walked up to the boys who were now
on their feet standing behind their table. Cursing, I asked,
"Where's your leader?"

A mean looking kid with dark glasses spoke up, "Fred-
dy's our leader."

"Which one of you is Freddy?"

A boy about 18 with rough complexion and kinky black
hair stepped out and said, "I'm Freddy, who the hell are
you?"

I still had my hands in my pockets, with the collar of the
raincoat pulled up around the back of my neck. "I'm
Nicky, President of the Mau Maus. You heard of the Mau
Maus? This is Willie the Butch, leader of the Hell Burners.
We're brother clubs now. We want to call off the fighting."

"Okay, man," said Freddy. "Come on over here and let's
talk about it."

We stepped to one side to talk but one of the Phantom
Lords cursed Willie. Before I could move, Willie pulled his
hand out of his pocket and flicked open a switchblade. In-
stead of backing off, the boy jabbed his umbrella toward
Willie. The metal tip, filed to a needle sharp point, slashed
through his raincoat grazing his ribs. Immediately, one of
the Hell Burners grabbed a heavy sugar container off the
counter and threw it at the boy with the umbrella, hitting
him on the shoulder and knocking him down.

Freddy began to shout, "Hey! Cool it!" But no one
heard him, as the boys surged toward each other. Freddy
turned to me, "Make 'em stop."

"Man, you make 'em stop. Your boys started it."

Just then someone hit me in the back of the head. I
heard broken glass tinkle as a bottle smashed against a
mirror behind the counter.

Outside a squad car screeched to a stop in the middle of
the street, red lights blinking. Two uniformed policemen
leaped out, leaving the doors of the car wide open as they
ran toward the candy store with billy clubs in their hands.

The other boys had seen them at the same time. As if by
a given signal, we all poured out the door and scattered
between the cars. A policeman was right behind me but I

turned over a big garbage can in the middle of the sidewalk, slowing him up enough to get away down an alley.

But the stage was set for an all out rumble.

The next night more than 100 Mau Maus gathered at the candy store in Hell Burner turf. Willie the Butch was there with more than 50 of his boys and we marched together down the middle of the street toward the candy store in Phantom Lord turf.

Charlie Cortez, one of the Mau Maus, had been high on heroin for the last week and tonight was in a mood for fighting. When we got to the candy store, he snatched the door open and grabbed one of the Phantom Lords who tried to break and run. He slashed at him with his knife but missed and shoved him backward toward me.

I was laughing. This was my kind of odds—about 150 to 15. I swung at the stumbling boy with a heavy lead pipe with a huge joint on one end. He screamed in pain as the pipe smashed across his shoulder. As he crumpled to the sidewalk, I hit him again, this time on the back of the head. He dropped heavily on the concrete as the blood seeped through a deep gash.

"Come on," someone screamed, "let's burn this whole turf." The boys scattered. Some of them headed into the candy store and the others surged into a pool hall next door. I got caught in the wave and was carried into the candy store. I still had my pipe in my hand and was swinging out at everything. The windows had already been broken and I could see the manager of the store huddling underneath the counter trying to protect himself. The boys had gone wild. They were tearing up everything. Someone turned over the juke box and I was on top of it with my pipe, smashing it to pieces. Others were behind the counter ripping the cabinets off the walls, breaking glasses and dishes. Someone cleaned out the cash register and then two of the boys heaved it through the broken plate glass window.

I ran into the street, my face covered with blood from a piece of flying glass. I was running up and down the street smashing my pipe against car windshields.

About fifty boys were inside the pool hall. They had turned over all the pool tables and broken the cue sticks.

Now they were back out on the street throwing pool balls at all the shops across the street.

A gang of boys had stopped a car in the middle of the street and were climbing all over it, jumping up and down on the hood and the roof until it was bent beyond shape. Everyone was laughing and shouting and destroying.

Sirens wailed as police cars converged from both ends of the street. Ordinarily, this would act as a signal for the boys to break and run. But the riot fever had taken control and we no longer cared.

A squad car worked its way to the middle of the block but the patrolmen were unable to get their doors open as the boys surged around the car, pummeling it with broken bottles, bricks and clubs as they smashed out the headlights and shattered the windows. The policemen, trapped inside, tried to call out on their radio for help, but we clambered onto the top of the car and snatched the antenna off. One of the boys kicked at the siren until it came loose and fell in the street.

More police cars screeched to a halt at the end of the block. It was bedlam. More than 150 boys were fighting, shouting, overturning cars, breaking glass. Policemen waded into the seething, screaming mob slashing out with their billy clubs. I saw Charlie struggling with two cops in the center of the street. I ran to help him but heard gunfire and knew it was time to beat it.

We scattered in all directions. Some of the boys ran down the streets and through the alleys. Others took off into the apartments, up the steps and onto the roof tops. In a matter of minutes the mob scene had cleared and there was nothing left but a block full of destruction. Not a car had gone undamaged. The candy store was completely demolished. So was the pool hall. All the windows had been broken in the bar across the street and most of the whiskey stolen out of the showcase. Someone had opened a car door, slashed the seats and then set the stuffing on fire. The police were trying to put out the fire but the car was still burning as we left.

Everyone escaped except Charlie Cortez and three Hell Burners. Gang law stated that if you were caught you had to bear the rap yourself. If you began to "sing" or "rat out" you would be punished by the gang. Or, if you were in prison, they would punish your family. Charlie was sentenced to three years and the others received sentences also.

But the Phantom Lords never came back into Hell Burner territory again.

7

Lucifer's Child

As the 2nd summer approached it seemed the entire ghetto was aflame with hate and violence. The gangs had retrenched during the winter and emerged in the spring with strongly organized forces. All that winter we had been making zip guns, stealing firearms, and storing up munitions. I had gained a reputation as the most feared gang leader in Brooklyn. I had been arrested 18 times and once that winter had spent 30 days in jail awaiting trial. But they never could make the charges stick.

As warm weather came we began to act like crazy wild people. The Dragons had been having a running battle with the Viceroys. The 1st of May, Mingo, President of the Chaplains, walked into a candy store carrying a sawed-off shotgun in his arm.

"Hey, baby," he said, pointing the shotgun across his arm at a boy sitting in a booth, "you Sawgrass?"

"Yeah man, that's me. What you gonna do about it?"

Mingo didn't answer. He just pulled the shotgun up into position and pointed it at his head. "Hey, fella," Sawgrass grinned weakly getting to his feet and backing up. "Don't point that thing at me. It might go off."

Mingo was high on heroin and just looked at him blankly as he pulled the trigger. The blast struck him just above the nose and blew the top of his head off. The rest of his body fell twitching on the floor. Blood, bone and pellets were smashed against the far side of the wall.

Mingo turned and walked out of the candy store. When the police caught up with him, he was walking down the street, the shotgun dangling from a limp hand. They shouted at him to stop. Instead, he turned and pointed the shotgun at the cops. They opened fire on him and he fell to the street riddled with bullets.

But inside everyone of us was a Mingo. It was as though the whole city were crazy.

That summer we declared war on the police. We wrote a letter to the cops at 88th Precinct and to the Housing Police. We told them we were declaring war on them and from that time on any cop who came into our turf would be killed as the enemy.

The police doubled their patrols, and often three men would walk the beat together. This didn't slow us down. We would gather on the roof tops and throw bricks, bottles, and garbage cans at them. When they stepped out to see who was throwing things, we would open fire. Our aim was very bad and our homemade zip guns were very inaccurate except in close fighting. Our fondest dream was to kill a cop.

One of our favorite tricks was to throw the gasoline bomb. We'd steal the gas from parked cars at night and store it in soda and wine bottles. We'd make a wick with a rag, light it and burst it on the side of a building or on a police car. It would explode in a mass of flames.

Sometimes this backfired. One afternoon Dan Brunson, a mamber of our gang, lit a gasoline bomb to throw at the police station. The wick burned too fast and the bomb exploded in his face. Before anyone could get to him he was covered with flaming gasoline. The cops rushed out and beat out the flames with their hands. One of them was badly burned while smothering the fire. They rushed Dan to the hospital but the doctors said it would be years before he could ever be normal again.

We eased off on our fighting the following week, but soon it resumed even more furiously.

Holidays were favorite times for the gangs to rumble. Easter, Memorial Day, and July 4th most of the 285 gangs in the city would assemble at Coney Island. Everyone wore his best clothes and tried to show off, which resulted in vicious and often fatal fights. That July 4th the Bishops killed Larry Stein, one of our guys. He was only 13 years old and five of them beat him to death with bicycle chains and then buried his body in the sand under the boardwalk. He wasn't found for almost a week.

When we got the news nearly 200 of us met in the basement of the school for a revenge meeting. The room was charged with hatred. Half the guys were drunk and wanted to go out that night and burn the Bishops' apartment houses and set fire to the Bedford Avenue section of Brooklyn. However, I was able to maintain order and we agreed to attend Larry's funeral the next afternoon and then meet again tomorrow night to make plans for a rumble.

The next afternoon we gathered at the cemetery for the burial. Two cars pulled up and a small group of mourners got out. I recognized Larry's mother and father and his 4 brothers. The Mau Maus had been hanging back in the cemetery and when the funeral party arrived we all moved forward—more than 200 boys and girls, most of us wearing our black jackets with the red double M on the back.

I stepped out to speak to Mrs. Stein. She saw me coming and began to scream. "Get them out of here! Get them out of here! Monsters. Witches." She turned and started to stagger back to the car but fainted and fell to the grass. Her husband knelt over her and the little brothers stood in stark horror looking at our gang as it moved out of the tombs to stand around the grave.

Mr. Stein looked up at me and cursed, "You're responsible for this. If it weren't for you and your filthy gang Larry would be alive today." He started toward me with hatred spitting from his eyes, but the funeral director grabbed him and pulled him back.

"Please wait on the other side of the grave," the funeral director said to me. "Give us a chance, won't you?"

I obliged and we dropped back beyond the grave while they revived Mrs. Stein and proceeded with the service.

That night we had our second meeting. This time nothing was going to stop us. We'd learned that afternoon that the GGI's had killed one of the Bishops and they were to have the funeral the next day. The boys wanted to bust up the funeral by throwing firebombs from the buildings. The intense gang loyalty in avenging this fallen gang member was astounding. They were seething with hatred and finally could not contain it any longer. It was Mannie who shouted that he was heading to the funeral parlor where the Bishop's body was awaiting burial. "Let's go burn that creepy place," he shouted. "If we wait until tomorrow it'll be too late. Let's go now."

"Yeah, yeah, yeah, let's go," they shouted in chorus. More than fifteen of them converged on the little negro funeral parlor, overturned caskets and slashed the curtains with their knives.

The service was held the next day under heavy police guard, but we felt avenged.

The rumbles in the streets were exceeded only by the nightmare of violence that seethed in my own heart. I was an animal, without conscience, morals, reason, or any sense of right and wrong. The gang supported me from their nightly robberies and Frank helped me some. But I preferred to make it on my own.

In the Spring of 1957 Frank came by and said that Mama and Papa were coming for a visit from Puerto Rico. He wanted me to come to his apartment the next night to see them. I refused. I had no need of them. They had rejected me and now I wanted nothing to do with them.

The next evening Frank brought Papa to my room. He said Mama refused to come since I did not want to see her.

Papa stood at the door a long time and looked at me as I sat on the side of my bed.

"Frank has told me about you," he said, his voice rising as he spoke until he was almost shouting when he finished. "He says you're a gang leader and the police are after you. This true?"

I didn't answer him but turned to Frank, who was standing beside him and snarled, "What the hell you been telling him? I told you I didn't want to see none of them."

"I told him the truth, Nicky," Frank said calmly, "maybe it's about time you faced the truth yourself."

"He has a demon," Papa said, staring at me without blinking his eyes. "He is possessed. I must release him."

I looked at Papa and laughed nervously. "Last year I thought I had a demon. But even the demons are afraid of me now."

Papa walked across the room and placed a heavy hand on my shoulder. He pushed me down until I had to kneel on the floor. He towered above me, his huge hands binding me like chains.

"I sense five evil spirits in him," Papa said. He motioned Frank to grab hold of my arms and hold them over my head. I struggled to get loose but they were too strong for me. "Five demons!" Papa chanted, "this is why he is delinquent! Today we shall cure him."

Clasping his hands on top of my head he exerted great pressure as he pressed down and twisted his hands, like he was trying to screw the top off a jar.

"Out! Out!" he screamed, "I command you to leave." Papa was speaking to the demon in my mind.

Then he took both hands and slapped me hard on the sides of the head, slapping my ears again and again. I could hear him screaming for the demons to come out of my ears.

Frank was holding my arms above my head as Papa put both his huge hands around my throat and began to choke me. "There's a demon in his tongue. Out demon, out." Then he shouted, "There it is. I see it coming out."

"His heart is black, too," he said, and hit me in the chest with his fist several times until I thought my ribs would cave in.

Finally, he grabbed my hips and pulled me to my feet, slapping his hand over my groin and commanding the evil spirits to leave my loins.

He released me and Frank backed away saying, "He has done you a great favor, Nicky. You've been very evil but he has made you clean."

Papa was standing in the middle of the room shaking like a leaf. I cursed and stormed out the door and ran down the stairs to the street. Two hours later I found a sailor sleeping off a drunk on a bench in Washington Park. I rolled him and took his wallet. If Papa had cast any demons out of me, it didn't take them very long to get back in. I was still Lucifer's child.

The nightmares grew worse. Papa's appearance seemed to intensify my fear of the future. Night after night I lay in my bed screaming as I awoke from one recurring nightmare after another. I redoubled my frenzied fighting trying to cover up the consuming fear within.

That summer our fights with the police became even more intense. Every night we were on the roof tops waiting for the cops to come by below. We would drop sand bags, throw bottles and rocks—but we needed guns, rifles in particular. And these cost money.

I had an idea for an easy setup for a robbery. I had noticed that every Saturday at 3 a.m. a man drove up to one of the apartments in a big black Cadillac. The guys watched him a lot and we had a lot of jokes about him. We knew he was from Jersey and that he always waited until Mario Silvario left for work. We figured he was sleeping with Mario's wife.

One night some of the guys dared Albert and me to spy on them. So we climbed out on the fire escape and watched him go to bed with Mrs. Silvario.

Every Saturday at 3 a.m. it was the same thing. He'd park his Cadillac, lock the doors and go up the stairs to Mario's apartment.

I told Mannie what an easy job I thought it would be and he agreed. We asked Willie the Butch to bring his revolver and meet us at 2 a.m.

When we got to the apartment, Willie was already there checking his revolver. He had taken all the bullets out and set them up in a line on the steps. Seeing us walk up he reloaded and stuck it in his belt.

Our plan was for Willie and Mannie to wait behind the building. When the man got out of his car, I was going to walk up to him and ask him a question. Then Willie and Mannie would come out and Willie would hold the gun on him while we searched him and took his money.

The clock on the big building in Flatbush at the corner of Houston chimed 3 a.m. and Willie wanted to check the gun again. This time he went back behind the building and came back in a few minutes whispering it was all set.

About 3:15 a.m. the Cadillac turned the corner and stopped in front of the building. Willie and Mannie crouched in the shadows and I pulled my raincoat around me and walked out onto the sidewalk. The man got out of his car. He was a big fellow, about 40 years old with an expensive coat and hat. He carefully locked his car and started toward the building. The streets were empty. Only the cars on the nearby thoroughfare broke the silence.

He saw me coming and stepped up his pace. "Hey, sir," I said, "I'm lost. Could you tell me the way to Lafayette Avenue?"

The man drew back and looked in all directions. "Beat it, kid," he said, "I don't want any trouble."

"Hey, man, all I want to know is the way to Lafayette

Avenue." I grinned and put my hand in my raincoat pocket like I had a gun pointing at him.

"Help! Robbers!!" he screamed backing off toward his car.

I pushed myself up against him, "Shut up, or I'll kill you."

He gasped and looked at me in disbelief. Then he started to shout, "Somebody help me! Help!"

Just then Willie threw his arm around the man's neck from behind and jabbed the barrel of the gun into the side of his face. "Make another sound and I'll kill you," Willie hissed.

The man stood frozen as Mannie and I began to frisk him.

In his coat pocket I found the biggest roll of bills I'd ever seen. They were rolled together with a rubber band around them. I guess he was taking it to Mario's wife.

"Hey, look, Willie. How about this? This guy's rich. Man, look at all this money."

I backed off laughing. We'd struck it rich. I was bebopping in the street and began to make fun of him. "Hey, man, if I let you sleep with my old lady will you give me some money every week?"

Mannie got in on the act and started to unbuckle the man's belt. "How about it, man? You won't mind if we take your pants off so all the ladies can see how handsome you are?"

The man clenched his teeth and started to moan. "Hey, man, we're doing you a favor," Mannie said. "Come on, let's get these pants down like a good little boy."

He pulled the buckle loose and the man started to scream again, "Help! Hel. . . ."

But I jumped forward and slapped my hand over his mouth. He viciously sunk his teeth into the heel of my palm. I jerked back shouting, "Shoot 'im, Willie! Burn 'em! He bit me."

Willie stepped back and with both hands pointed the revolver at the man's back and pulled the trigger. I heard the pin snap forward but nothing happened.

I hit the man as hard as I could in the stomach with my good hand. He bent forward and I hit him on the side of the head with my other hand but it hurt so badly I thought

I was going to faint. I moved to one side circling him, "Shoot 'im, Willie. Let 'im have it."

Willie pulled the trigger again. Stilll nothing happened. He kept trying but it wouldn't go off.

I grabbed the gun from Willie and hit the man in the face. There was a crunching sound of metal against bone. The flesh opened up and I glimpsed the stark white of his cheekbone, framed by scarlet red. He was trying to scream when I hit him again, on top of the head. He crumpled into the gutter, one hand dangling into the open drain along the curb.

We didn't wait. Lights were coming on in the apartment windows and we could hear somebody shouting. We ran down the street and cut into an alley that led behind the school. I was pulling my raincoat off as I ran and stuffed it into a garbage can.

We separated at the next street. I ran back to my street and up the stairs to my room. Once inside, I locked the door and stood in the darkness panting and laughing. This was the life.

I turned on the light and looked at my hand. I could see the man's teeth marks in the heel of my palm. I washed it out with some wine and wrapped my handkerchief around it.

I turned off the light and flopped on my bed. The police sirens wailed in the distance and I laughed to myself. "What a bundle," I thought as I felt in my pocket for the roll of bills.

God! It wasn't there! I jumped to my feet frantically searching all my pockets. Suddenly, it hit me. I had stuck it in my raincoat pocket when the fight began. Oh, no! I had stuffed the raincoat in the trash can. And the gun! Willie's gun was gone too. I must have dropped it after I'd hit the man.

I couldn't go back down there now. The place would be crawling with cops. I'd have to wait until morning, but the garbage man would have come by then and the coat and money would be gone.

I fell back on the bed and pounded the mattress with my fist. All that trouble, and nothing to show for it.

8

The Laugh of Satan

During the two year period I had been leader of the Mau Maus seventeen people had been killed. I had been arrested more times than I could remember. We lived—all of us in the gangs—as though there were no law. Nothing was sacred, except our loyalty to each other—especially the bond of loyalty that I felt toward Israel and Mannie.

One night Israel sneaked up to my room in the middle of the night and threw a pigeon through the door. He stood outside and laughed as he heard my frightened screams. When he opened the door and flipped on the light I was under the bed. I tried to cover up my fear by laughing as he threw the pigeon out the window. But after he left, I lay trembling on the bed, the sound of flapping wings ringing in my ears. When I finally drifted into a fitful slumber I dreamt of falling. I awoke thinking I had heard the laugh of Satan.

The next morning Israel returned to tell me Mannie had been stabbed and was in the hospital.

"Whatsamatter, Nicky?" he said, after he had finished telling me about the stabbing. "How come you're acting like that?"

My stomach was tied in a knot and I could feel the blood draining from my face. Mannie and Israel were the only friends I had. Now suddenly I felt some of my security slipping away as Israel told me how close Mannie had come to being killed.

I shook my head, "I'm okay. Just mad. I'll get in to see him and we'll find out who did it and burn him good."

That afternoon I tried to get in the hospital but there were two uniformed policemen at the door. I climbed up the fire escape and pecked on the window until Mannie unlocked it from the other side. He was weak and barely able to crawl back into bed.

"Who did it, baby?" I asked. "No one's gonna stab you and get away with it."

"It was the Bishops. They caught me by myself and got me twice, once in the leg and once in the side."

"Which one?" I asked. "Do you know which one did it?"

"Yeah. It was that guy that they call Joe. He's their new vice president. He act like a big shot all the time. When he run away he said they coming back to kill me. That's why the cops are out there."

"Well, just you get well, baby. And when you get out we'll get that dirty nigger."

I crawled back down the fire escape and that night met with Israel and Homer Belanchi, our war councilor, to make plans for revenge. We decided on a kidnapping.

The next day Homer stole a car. We hid it behind an old warehouse for two weeks until Mannie was out of the hospital.

It was the week before Christmas 1957, when we made our move. Homer drove the car and we picked up Mannie. He was still limping on a cane. Augie, Paco and I were in the back seat. We cruised down St. Edward Street past the Catholic Center. There was a Christmas dance at the Center that night and two uniformed policemen were standing guard at the door. We didn't see any Bishops hanging around so we drove down to the candy store and parked across the street. It was almost 11:00 p.m. and we told Mannie to wait in the car.

We crossed the street and walked into the candy store. There were several Bishops in the store and I said, "Hey you guys, we're looking for our friend the Vice President of the Bishops. We heard he wants to make peace and we came to talk to him about it. Is he around?"

One of the Bishops said, "You mean Joe? Yeah, he's back there in the corner kissing his girl."

We sauntered back to where Joe was sitting on the floor beside his girl. He looked up and Augie said, "Man, we are the people. The Mau Maus. We've come for you."

Joe tried to climb to his feet but Augie put his foot against his shoulder and pushed him back down. Both of us had pistols in our pockets and he could see we had them pointed at him.

He began to scream. Augie pulled his gun and pointed it at the other boys in the store. "Don't move. Any of you. First one to move is a dead man."

The owner looked like he was going to panic. "We ain't gonna do anything to you, Pops," Augie said. "Just hold still and we'll be outta here in a minute."

I spoke to Joe, who was still sitting on the floor beside the terrified girl. "Hey, Punk, you got two choices. Either you go with us now or we kill you where you sit. You want a minute to think about it?"

The boy started to stammer something and I said, "Good, glad you thought it over." I jerked him to his feet and we walked out the door while Israel held his gun on the other boys in the store.

"You tell the Bishops we'll bring him back after we teach him a lesson about stabbing a Mau Mau," Augie said. We closed the door behind us and forced him to run across the street where we piled into the car. He sat in the back between Augie and me while we held our guns on him. Homer started the car and we drove to an abandoned building near the Manhattan Bridge.

We took him inside and tied him to a chair with a gag in his mouth.

"Maybe we kill you fast. Maybe we just let you stay here the rest of your life," I sneered at him. Augie spat in his face and we walked out, bolting the door behind us. It was midnight.

We didn't go back for two nights. When we did we took 25 of the Mau Maus with us. Joe was lying on his side still tied to the chair. He had tried to escape but was too tightly bound. We sat him upright and flipped on the light. He had been two full days without water or food. The building was freezing. He blinked in fear and horror as we stood around him.

I called Mannie to come and stand before him. "Mannie, is this the boy who stabbed you and threatened to kill you?"

Mannie limped up on his cane. "That's him. He's the one."

I pulled the gag off his mouth. His lips and tongue were

puffed and cracked. His throat was dry and he made grating, gasping noises as he tried to talk.

"See, he admits he's the one," I said laughing.

Augie grabbed his long hair and pulled his head backward. Mannie flicked the ash off his cigarette and held it close to the boy's throat. Joe's eyes were wild with fear and Mannie laughed as he gently touched the glowing coal against the tender skin. He screamed out in pain and Mannie pulled it away.

"Again," Augie said to Mannie. "He stabbed you twice."

This time Mannie slowly ground the cigarette out on the boy's mouth, deliberately forcing it between his clenched cracked lips. The boy's chin quivered slightly as he ran his parched tongue across the angry red blisters in a feeble attempt to get rid of the ash and shreds of tobacco which clung to them.

"Now, boys, it's your turn," Augie said.

Each boy in the room lit a cigarette and moved toward him while Augie grabbed his hair again and held his head backward. He screamed with fear, his throat making only funny grating noises like sandpaper scraped over screen wire. The boys pressed in on him, each one grinding his cigarette out against his face and neck. He screamed over and over until he fainted from the pain.

We untied him and he slumped to the floor in the dirt and cobwebs. Cursing loudly the boys kicked him with their pointed shoes, breaking his ribs and jaw. We then dumped him in the back of the car and drove to the candy store in Bishop turf. Augie wrote a note and pinned it to his back: "Nobody hurts a Mau Mau and gets away with it." We drove slowly by the store and rolled his unconscious body into the street. Then we roared away.

Christmas day I met Mannie in Gino's. We were sitting on a stool at the counter smoking cigarettes and laughing about the week before.

I looked up and saw five of the Bishops crossing the street. I glanced around and even though we were in the heart of Mau Mau turf, we were alone. I poked Mannie, "Bishops, man. Let's blow this place."

But it was too late. They saw us duck behind the counter to leave by the side door. We had a head start and burst out the door and across the street into an alley. We were running as fast as we could but in his weakened condition, Mannie was falling behind. When we rounded the corner of the alley and out into the street—they met us head on.

I put my head down and ran right through them. They were surprised at my daring and not prepared for the attack. I hit one of them in the stomach with my head and he fell backward to the sidewalk, skidding along on the seat of his pants. I put my hand on the hood of a parked car and vaulted over it into the street. A delivery truck rumbled down the street and harshly blew his horn as I sped toward safety. I hoped Mannie had taken advantage of my attack and was following.

Suddenly, I realized Mannie hadn't caught up. I glanced back. None of the Bishops were following me. I stopped running and stepped back out in the street to see what had happened. Back at the mouth of the alley I saw all five of them had Mannie crouched against the wall hitting him with their fists and kicking him in the stomach and groin.

I saw a quick flash of light and knew it was the reflection of the sun on a knife blade. I ran back fumbling for my knife and shouting, "Bastards! You filthy pigs! Leave him alone. I gonna kill you."

But it was too late. I saw the boy with the knife pull his arm back and with an underhand gesture jab the knife toward Mannie's ribs with great force. Mannie gasped and I saw him jerk upright. He remained erect against the wall for a short moment, and then started to collapse face first toward the concrete. As he fell, the boy with the knife viciously plunged it once more into his chest.

I had paused at the curb. I didn't believe they would try to kill him. Now I was like a wild man. I rushed into the mob slashing with my knife and swinging with my fist. They scattered and ran in both directions down the street. Mannie was left lying on the sidewalk, blood running out of his mouth and nose and a puddle beginning to form where it seeped out from under his leather jacket.

He was lying on his stomach with his face turned sharply at the neck looking up at me with terror filled eyes. He tried to speak but when he opened his mouth nothing came out but little bubbles of blood.

I knelt and turned him over on his back. I picked up his head and nestled him in my lap, cuddling his head against my leather jacket. His blood stained my pants and was warm and sticky on my hands.

He kept trying to say something. His eyes were wide with terror. But when he opened his lips to talk, all I could hear was a gurgle in his lungs. He kept blowing little blood bubbles with his lips.

"Mannie, Mannie," I screamed. "Don't die, Mannie. Don't die, Mannie."

He opened his mouth once, ever so slightly, and the sound of escaping air came out. It sounded like the soft hiss of a tire as it settles flat against the street. His head rolled in my arms and I felt his chest collapse under his jacket.

I stared at his unblinking eyes. He was dead!

"Mannie! Mannie! Mannie!" I was screaming at the top of my lungs, my own voice filled with the stark horror of the reality I had just experienced.

I heard voices down the street. A woman screamed, "Hey, what's going on down there?"

I couldn't stay. With my police record they would try to blame me. There was nothing else I could do now. The voices grew louder. I scrambled to my feet. Mannie's limp body dropped heavily back on the sidewalk. The hollow sound of his head cracking against the hard concrete echoed with every step as I raced down the back alley and out onto the next street. In my mind I could picture Mannie lying there on the sidewalk, his face turned up at me with those terrified eyes glazed open in death. I was scared.

I ran all the way to my apartment. I slammed the door behind me and grabbed my revolver out of the closet. My breath came in great gulps as I sat trembling on the side of the bed with my pistol aimed at the closed door. I was petrified with fear.

I had never seen death so close up—at least not face to face. He was my friend. One minute he was laughing and talking. The next he was lying on the street with blood bubbling out his mouth. . . . I couldn't cope with this. I had thought I was brave—unafraid of anything. But death was too much for me. I began to get sick at my stomach. Great waves of nausea swept over me and I gagged over and over. I wanted to cry, but didn't know how.

I jumped to my feet and ran against the wall. "I'm not afraid! I'm not afraid!" I screamed over and over.

I was like a man possessed with demons. I looked at my hands. I could see the dried blood against my skin and under my fingernails. Again the image flashed through my mind of his cracked lips and glazed eyes.

I began to hit my head against the wall, screaming, "Nobody can hurt me! Nobody can hurt me. Nobody . . ."

In exhaustion, I fell to the floor and gasped for breath. Fear! Stark, terrifying, indefensible, unconquerable fear! It was like a nightmare come true. I rolled over and over on the floor hugging my chest with both arms and moaning and screaming. The walls of the room seemed to close in toward me and the ceiling moved upward, stretching out until it was 10 miles away. I lay in the bottom of the tiny rectangle looking up at the door and window which were thousands of feet above me. I was cramped and caught in the bottom of what was like a square soda straw that was ten miles high with no way of escape.

Then, from above, a thick oozy black cloud appeared and began to settle down the straw toward me. I was suffocating. I opened my mouth to scream but nothing came out but bubbles of blood. I was clawing at the walls trying to escape, trying to climb out. But my neck kept flopping over to one side and I could sense my head hitting the floor with a sound like Mannie's when it struck the concrete as he rolled out of my lap.

The black cloud descended and I lay on my back with hands and feet extended upward trying to ward it off. It was the cloud of death—death—death—and it was coming after me. I could hear the soft hiss of air escaping from my deflating lungs. I gagged and tried to scream, but only more bubbles and then that low gurgle I had heard in Mannie's chest as the blood gushed through his lungs and up into his throat. I heard it in my own chest. Suddenly, the black cloud was upon me and I heard a hollow laugh echoing back up the sides of that square straw where I lay. Over and over it echoed. DEATH . . . Death . . . Death . . . It was the laugh of Satan.

When I awoke it was morning. The sun was trying to peek into my dirty window. I was still on the floor, cramped, sore and cold. The first thing I noticed were my hands, still covered with dried caked blood.

9

Into the Pit

Three days before Easter four of us were on the corner of Auburn and St. Edward in front of St. Edward-St. Michael Church. We knew that the priests collected a lot of money during the Easter week special services and we were making plans to break into the church.

A policeman came out of the Housing Precinct Station across the street and saw us leaning up against the iron spike fence around the church. He crossed the street and said, "Get out of here, you Puerto Rican pigs." We just stood there with our arms draped across the top of the fence and looked at him with blank stares.

He said it again. "You Spics, I said clear out of here." The other boys scattered but I held my ground. The cop glared at me, "I said move, you dirty Spic, move." He drew back his billy club as if to hit me.

I spit on him. He swung at me with his club and I ducked as it smashed into the fence. I charged into him and he grabbed me around the neck. He was twice as big as I, but I was going to kill him if I could. I was reaching for my knife when I felt him unbuckle his holster and reach for his revolver. He was calling for help at the same time.

I quickly backed away and put my hands up. "I surrender! I surrender!"

Police poured out the door of the Housing Precinct and rushed across the street. They grabbed hold of me and dragged me back across the street, up the steps and into the station.

The cop who had struggled with me slapped my face hard. I could taste the blood from my lips.

"You're a big man with a gun, but inside you're a coward just like all the rest of these filthy cops," I said.

He hit me again and I pretended to faint and fell to the floor.

"Get up, you dirty pig. This time we're going to send you away for good."

As they dragged me into the other room I heard the desk sergeant mutter, "That kid must be out of his mind. Man, they ought to put him away for good before he kills somebody."

I had been picked up by the police many times before, but they never had been able to hold me. No one would ever testify against me because they knew when I got out I would kill them, or the Mau Maus would kill them for me.

This time they took me across town and put me in a cell. The jailer pushed me as I went into the cell and I turned and charged at him with both fists. He pulled me out in the corridor and another cop held me while he beat me with his fists.

"The only way to handle these S.O.B.'s is to beat the hell out of 'em," he said. "They're all a bunch of stinking, filthy pigs. We got a jail full of niggers, wops, and spics. You're just like all the rest and if you get out of line, we'll make you wish you were dead."

They pushed me back into the cell and I lay on the hard floor cursing them. "Okay, punk," the turnkey said as he closed the cell door, "Why don't you get up and jitterbug for us now? Not so tough are you?" I bit my lips and didn't reply. But I knew I would kill him when I got out.

The next day the jailer came back to my cell. When he opened the door, I charged him again knocking him back across the corridor. He slapped me in the head with his keys. I felt the blood running from a cut over my eye.

"Go ahead, hit me," I screamed. "But one day I'm gonna come to your house and kill your wife and children. Just you wait and see."

I was only being booked on a minor offense of resisting arrest and failing to obey an officer. But I was making it worse. The jailer knocked me back in the cell and locked the door.

"Alright, Spic, you can stay there and rot!"

My hearing came up the following week. I was hand-cuffed and marched into the courtroom. I sat in a chair while the policeman began reading off the charges.

The judge, a stern faced man in his 50's with rimless glasses, said, "Wait a minute, haven't I had this boy before in this court?"

"Yes, your honor," the policeman answered, "this is his third appearance in this court. Besides this, he has 21 arrests in his record and has been charged with everything from robbery to assault with intent to kill."

The judge turned and looked at me.

"How old are you, young man?"

I slouched down in my chair and looked at the floor.

"Stand up when I speak to you!" the judge snapped.

I stood to my feet and looked at him.

"I said, how old are you?" he repeated firmly.

"Eighteen," I answered.

"You're eighteen and you've been arrested 21 times and have been in this court three times. Why aren't your parents with you?"

"They're in Puerto Rico," I answered.

"Who do you live with?"

"With nobody. I don't need nobody. I live with myself."

"How long have you lived by yourself?"

"Ever since I came to New York 3 years ago."

"Your honor," the officer interrupted, "he's no good. He's the President of the Mau Maus. He's the heart of all the trouble we've had in the housing project. I've never seen a kid as mean and vicious as this one. He's like an animal and the only thing to do with a mad dog is to pen him up. I'd like to recommend, your honor, that you put him in prison until he's 21. Maybe by then we can restore some order in Ft. Greene."

The judge turned and looked at the officer. "You say he's like an animal, eh? A mad dog, you say."

"That's right, your honor. And if you turned him loose he'd kill someone before dark."

"Yes, I believe you're right," the judge said, looking back at me. "But I think we need at least to try to find out what makes him like an animal. Why is he so vicious? Why does he want to hate and steal and fight and kill? We have hundreds just like him coming through our courts every day and I think the state has something of an obligation to try to salvage some of these boys—not just lock them up for the rest of their lives. And I believe, that deep down in the heart of this vicious 'mad dog' there's a soul that can be saved."

He turned to the officer, "Do you think we ought to try?"

"I don't know, your honor," said the policeman. "These kids have killed three officers in the last two years and we've had almost 50 murders down there since I've been on that beat. The only thing they respond to is force. And I know if you turn him loose we'll just have to lock him back up again—only the next time it will probably be for murder."

The judge glanced down at the sheet of paper in front of him.

"Cruz, is it? Come up here Nicky Cruz and stand before the bench."

I got up and walked to the front of the courtroom. I could feel my knees beginning to shake.

The judge leaned over the desk and looked straight at me.

"Nicky, I've got a boy just about your age. He goes to school. He lives in a good house in a nice neighborhood. He doesn't get into trouble. He plays baseball on the school team and makes good grades. He's not a mad dog like you are. And the reason he isn't a mad dog is because he has someone to love him. Obviously, you don't have anyone to love you—and you don't love anyone either. You don't have the capacity to love. You're sick, Nicky, and I want to know why. I want to know what it is that makes you hate so much. You're not normal like other boys. The officer is right. You're an animal. You live like an animal and you act like an animal. I ought to treat you like an animal, but I'm going to find out why you're so abnormal. I'm going to put you under the custody of our court psychologist, Dr. John Goodman. I'm not qualified to determine whether or not you're psychotic. He will examine you and make the final decision."

I nodded. I didn't know whether he was going to turn me loose or keep me in jail, but I did understand that he wasn't going to send me to prison, at least not right then.

"One more thing, Nicky," the judge said, "if you get into any more trouble, if I get a single complaint about you, if you misbehave at all, then I'm going to assume that you are entirely incapable of understanding directions and responding to responsibility and I will send you immediately to Elmira to the work farm. Understand?"

"Yes, sir," I answered. And I was surprised at myself. It was the first time I had ever said "sir" to any man. But it just seemed the right thing to do in this case.

The next morning the court psychologist, Dr. John Goodman, came to my cell. He was a big man with premature gray temples and a deep scar on his face. His shirt collar was frayed and his shoes unshined.

"I've been assigned to review your case," he said, sitting down on my bunk and crossing his legs. "This means we'll have to spend some time together."

"Sure, big man, anything you say."

"Listen, punk, I talk to 20 kids a day like you. You smart your mouth off at me and you'll wish you hadn't."

I was taken aback by his abrupt manner but sneered arrogantly, "You talk mighty big for a headshrinker. Maybe you like to have a visit from the Mau Maus one of these nights."

Before I could move the doctor had hold of the front of my shirt and almost lifted me off the floor. "Let me tell you something, squirt. I spent 4 years in the gangs and three years in the Marines before going to college. See this scar?" He twisted his head so I could see the deep scar running from the point of his cheekbone into his collar. "I got that in the gangs, but not until I had almost killed 6 other punks with a baseball bat. Now if you want to play rough, you've got the right man."

He shoved me backward and I stumbled against the cot and sat down.

I spat on the floor, but said no more.

His voice returned to its matter-of-fact tone as he said, "Tomorrow morning I have to make a trip up to Bear Mountain. You can ride along and we'll talk."

All the next day I was under the informal examination of the psychologist. We drove out of the city into upper New York state. It was my first trip out of the asphalt jungle since I had landed from Puerto Rico three years before. I felt a tinge of excitement but remained sullen and arrogant when he asked me questions.

After a brief stop at the clinic he took me by the zoo in the public park. We walked down the path in front of the cages. I stopped and looked at the wild animals pacing back and forth behind bars.

"Do you like zoos, Nicky?" he asked.

"I hate 'em," I answered, turning away from the cages and walking back down the path.

"Oh? Why's that?"

"I hate them stinking animals. Always pacing. Always wanting out."

We sat on a park bench and talked. Dr. John pulled some notebooks out of his brief case and asked me to draw some pictures. Horses. Cows. Houses. I drew a picture of a house with a huge door in the front.

"Why did you put such a big door on the house?" he asked.

"So the stupid headshrinker can get in," I answered.

"I won't accept that. Give me another answer."

"Alright, so I can get out in a hurry in case someone's chasing me."

"Most people draw doors to get in."

"Not me, I'm trying to get out."

"Now draw me a picture of a tree," he said.

I drew a tree. Then I thought it wasn't right to have a tree without a bird, so I drew a bird in the top of the tree.

Dr. Goodman looked at the picture and said, "Do you like birds, Nicky?"

"I hate 'em."

"It seems to me you hate everything."

"Yeah. Maybe I do. But I hate birds most of all."

"Why?" he asked, "because they're free?"

In the distance I could hear the dark rumbling of thunder.

This man was beginning to scare me with his questions. I took my pencil and bored a hole through the picture of the bird. "So, forget about the bird. I just killed him."

"You think you can get rid of everything you're afraid of by killing them, don't you."

"Who the hell do you think you are, you stupid quack?" I screamed. "You think you can get me to draw a stupid picture and ask me some dumb questions and know all about me? I ain't afraid of nobody. Everybody's afraid of me. Just ask the Bishops, they'll tell you about me. There ain't no gang in New York that wants to rumble with the Mau Maus. I ain't afraid of nobody." My voice had reached a fever pitch as I stood to my feet in front of him.

Dr. Goodman kept making notes in his pad. "Sit down, Nicky," he said, glancing up, "you don't have to impress me."

"Listen, man, you keep picking on me and you'll wind up a dead man."

The rumbling on the horizon grew louder as I stood shaking in front of him. Dr. Goodman looked up at me and started to say something, but rain drops began to splatter on the path beside us. He shook his head. "We'd better go before we get wet," he said.

We slammed the car doors just as the first huge drops of heavy rain splashed on the windshield. Dr. John sat silently for a long time before starting the car and pulling out on the road. "I don't know, Nicky," he said, "I just don't know."

The trip back was misery. The rain was pelting the car without mercy. Dr. John drove silently. I was lost in thought. I hated going back to the city. I dreaded the thought of going back to jail. I couldn't stand to be caged like a wild animal.

The rain quit but the sun had already gone down as we drove past the hundreds of blocks of towering, grimy apartments. I felt like I was sinking into a pit. I wanted to get out and run. But instead of turning toward the jail, Dr. John slowed down and turned on Lafayette toward the Ft. Greene project.

"Ain't you taking me to jail?" I asked, puzzled.

"No, I have the prerogative of locking you up or turning you loose. I don't think jail will do you any good."

"Yeah man, now you're on my beam," I grinned.

"No, you don't understand what I mean. I don't think anything will do you any good."

"What do you mean, Doc, you think I'm hopeless?" I laughed.

He pulled his car up at the corner of Lafayette and Ft. Greene Place. "That's exactly right, Nicky. I've worked with kids like you for years. I used to live in the ghetto. But I've never seen a kid as hard, cold, and savage as you. You haven't responded to a thing I've said. You hate everyone and you're afraid of anyone that threatens your security."

I opened the door and got out. "Well, you can go to hell, Doc. I don't need you or nobody."

"Nicky," he said, as I started to walk away from the car. "I'll give it to you straight. You're doomed. There's no hope for you. And unless you change you're on a one way street to jail, the electric chair, and hell."

"Yeah? Well, I'll see you there," I said.

"Where?" he said.

"In hell, man," I said laughing.

He shook his head and drove off into the night. I tried to keep laughing but the sound died in my throat.

I stood on the street corner with my hands in the pockets of my raincoat. It was 7 p.m. and the streets were full of nameless faces with hurrying legs . . . moving, moving, moving. I felt like a leaf on the sea of humanity, being blown in every direction by my own senseless passions. I looked at the people. Everyone was moving. Some were running. It was May but the wind was cold. It whipped my legs and made me cold inside.

The words of the psychologist kept running through my mind like a stuck record, "You're on a one way street to jail, the electric chair, and hell."

I had never looked at myself before. Not really. Oh, I liked to look at myself in the mirror. I had always been a clean boy, which is a bit unusual for most Puerto Ricans in my section. Unlike most of the guys in the gang, I took pride in the way I dressed. I liked to wear a tie and colored shirt. I always tried to keep my slacks pressed and used lots of lotion on my face. I never did like to smoke too much because it made my breath smell bad.

But inside I suddenly felt dirty. The Nicky I saw in the mirror wasn't the real Nicky. And the Nicky I was looking at now was dirty . . . filthy . . . lost.

The juke box in Papa John's was blaring forth with a loud bebop tune. The traffic in the street was bumper-to-bumper. Horns were blowing, whistles shrilling, people shouting. I looked at their blank nameless faces. No one was smiling. Everyone was in a hurry. Some of the creeps were drunk. Most of the goofeys in front of the bar were hopped up. This was the real Brooklyn. This was the real Nicky.

I started up the street toward my room on Ft. Greene. The newspapers were whipping against the iron fence and the iron grates in front of the stores. There were broken bottles and empty beer cans along the sidewalk. The smell of greasy food drifted down the street and made me sick at my stomach. The sidewalks shook beneath my feet as the subways rattled and faded into the dark unknown.

I caught up with an old wretch of a woman. I say "old" but from the rear I couldn't tell her age. She was short, shorter than I. And she had a black scarf pulled tight around her head. Her reddish yellow hair that had been dyed and dyed some more, stuck out around the edges. She had on an old Navy peajacket that was about six sizes too large for her. Her scrawny legs covered with black slacks stuck out like toothpicks below the hemline of the peajacket. She had on men's shoes without any socks.

I hated her. She symbolized all the dirt and filth in my life. I reached in my pocket for my blade. I wasn't kidding this time. I kept wondering to myself how hard I would have to shove it to get the blade to go through the hard felt of the peajacket and into her back. It gave me a warm sticky feeling inside to imagine the blood dripping out from under the edge of the jacket and puddling on the street.

Just then a small dog came running down the street toward us and swerved to miss her. She turned and stared at him with empty ageless eyes. I recognized her as one of the burned out whores who used to live on my block. From the look on her face, the droopy eyelids, and the blank stare in her eyes, I could tell she was high.

I turned loose of the blade, my mind now back on myself, and started to pass her. As I did, I saw her vacant eyes watching a bright red balloon as it bounced before the wind down the middle of the street.

A balloon. My first instinct was to dash into the street and step on it. I hated it. Damn, I hated it! It was free.

Suddenly, a huge wave of compassion swept over me. I identified with that stupid bouncing balloon. It's a strange thing that the first time I was to feel pity in all my life it was to be for an inanimate object being blown before the wind, going nowhere.

So, instead of stepping into the street and stomping on it, I passed the old woman by and speeded up to keep up with the balloon as it bounced and rolled down the dirty street.

It seemed to be strangely out of place in that filthy setting. All around it were papers and trash being blown by the cold wind also. On the sidewalk were the broken wine bottles and crushed beer cans. Towering up on each side were the dark dismal concrete and stone walls of the inescapable prison where I lived. And here, in the midst of all this was a free, red balloon, being blown before the invisible forces of the winds of nature.

What was it about that stupid balloon that interested me? I quickened my pace to keep up with it. I found myself hoping it wouldn't hit a piece of broken glass and explode. And yet knowing it could not possibly last. It was too delicate. It was too clean. It was too tender and pure to continue to exist in the midst of all this hell.

I held my breath each time it bounced in the air and came back down in the street. Waiting for that final, irrevocable explosion. And yet it continued on its merry course in the middle of the street. I kept thinking, "Maybe it will make it. Maybe it can get all the way down the block and be blown free into the park. Maybe it has a chance after all."

I was almost praying for it. But then the dejection returned as I thought of the park. That stinking, stupid park. What if it does make it to the park? What then? There's nothing for it there. It will bounce against that rusty fence and explode. Or even if it makes it over the fence and gets inside, it will fall on some of those stickers in the grass and weeds and be gone.

"Or," I thought to myself, "even if somebody picks it up, all they'll do is carry it to their filthy apartment and it will be imprisoned the rest of its life. There is no hope. No hope for it—or for me."

Suddenly, without warning, a police van rolled down the street. Before I could break away from my chain of thought it was on top of the balloon and I heard the pitiful "pop" as the van mercilessly ground it into the pavement. The van was gone—down the street and around the block. It didn't even know what it had done, and even had it known it wouldn't have cared. I wanted to run after the van and shout, "You dirty coppers. Don't you care?" I wanted to kill them for crushing me into the street.

But the life was gone out of me. I stood on the curb and looked into the dark street but there was no sign of the balloon. It had been ground into the trash and rubble in the middle of Ft. Greene and had become like all the other dirt in Brooklyn.

I turned back to my steps and sat down. The old whore shuffled on down the street into the darkness. The wind still whistled 'and the papers and trash kept blowing down the street and sticking on the fence around the park. Another subway rattled by underneath and rumbled into the darkness. I was afraid. Me, Nicky. I was afraid. I was shaking not with the cold, but from the inside out. I put my head in my hands and thought, "It's useless. I'm doomed. It's just like Dr. John said. There's no hope for Nicky except jail, the electric chair, and hell."

After that I didn't seem to care any more. I turned the presidency of the gang back over to Israel. I was in the pit as deep as I could get. There was no hope any more. I might as well become like all the others in the ghetto and turn to the needle. And I was tired of running. What was it the judge said I needed? Love! But where can you find love in the pit?

10

The Encounter

It was a hot Friday afternoon in July, 1958. Israel, Lydia, and I were sitting on the steps in front of my apartment when some of the kids came running down the street. "Hey, What's going on," I shouted at them.

"There's a circus down at the school," one of the kids shouted back.

Excitement in Brooklyn is sparse and far between. This is one of the reasons that we had to provide our own excitement in the form of fights, narcotics, and sex. Anything was better than the boredom of sitting around. So we headed across the park toward the school on St. Edward Street.

When we arrived a large crowd had formed in front of P.S. 67. We elbowed our way through the crowd, pushing the little kids to the ground so we could see what was taking place.

A man was standing on the fireplug blowing "Onward Christian Soldiers" on a trumpet. He kept playing the same song over and over again. Next to him, standing on the sidewalk, was another man. The skinniest, weakest, puniest looking man I had ever seen. Above them fluttered an American flag on a stick.

The trumpet player finally stopped and the crowd began to shout at him. Almost 100 boys and girls had gathered, blocking the street and sidewalk.

The skinny man had a piano stool that he had gotten out of the school. He climbed up on it and opened a black book. We began to shout and holler at him. He stood there with his head bowed and we could see that he was afraid. The shouting became louder. The crowd was packed in tight and I was standing with an arm around Lydia. She was giggling as I tried to reach around her shoulder and feel under her sweater.

Suddenly, I realized that everything had grown quiet. I shifted my attention from Lydia and looked up at the man on the piano bench. He was standing with his head bowed, his black book open in his hands in front of him. An eerie feeling swept over me, like I used to have back home when my father practiced his witchcraft. Everything got strangely quiet, even the cars on Park Avenue, just half a block away, didn't seem to be making any noise. It was an unearthly quiet. I was afraid.

The old fear that I hadn't felt since joining the Mau Maus suddenly swept over me. It was the fear I had battled in court in front of the judge. It was the fear I felt the night I walked home after my day with the court psychologist. Each time I had been able to push it aside, to run from it. But now, it crept into my heart and body and I could feel it grabbing hold of my very soul. I wanted to break and run but everybody else was listening—waiting.

Suddenly, the skinny man raised his head and in a voice so faint you could hardly hear him, he began to read from the black book . . . "For God so loved the world that He gave His only begotten son, that whosoever believeth in Him, should not perish, but have everlasting life."

I was shaking with fear. This guy had to be some kind of priest or witch or something. He was talking about love. I knew about "love." I was an expert. I reached over and pinched Lydia's hip. She looked at me. "Listen to him, Nicky." I scowled and turned my head back toward the skinny man. He said something about asking for a miracle to happen. I didn't know what a miracle was, but everyone else was listening and I didn't want to be different.

He had finished speaking and was standing up there waiting for something to happen. Then, he said he wanted to talk to the presidents and vice presidents of the gangs. I began to sense that this man was dangerous. He was invading our world and I didn't want any strangers intruding.

He continued, "If you're so big and tough, you wouldn't be afraid of coming up here and shaking hands with a skinny preacher, would you?"

There was a stir in the crowd. Someone called out from the rear, "Hey, Buckboard, whatsamatter, you scared?" He was referring to Buckboard, the president of the Chaplains, our brother gang.

I heard a movement in the rear of the crowd and looked up and there came Buckboard along with Stagecoach and two other Negro members of the gang. They were walking toward the skinny preacher, who had now gotten down off the stool and was standing to meet them.

I grew more nervous. I didn't like this at all. I glanced around but everyone seemed to be smiling and were opening up for Buckboard and Stagecoach to come through.

They shook hands and then the preacher and the trumpet player took Buckboard and Stagecoach and the other two boys over to the doorway of the school. They stood there talking and I walked away from Lydia and got close to Israel. "What're they doing?" I asked him. Israel didn't answer. He had a funny look on his face.

Suddenly, I saw the whole bunch of them get on their knees right there in the street. Buckboard and Stagecoach had taken off their hats and were holding them in their hands and kneeling down on the sidewalk.

When they got up, they started walking back toward the crowd. I shouted at Buckboard, "Hey, Buckboard, you got religion now?" Buckboard was a big boy, about 6'2" and weighed close to 200 pounds. He turned and looked at me in a way I had never seen him look before. His face was serious, dead serious. His eyes pierced deep into mine and I understood what he meant, even though I didn't understand what had happened to him. He said with his eyes, "You better lay off, Nicky, this ain't no time for fooling around."

Suddenly, someone yelled at me. "Hey, Nicky, you gonna let those niggers show you up? You afraid to go up, too?"

Israel punched me and nodded his head in the direction of the two men. "Come on, Nicky, let's go." I could see that he was serious and I pulled back. There was something sinister about this whole thing . . . something dangerous and deceptive. It smacked of something I was deathly afraid of.

The crowd began to hoot and shout. "Hey, look at our leader. He's afraid of the skinny preacher."

Israel pulled at my jacket. "Come on, Nicky, let's go." I

had no choice but to go forward and stand in front of the two men.

Israel shook hands with the two men. I was still afraid, hanging back. The skinny man walked over to me and stuck out his hand. "Nicky, my name is David Wilkerson. I'm a preacher from Pennsylvania."

I just stared at him and said, "Go to hell, preacher."

"You don't like me, Nicky," he said, "but I feel different about you. I love you. And not only that, I've come to tell you about Jesus who loves you, too."

I felt like a trapped animal about to be caged. Behind me was the crowd. In front of me was the smiling face of this skinny man talking about love. No one loved me. No one ever had. As I stood there my mind raced back to that time so many years ago when I had heard my mother say, "I don't love you, Nicky." I thought, "If your own mother doesn't love you then no one loves you—or ever will."

The preacher just stood there, smiling, with his hand stuck out. I always prided myself on not being afraid. But I was afraid. Deeply afraid that this man was going to put me in a cage. He was going to take away my friends. He was going to upset everything and because of this I hated him.

"You come near me, Preacher, and I'll kill you," I said, shrinking back toward the protection of the crowd. I was afraid, and I didn't know how to deal with it.

The fear overwhelmed me. I was close to panic. I snarled at him and turned and walked back through the crowd. "This man's a Communist, boys," I shouted. "Leave him alone. He's a Communist."

I didn't know what a Communist was, but I knew it was something everyone was supposed to be against. I was running, and I knew it. But I couldn't fight this kind of approach. If he had come at me with a knife, I would have fought him. If he had come begging and pleading, I would have laughed at him and kicked him in the teeth. But he came saying, "I love you." And I had never come up against this kind of approach before.

I barged through the crowd with my head up and chest out. I reached out and grabbed Lydia by the arm and pulled her away with me and we started up St. Edward, away from the school.

Some of the boys followed and we went down into the

basement and I turned the phonograph on as loud as it
would play. I was trying to drown out the sound of those
words "Jesus loves you." Why would something like that
bug me so badly? I danced a while with Lydia and drank a
half bottle of cheap wine and smoked a pack of cigarettes.
Chain smoking—lighting one from the tip of the other.
Lydia could sense I was nervous. "Nicky, maybe you ought
to talk to the preacher. Being a Christian may not be as
bad as you think." I stared at her and she dropped her
head.

I was miserable. And afraid. Suddenly, there was a com-
motion at the door and I looked up and saw the skinny
preacher walk in. He seemed so out of place, with his nice
suit and white shirt and neat tie, walking into this filthy
basement room. He asked one of the boys, "Where's
Nicky?"

The boy pointed across the room where I was sitting
with my head in my hands, cigarette dangling out of my
mouth.

Wilkerson walked across the room like the place be-
longed to him. He had a big smile on his face. He stuck
out his hand again and said, "Nicky, I just wanted to shake
hands with you and . . ." Before he could finish, I slapped
him in the face—hard. He tried to force his grin but it was
obvious that I had made an impression on him. He held his
ground and the fear once again welled up inside me so
that I was sick to my stomach. I did the only thing I knew
to retaliate. I spit on him.

"Nicky, they spit on Jesus, too, and he prayed, 'Father
forgive them, for they know not what they do'." I
screamed at him, cursing. "Get the hell out of here!" and I
pushed him backwards toward the door.

"Nicky, before I leave let me tell you just one thing.
Jesus loves you."

"Get out, you crazy priest. You don't know what you're
talking about. I'll give you 24 hours to get off my turf or
I'll kill you."

Wilkerson backed out the door, still smiling. "Re-
member, Nicky, Jesus loves you." It was more than I could
take. I reached down and picked up the empty wine bottle
and smashed it to the floor. I had never felt so frustrated,
so desperate, so completely undone.

I stomped out the door, my pride welling up inside of

me. I was aware that all the other guys knew that this guy had really gotten under my skin. The only way I knew to fool them was to act tough. If I showed my true emotions, for even a moment, I felt I would lose all respect from the gang.

"That stupid, crazy witch," I said, "if he comes back here, I'll set him on fire." I slammed the door shut behind me and stood on the sidewalk looking after him as he walked briskly away. "Cocky," I thought. Yet, I knew deep inside there was something real about this strange man.

I turned and walked in the other direction. Stopping by the pool parlor, I ordered a rack of balls and tried to concentrate on the tip of my pool cue. But all I could hear in my mind was the voice of that skinny preacher and the words, "Jesus loves you."

"I don't care," I thought, "he ain't going to scare me. Nobody's gonna scare me."

I scratched the next two shots and threw the stick on the table. "Jesus loves you," the words rang over and over in my ears. I told the boys that I was sick and I crept back to my apartment.

I was afraid that I really was sick. I had never gone to my room this early. It was 10:30 and I always waited until 3 or 4 a.m. before coming to bed. I closed the door behind me and locked it. I was shaking as I crossed the room and turned on the little lamp on the table beside my bed. I took my gun out of the closet and put two bullets in the magazine and laid it on the table beside my bed. I kicked off my shoes and changed clothes. Laying my pack of cigarettes on the table, I lay back on the bed and looked at the ceiling. I could hear those words of David Wilkerson over and over, "Jesus loves you, Nicky, Jesus loves you."

I reached up and flipped off the light and lit a cigarette. I was chain smoking again. I couldn't rest. I twisted one way and then another. I couldn't sleep. The hours went by. I finally got up and turned on the light and looked at my watch. 5 a.m. I had turned on the bed all night long.

Getting up, I dressed and put my gun back in the closet. I took my cigarettes and walked down the two flights of stairs and opened the front door of the apartment. The sky was just beginning to turn gray. In the distance, I could hear the sounds of the great city as it yawned and stretched to life.

I sat on the front steps with my head in my hands. "Jesus loves you . . . Jesus loves you . . . Jesus loves you."

I heard a car pull up in front of the apartment and heard the door slam shut. A hand clapped me on the shoulder. I lifted my weary head and saw the skinny preacher standing in front of me. He was still smiling and he said, "Hi, Nicky. Do you remember what I told you last night? I just wanted to come by and tell you again. Nicky, Jesus loves you."

I jumped to my feet and made a motion for him. Wilkerson had obviously wised up and he jumped back out of my reach. I stood there snarling at him like an animal preparing to leap. Wilkerson looked me straight in the eye and said, "You could kill me, Nicky. You could cut me in a thousand pieces and lay them out on the street. But every piece would cry out, Jesus loves you. And you'll never be able to run from that."

I tried to stare him down, but he kept talking. "Nicky, I'm not scared of you. You talk tough but inside you're just like all the rest of us. You're afraid. You're sick of your sin. You're lonely. But Jesus loves you."

Something clicked. How did he know that I was lonely? I didn't know what he was talking about when he said sin. I was afraid to admit my fear. But how did he know I was lonely? The gang was always with me. I had any of the girls I wanted. People were afraid of me—they would see me coming and move off the sidewalk and into the street. I had been the leader of the gang. How could anyone think I was lonely. And yet I was. And now this preacher knew it.

I tried to get smart. "You believe you're going to change me just like that?" I said, snapping my fingers. "You think I'm going to hear you and pick up a Bible and walk around like a preacher and people are going to start saying Nicky Cruz—angel—saint?" But I realized that he meant business. That he was sincere.

"Nicky, you didn't sleep much last night, did you?" Again, I was amazed. How did he know that I hadn't slept?

Wilkerson continued, "I didn't sleep much last night either, Nicky. I stayed awake most of the night praying for you. But before I did, I talked to some of your boys. They tell me that no one can get close to you. They are all afraid of you. But Nicky, I've come to tell you that somebody does care. Jesus cares. He loves you." And then he looked me straight in the face, "One day, soon, Nicky, God's Spirit is going to deal with you. One day, Nicky, you are going to stop running and come running to Him."

I said no more. I got to my feet and turned my back on him and walked back into the apartment, shutting the door behind me. I climbed the steps to my room and sat on the side of the bed looking out the window. His car was already gone when I looked down. In the east, the sky was beginning to turn a rosy hue. The huge building across the street that housed Brooklyn Tech blocked my view of the horizon. But suddenly, like catching a whiff of the sea when you're still miles up the river, I had a feeling there was more to life than this. More than these towering concrete buildings—these prison walls of glass and stone.

I thought of his words, "One day you will stop running, and come running to Him." I didn't even know who He was. But I thought, sitting there on the side of my bed looking out over the trash-filled street with the sound of the trucks grinding and roaring down the thoroughfare, that He must be something like the sun rising out of the ocean on a cloudless day. Or maybe something like the morning star that still hung in the dawning sky. Maybe . . . Someday. . . .

The time was closer than I knew.

In the days ahead I couldn't escape my encounter with the man that represented God. It was Israel that bugged me constantly about him. Every time I saw him he said something about God.

"Damn it, Israel, if you don't shut up about that God stuff I'm gonna kill you."

But Israel kept talking about it and I suspected he was seeing Wilkerson on the side. But I didn't like it. I sensed this was one man who could possibly destroy our gang. Now that Mannie was gone only Israel was left. And even he seemed to be drifting in another direction. His constant references to Wilkerson and his constant desire to force me to talk drove me to the brink of despair.

I could take no more. The night before the 4th of July when all the gangs were supposed to converge on Coney

Island, Israel spent the night with me. He talked long into the night trying to convince me to stay away from Coney Island the next night and go talk to Wilkerson instead. I put my hands over my ears trying to drown out his constant chatter. Eventually, he dropped off to sleep. I lay in bed staring at the dark ceiling, the fear almost consuming me. I had to stop it. I had to shut Israel up. I couldn't stand to hear any more about Wilkerson.

I reached under my mattress and closed my hand on the wooden handle of the icepick I had hidden there. I could hear Israel breathing deeply in the bed next to me. The more I thought about him bugging me about God the more it infuriated me.

I could stand it no more. "This will teach you to bug me," I screamed as I snatched the icepick from under the mattress and plunged it toward Israel's back.

The screaming aroused him and he jerked upright in the bed just as the icepick plunged deep into the mattress behind him.

I pulled it out and tried to swing it again shouting, "I told you to shut up about God. Why didn't you shut up? Why? Why? Why?"

Israel grabbed me and we grappled, rolling off the bed onto the floor as I stabbed blindly at him.

He shoved me backward and fell on top of me, straddling my chest with his body, holding my hands over my head against the floor.

"Why couldn't you shut up?" I kept screaming.

"What's wrong with you?" Israel was yelling, trying to hold me down. "You're crazy. It's me. Your friend. What's wrong with you?"

Suddenly I realized he was crying as he yelled and struggled with me. Tears were streaming down his face. "Nicky. Nicky. Stop. I'm your friend. Don't make me hurt you. Please stop. I'm your friend. I love you."

He had said it. It swept over me like he had poured icewater in my face. He had said it just like Wilkerson had said it. I relaxed my grip on the icepick and he snatched it out of my hand. I had never seen him cry before. Why was he crying?

He held the icepick poised over my face. His hand was gripping it so tightly I could see the white of his knuckles in the dim light. He was shaking as his muscles tensed. For a moment I thought he was going to stab me in the head with it, then he viciously slung it across the room. He was still crying as he released me and threw himself on his bed.

I rolled over, frustrated, confused and exhausted. What was wrong with me? I'd just tried to kill my best friend!

I ran from the room and up the steps to the rooftop. Outside it was dark and sultry. I made my way across the roof to the place where old man Gonzales kept his pigeons in a cage. I pried the cage open and grabbed a bird. The others fluttered and flapped and flew off into the night.

I held the pigeon tightly against my bare chest and made my way to the air ventilator and sat down.

Birds! I hated them. So free. God I hated those who were free. Wilkerson was free. Israel was approaching freedom. I could sense it. This bird was free but I was trapped in my cage of hate and fear.

I felt my fingers tighten around the bird's head, stretching it away from his body. "I'm not afraid."

The bird gave a small pitiful squeak and I felt his body quiver as the bones in his neck separated. "See, Mama, I'm not afraid."

I went out of control. I twisted his neck back and forth until I felt the skin and bones separate and with a vicious yank I ripped his head from his body. The warm blood squirted into my hands, dripping on my knees and onto the tarred rooftop. I held the gory head in my hand and looked at it crying, "Now, you're not free. No one is free."

Slinging the head off the roof top, I smashed the still quivering body against the roof. At last, that damned bird was dead, never to haunt my dreams again.

I stayed on the roof top, intermittently sleeping and waking. Each time I'd sleep the nightmare would reoccur, more horrible than ever before. At dawn I returned to my room. Israel was gone.

I spent most of the next day looking for him. I finally found him sitting alone in the basement room where we held our gigs. All the others had gone to Coney Island.

"Hey man, I'm sorry about last night," I began.

"Forget it," Israel said with a weak grin.

"No baby, I'm sorry. That's not like me. Something's wrong with me."

Israel got up and faked a punch at my jaw. "Sure, baby. You're just like me, nuts."

I spent the rest of the afternoon with him. It was the first time in 3 years I missed Coney Island on July 4.

During the second week of July, 1958, Israel came by and told me about Wilkerson's big meeting over at St. Nicholas Arena. In fact, Wilkerson had been down and talked to Israel, inviting the Mau Maus to the meeting. There was to be a special bus for us in front of P.S. 67, and they were going to have special seats reserved for us at the front of the auditorium. Israel had told Wilkerson that he'd make sure the Mau Maus were there.

I shook my head and started to get up from the steps and walk back inside. I wanted nothing to do with it. The waves of fear started over me again and I choked up so tight I had trouble speaking.

"Hey man," Israel called as I started to turn away, "You ain't chicken are you?"

Israel had hit me at the only chink in my armor—in my only tender place. I turned back at him, "Nicky ain't afraid of no-one . . . that skinny preacher . . . you . . . not even God."

Israel just stood there with a little smile playing across his handsome face. "Sounds to me like you're scared of something. How come you don't want to go?"

I remembered Buckboard and Stagecoach kneeling there on the sidewalk in front of the school. I knew that if it could happen to them . . . The only thing I knew to do was run—keep running. But to run now, in the face of Israel's challenge, would make it seem like I was afraid. Really afraid.

"What time that bus supposed to be there?" I asked.

"7:00 p.m.," Israel answered. "The meeting starts at 7:30. You gonna come?"

"Yeah man! You think I'm chicken or something? Let's get the whole gang and go over there and burn that joint good."

Israel nodded and walked off down the street, swinging his hips and jitterbugging. I turned and climbed the steps to my room, three floors above the sidewalk. I felt sick.

I locked the door behind me and flopped on my back on the bed. I reached for a reefer. Maybe this would help. I was out, so I smoked a regular cigarette.

Thoughts flooded my mind like water rushing through a flood gate at the tide basin. I was scared. The cigarette shook and the ashes fell off onto my shirt and tumbled down onto the dirty bed sheets. I was scared to get on that bus. I hated to leave my own turf. The thought of having to travel away from the little plot of familiar territory put terror into my heart. I was afraid if I found myself in a large crowd of people I would be swallowed up and become a blob—a nothing. I knew that once I got to the arena I would have to do something to call attention to myself.

But most of all, I was afraid of what I had seen out there on the street that day. I was afraid that someone or something bigger and more powerful than I would force me to my knees in front of people and that I would cry. I was desperately afraid of tears. Tears were the ultimate sign of weakness, failure, softness, and childishness. I hadn't cried since I was eight years old. Something made Israel cry. Not me—ever.

Yet, if I didn't go, I would be branded a chicken by Israel and the rest of the gang. I had no choice.

It was hot that July night when we scrambled on board the bus. There were a couple of men dressed in suits and ties who were supposed to keep order. They might as well have stayed at home. The noise on the bus was deafening.

I felt better once I was with my crowd. It was the loneliness of my room that depressed me. But on the bus it was different. More than 50 Mau Maus crowded onto the bus. The harried men tried to keep order but finally gave up and let us take over. The gang was pulling at each other, shouting obscenities, opening windows, smoking, drinking wine, pulling the bell cord, and shouting for the bus to get under way.

When we arrived at the arena, we opened the emergency doors and some even crawled out the windows. There were several teenage girls standing around in front of the arena with tight shorts and brief halters. Cries such as, "Hey Baby, how about a piece?" and "Come on in with me, Chick, we're heading for a real gig," punctuated the night. Some of the girls joined us as we marched in.

Israel and I led the parade into the arena. An usher tried to stop us at the inner door. Inside, we would see people turning around and looking at us as we stormed into the foyer.

"Hey man, let us in," Israel said. "We are the People.

The Mau Maus. The Priest himself invited me. We got reserved seats."

Down front, a member of the Chaplains saw us and stood up and shouted, "Hey, Nicky, baby. Come on down. These seats are for you." We pushed by the startled and helpless usher and swaggered into the arena.

We were dressed in our Mau Mau uniforms. None of us removed our black hats. We paraded down the aisle, tapping loudly with our canes and shouting and whistling to the crowd.

Looking out over the crowd, I could see members of rival gangs. There were Bishops, GGI's, as well as some of the Phantom Lords from The Bedford Avenue Park. The arena was almost full and it had all the makings of a full scale rumble. This might not be so bad after all.

The din of noise was deafening. We took our seats and joined in, whistling and shouting and tapping our canes against the floor.

To one side, a girl started playing the organ. A young Puerto Rican kid stood up and clasped his hands to his chest and threw back his head. "Oh Jeee—sus," he shouted. "Save my big, black soul." And he collapsed into his chair amid howls and gales of laughter from the gangs.

Several boys and girls stood up near the organ and went into the fish. The girls shaking their hips at double beat to the time of the music and the boys jitterbugging around them. Applause and shouts of approval greeted their performances. Things were beginning to get out of hand.

Suddenly, a girl walked out on the stage. She walked to the center and stood behind the microphone, her hands clasped in front of her, waiting for the noise to subside.

It grew louder. "Hey, baby, wiggle it a little bit," someone shouted. "How about a date, Honey?" A lanky kid I had never seen before stood up and closed his eyes and held out his arms and said in an Al Jolsen accent, "Maaammy!" The crowd increased its clapping and whistling.

The girl began to sing. Even from our vantage point in the third row, it was impossible to hear her over the din of the crowd. As she sang, several boys and girls got up on the seats and began gyrating and dancing. The girls in their short shorts and brief halters and the boys with their black Mau Mau jackets, pointed shoes, and pointed alpine hats covered with matches and decorated in front with a silver star.

The girl finished her song and glanced nervously toward the wings. We began to cheer and clap and call for another song. However, she walked off the stage and suddenly the skinny preacher stepped forward.

I hadn't seen him since that early morning encounter several weeks before. My heart skipped a beat and the fear came flooding back. It was like a dark forboding cloud that settled on every aspect of my personality. Israel was on his feet. "Hey, Davie! Here I 'am. See, I told you I'd come. And look who's here," he said, pointing to me.

I knew I had to do something or I was going to crack from the fear. I jumped to my feet and shouted, "Hey Preach . . . whatcha gonna do . . . convert us or something?"

The Mau Maus joined in the laughter and I sat back down, feeling better. They still recognized me. Despite the fact that I was petrified with fear, and had relinquished the presidency to Israel; I was still their leader and they still laughed at my jokes. I was back in control of the situation.

Wilkerson began to speak: "This is the last night of our city wide youth crusade. Tonight, we're going to do something different. I'm going to ask my friends, the Mau Maus, to receive the offering."

Pandemonium broke loose. Gang members all over the auditorium knew our reputation. For the Mau Maus to take up the offering was like asking Jack the Ripper to baby sit. The people began to laugh and shout.

But I was on my feet in a second. I'd been waiting for some opportunity to show off, to draw attention to myself in a big way. This was it. I couldn't believe that the preacher would call on us, but if he wanted us to do it, we'd really do it.

I pointed at five others, including Israel. "You, you, you . . . let's go." The six of us walked to the front and lined up in front of the stage. Behind us things got quiet—deathly quiet.

Wilkerson bent down and handed each one of us a big ice cream carton. "Now," he said, "I want you to line up here in front of the platform. The organ will play and I'm going to ask the people to come forward and give their offering. When it is finished, I want you to come around behind that curtain and up onto the stage. I'll wait here until you bring me the offering."

It was too good to be true. There was no doubt in anyone's mind what we would do. Anyone who didn't take advantage of a situation like this was a fool.

The offering was large. The aisles were full of people who were coming to the front. Many of the adults put in large bills and others put in checks. If we were going to receive the offering, I was determined to make it a good one. Some of the gang members came forward, jitterbugging and dancing down the aisles and either pretended to put in money or tried to take some out of the cartons. When this happened, I'd put my hand in my pocket like I was going for my knife and say, "Hey, wait a minute, baby. You forgot to put anything in."

They would begin to laugh until they saw I was serious. "Man, the priest said give . . . you gonna give or do I have to get my boys to cut it out of you?"

Nearly everyone made some kind of a contribution.

When all had come forward, I motioned with my head and we all marched out the right side of the auditorium through the drapes that hung along the wall. Right above our heads was a huge red-lettered sign that said, "EXIT". It was noticeable to everyone and as we disappeared behind the curtain, the laughter began. It was low at first, just a few snickers, Then, we could hear it rising to a crescendo until the whole auditorium was engulfed in gales of laughter at the poor preacher who had been duped by the Mau Maus.

We gathered behind the curtain. The boys looked at me expectantly, waiting for me to tell them what to do. I could talk to them with my eyes. They were looking for a sign, for a flick of my eyes toward the exit that would say, "Let's run. Let's take this money and bug out of here."

But something inside me was tugging in the other direction. The preacher had singled me out and had shown confidence in me. I could do what was expected of me by the crowd, or I could do what he trusted me to do. The preacher's trust ignited a spark inside of me. Instead of flicking my eyes toward the exit door, I shook my head "no." "Come on," I said. "Let's take the loot to the skinny priest."

The boys couldn't believe me, but they had to do what I told them to do. There were two boys ahead of me as we started up the steps behind the platform. One of them reached into the ice cream bucket and took out a $20 bill and stuffed it into the pocket of his jacket.

"Hey, you! What the hell you think you're doing? Put that money back. That belongs to the priest."

The boys turned and looked at me in unbelief. "Hey, Nicky. Don't get so excited. Look at all this dough. No one'll know. Come on! There's plenty for all of us and him too."

I reached in my pocket and in a deft movement pulled out my knife. Flicking the switchblade open I said, "Man, this gonna be your cemetery unless you put it back."

There was no more argument. He humbly returned the wadded bill to the bucket. "Wait a minute, we're not finished," I said. "How much money you have in your pocket, bright boy?"

"Aw, Nicky, come on," he stuttered. "That's my money. My mother gave it to me to buy some slacks."

"How much?" I asked again, pointing the gleaming tip of the knife at his adam's apple.

He flushed and reached in and pulled out two $10's and a $5. I said, "In the bucket."

"Man, you crazy or something. My old woman'll skin me alive if I lose this." He was almost screaming.

"Well, I'll tell you something, bright boy. I'm gonna skin you alive right here if you don't. In the bucket!"

He looked at me again in disbelief. The knife convinced him I meant business. He wadded it up and threw it in the bucket.

"Now, let's go," I said.

We walked single file out onto the stage. A lot of kids began to boo. They thought we had made a fool out of the preacher and were sorry we hadn't ducked out the door as they would have done. But it gave a warm, satisfying feeling to know I had done something right. Something honorable. For the first time in all my life I had done right because I wanted to do right. I liked the feeling.

"Here, Priest!" I said, "this is yours." I was nervous standing there in front of the crowd. But as I handed him the money the room grew quiet again.

Wilkerson took the cartons from us and looked me

straight in the eye. "Thank you, Nicky. I knew I could count on you." We turned and filed back to our seats. The auditorium was quiet enough to hear a pin drop.

Wilkerson began to preach.

He spoke for about 15 minutes. Everyone was quiet but I didn't hear a single word. I kept remembering that warm feeling I had when I handed him the money. Inside, I was reproaching myself for not having taken off with the loot. But something had come alive inside of me and I could feel it growing. It was a feeling of goodness—of nobleness —of righteousness. A feeling I had never experienced before.

I was interrupted in my chain of thought by a disturbance behind me. Wilkerson had reached a point in his sermon telling us we ought to love one another. He was saying that the Puerto Rican ought to love the Italian and the Italian ought to love the Negro and the Negro ought to love the Whites and we all ought to love one another.

Augie stood up behind me. "Hey Preach. You some kind of a nut or something. You want me to love them Dagos? You're crazy! Looky here." And he pulled up his shirt and pointed to a huge crimson scar on his side. "Two months ago one of them filthy Guineas put a bullet in me. You think I can forget that? I'll kill that S.O.B. if I see him again."

"Yeah," a boy from the Italian section jumped to his feet and ripped open his shirt. "See this?" He pointed to a jagged scar around his shoulder and down onto his chest. One of them nigger gangs cut me with a razor. I'll love them alright—with a lead pipe."

A colored boy in the back stood up and with venom in his voice hollered, "Hey, Guinea, you wanta try it now?"

The room was suddenly charged with hatred. A colored boy from the Chaplains got up, turning over chairs. He was trying to work his way out from the row of chairs heading toward the Phantom Lord section. I could sense a rumble.

A newspaper photographer ran down the aisle with his camera. Stopping at the front, he turned and began to take pictures.

Israel spoke quickly to three of the boys at the end of the row. "Get him!" They jumped to their feet and struggled with the photographer. One of the boys managed to snatch his camera out of his hands and threw it to the floor. As the photographer bent to pick it up, a boy from across the aisle kicked it down the aisle toward the front of the room. The photographer scrambled after it on his hands and knees. Just as he reached out his hand for it, another boy kicked it away from him toward the far wall. The photographer was on his feet running after the camera, but before he could get to it, another boy kicked it hard and it slid across the tile floor and smashed into the concrete wall, broken and useless.

All of us were on our feet. The room was charged with hatred. I was looking for a way out into the aisle. A full scale riot was building.

Suddenly I had a compelling urge to look at Wilkerson. He was standing calmly on the stage. His head bowed. His hands clasped tightly in front of his chest. His knuckles showed white against the skin. I could see his lips moving. I knew he was praying.

Something clutched at my heart. I stopped and looked at myself. All around me the bedlam continued but I was looking inward. Here was this skinny man, unafraid, in the midst of all this danger. Where did he get his power? Why wasn't he afraid like all the rest of us? I felt shame. Embarrassment. Guilt.

The only thing I knew about God at all was what I had learned from seeing this man. I thought about my one other exposure to God. When I was a child my parents had taken me to church. It was full of people. The priest mumbled and the people chanted back at him. It was a miserable hour. Nothing seemed to apply to me. I never went back.

I slumped down in my chair. All around me the pandemonium continued. Israel was standing up looking backward. He was shouting, "Hey! Cool it! Let's hear what the preacher has to say."

The Mau Maus sat down. Israel continued to shout for quiet. The noise died. Like a fog moving in from the sea the silence swept toward the back of the room and then up into the balconies. Again, that deathly hush hung over the arena.

Something was happening to me. I was remembering. I remembered my childhood. I remembered the hate for my mother. I remembered the first days in New York when I ran like a wild animal set free from a cage. It was as though I were sitting in a movie and my actions were flashing in front of my eyes. I saw the girls . . . the lust . . . the sex. I saw the stabbings . . . the hurt . . . the hatred. It was almost more than I could stand. I was completely oblivious to what was going on around me. All I could do was remember. And the more I remembered the greater the feelings of guilt and shame. I was afraid to open my eyes for fear someone would be able to look inside and see what I was seeing. It was repulsive.

Wilkerson was speaking again. He said something about repenting for your sin. I was under the influence of a power a million times stronger than any drug. I was not responsible for my movements, actions or words. It was as though I had been caught in a wild torrent of a rampaging river. I was powerless to resist. I didn't understand what was taking place within me. I only knew the fear was gone.

Beside me I heard Israel blow his nose. Behind me I heard people crying. Something was sweeping through that massive arena like the wind moving through the tops of the trees. Even the curtains on the side of the auditorium began to move and rustle as if stirred by a mysterious breath.

Wilkerson was speaking again. "He's here! He's in this room. He's come especially for you. If you want your life changed, now is the time." Then he shouted with authority: "Stand up! Those who will receive Jesus Christ and be changed—stand up! Come forward!"

I felt Israel stand to his feet. "Boys, I'm going up. Who's with me?"

I was on my feet. I turned to the gang and waved them on with my hand. "Let's go." There was a spontaneous movement out of the chairs and toward the front. More than 25 of the Mau Maus responded. Behind us about 30 boys from other gangs followed our example.

We stood around the bottom of the stage looking up at Wilkerson. He dismissed the service and told us to follow him to the back rooms for counseling.

Israel was in front of me, his head bowed, his handkerchief to his face. We went through the door and into a hallway that led to the dressing rooms.

Several of the gang members were standing around in

the hallway giggling. "Hey, Nicky, what's the matter, baby, you got religion?" I looked up and one of the girls stepped forward in front of us. She pulled her halter up and exposed her bare breast for us to see. "You go in there, honey, and you can kiss this goodby."

I realize now they were jealous. They felt we were going to share our love with God and they wanted it all for themselves. This was all they knew about love. It was all I knew about love. But at the moment it made no difference. I pushed her away spitting on the floor and said, "You make me sick." Nothing else mattered at the moment except the fact that I wanted to be a follower of Jesus Christ —whoever He was.

A man talked to us about the Christian way of life. Then Wilkerson came in. "All right, fellows," he said, "kneel down right here on the floor."

I thought he was crazy. I never had knelt down in front of anyone. But an invisible force pressed down on me. I felt my knees buckling. I couldn't remain erect. It was as though a giant hand were pushing me downward until my knees hit the floor.

The touch of the hard floor brought me back to reality. It was summer. It was time for the rumbles. I opened my eyes and thought to myself. "What're you doing here?" Israel was beside me, weeping, loudly. In the midst of all this tension I giggled.

"Hey, Israel, you're bugging me with that crying." Israel looked up and smiled through the tears. But as we looked at each other I had a strange sensation. I felt the tears welling up in my eyes and suddenly they spilled over the sides and dripped down my cheeks. I was crying. For the first time since I cried my heart out under the house in Puerto Rico—I was crying.

Israel and I were both on our knees, side by side, with tears streaming down our faces, yet laughing at the same time. It was an indescribably exotic feeling.

Tears and laughter. I was happy, yet I was crying. Something was taking place in my life that I had absolutely no control over . . . and I was happy about it.

Suddenly I felt Wilkerson's hand on my head. He was praying—praying for me. The tears flowed more freely as I bowed my head and the shame and repentance and the

wonderful joy of salvation mixed their ingredients in my
soul.

"Go on, Nicky," Wilkerson said, "Go ahead and cry.
Pour it out to God. Call on Him."

I opened my mouth but the words that came out were
not mine. "O God, if you love me, come into my life. I'm
tired of running. Come into my life and change me. Please
change me."

That's all it was. But I felt myself being picked up and
swept heavenward.

Marijuana! Sex! Blood! All the sadistic, immoral thrills
of a million lifetimes put together could not begin to equal
what I felt. I was literally baptized with love.

After the emotional crisis passed, Wilkerson quoted
some Scripture to us. "If any man be in Christ, he is a new
creature: old things are passed away; behold all things are
become new." (II Cor. 5:17).

It made sense. For the first time in my life it made
sense. I had become new. I was Nicky and yet I was not
Nicky. The old way of life had disappeared. It was as
though I had died to the old way—and yet I was alive in a
new kind of way.

Happiness. Joy. Gladness. Release. Relief. Freedom.
Wonderful, wonderful freedom.

I had stopped running.

All my fear was gone. All my anxieties were gone. All
my hatred was gone. I was in love with God . . . with Jesus
Christ . . . and with those around me. I even loved myself.
The hatred I'd had for myself had turned to love. I sud-
denly realized that the reason I had treated myself in such
a shoddy way was I didn't really love myself as God in-
tended for me to love myself.

Israel and I embraced. The tears running down our
faces and wetting each other's shirts. I loved him. He was
my brother.

Wilkerson had stepped out but was now back in the
room. I loved him, too. That skinny, grinning preacher I
had spit on just a few weeks before—I loved him.

"Nicky, Israel," he said, "I want to give you a Bible. I
have other Bibles for the Mau Maus, too. Come with me
and I'll get them for you."

We followed him to another room. There in boxes on the
floor were copies of the black book. He bent over and

picked up a pocket sized edition of the New Testament and started to pass it to us. "Hey, Davie," I asked, "what about these big books? Could we have the big ones? We want everyone to know we're Christians now."

Wilkerson looked surprised. The "big books" were just that. They were giant sized editions of the Bible. But the boys wanted them and he was willing to give them to us.

"Man," Israel said, grinning at me, "How about that? A twenty-five-pound Bible!" It felt like it, too. But the weight of it was small in comparison to the weight that had been lifted from my heart that night as the sin was removed and the love flowed in.

Late that night I climbed my steps to my room as a new person. It was a little after 11:00 P.M. which was early for me—but I was anxious to get back to my room. There was no more need to run. The streets had no appeal to me. I had no more need to be recognized as the gang leader. I had no more fear of the night.

I went to my closet and took off my Mau Mau jacket and shoes and put them in a bag. "No more," I thought to myself. "No longer will I need these." I reached up to the shelf and took down my revolver. By force of habit I started to put the shells in the magazine so I could sleep with the gun on my night stand. But suddenly I remembered. Jesus loves me. He will protect me. I took the bullets and placed them back in the small box and put the gun back on the shelf. In the morning I would turn it in to the police.

I walked by the mirror. I couldn't believe what I saw. There was a light coming from my face I had never seen before. I smiled at myself. "Hey, Nicky. Look how handsome you are. Too bad you have to give up all the girls now that you are so handsome." I broke out laughing at the irony of it all. But I was happy. The burden of fear was gone. I could laugh.

I knelt beside the bed and threw my head back. "Jesus. . . ." Nothing else came out. "Jesus. . . ." And finally the words came. "Thank you, Jesus . . . thank you."

That night, for the first time in my memory, I put my head on my pillow and slept nine beautiful hours. No tossing on the bed. No fear of sounds outside my room. The nightmares were gone.

11

Out of the Wilderness

Early the next morning I was out on the street rounding up the guys who had gone forward the night before. I told them to bring their guns and bullets and meet me in Washington Park. We were going to march on the police station.

Going back to my room I stuck my revolver in my belt and picking up my big Bible I started back to Washington Park to meet the others.

Walking down Ft. Greene Place I came face to face with an old Italian woman I had seen before. In the past she had crossed the street when she saw me coming. This time I held up my big black book that said, "Holy Bible" on the cover in gold letters as I approached.

She stared at the Bible, "Where'd you steal that Bible?"

I grinned, "I didn't steal it. A preacher gave it to me."

She shook her head, "Don't you know you shouldn't lie about sacred things? God will punish you for this."

"I'm not lying. And God is not going to punish me because he has forgiven me. I'm heading to the police station now to give them my gun." I pulled back my shirt so she could see the gun stuck in my belt.

Her eyes moved slowly from the gun to the Bible and lingered in disbelief. "Hallelujah!" she screamed as her face broke into a wreath of smiles. Throwing up her arms she shouted again, "Hallelujah!"

I grinned and ran past her toward Washington Park.

About 25 of the Mau Maus were there. Israel had them organized and we marched down St. Edward to the Housing Police Station on the corner of Auburn Street.

We didn't stop to think what it must have looked like to the police. Twenty-five of the toughest gang members in Brooklyn were marching down the middle of the street carrying an arsenal of weapons and ammunition. I have thanked the Lord many times that they didn't see us until we were at the door. Had they seen us a block away they would have barricaded the doors and probably shot us down in the street.

When we walked in the Desk Sergeant jumped to his feet and reached for his pistol. "What's going on here? What're you guys up to?"

"Hey, easy man," Israel said. "We ain't coming to cause no trouble. We come to turn in our guns."

"You've what?" the sergeant shouted. "What the hell is going on here anyway?" He turned and shouted over his shoulder, "Lieutenant, you better get in here right away."

The lieutenant appeared at the door, "What are these kids doing here?" he asked the sergeant. "What's this all about?"

Israel turned to the lieutenant, "We've all given our hearts to God and now we want to give our guns to the police."

"Yeah," one of the guys chimed in, "maybe you can use them to shoot the bad kids with."

We all laughed and the lieutenant turned to the sergeant. "Is this on the level? Better get some of the guys to check outside. We might be in for an ambush or something."

I stepped up. "Hey, Lieutenant, looky here." I held up my Bible. "The preacher gave us these Bibles last night after we all turned our hearts over to Christ. We're not gonna be gang members any longer. Now, we're Christians."

"What preacher?" the lieutenant asked.

"Man, Davie Wilkerson. That skinny preacher who's been hanging around talking to all the gangs. We had a big meeting over at St. Nicholas Arena last night and we all came to God. If you don't believe us, call him."

The lieutenant turned to the sergeant. "You got that preacher's number?"

"Yes sir, he's staying with a Mrs. Ortez."

"Call him and tell him to get over here as quick as he can. We may be in for big trouble. If this is something he's stirred up, I'll have him in jail so fast it'll make his head swim."

The sergeant placed the call and handed the phone to

the lieutenant. "Reverend Wilkerson? You better get down here right away. I've got a room full of Mau Maus and I don't know what's going on." There was a pause and then the lieutenant hung up. "He's on his way. But before he gets here I want your guns—all of them."

"Sure, General," Israel said, "that's what we came down here for." Then turning to the gang he said, "Alright you guys. Bring your guns up here and lay them on the counter. Leave your bullets too."

The policemen couldn't believe their eyes. By this time 4 other cops had come in and they stood there in unbelief while the stack of pistols, zip guns, and homemade rifles grew higher.

When we finished the lieutenant just shook his head. Turning to Israel he said, "Alright. Now suppose you tell me what's really going on."

Israel again related what had taken place at St. Nicholas Arena. He told him we had become Christians and that we were going to live a different kind of life. He then asked the lieutenant if he would autograph his Bible.

This seemed like a great idea and all of us crowded around asking the cops to autograph our Bibles.

Just then David pushed through the door. He took one look at all of us and walked straight up to the lieutenant. The lieutenant asked all the other officers to come into the room.

"Reverend," he said, "I want to shake your hand." Wilkerson glanced around with a quizzical look on his face but stuck out his hand while the policemen pumped it firmly.

"How did you do it?" he asked. "These boys declare war on us and have given us nothing but trouble for years. Then this morning they all troop in here and you know what they want?"

Wilkerson shook his head.

"They want us to autograph their Bibles!"

Wilkerson was speechless. "You asked these policemen to what?" he stammered.

I opened my Bible and showed him the lieutenant's autograph on the flyleaf. "Well, praise the Lord!" David said. "See, lieutenant, God is at work here in Ft. Greene!"

We all stepped out on the street and left the sergeant shaking his head in wonder at the pile of guns stacked on the counter in front of him.

We clamored around Wilkerson. Israel spoke up, "Hey, Davie, I been reading my Bible most of the night. Look! I'm in the Bible. Here's my name all over the place. See? Israel. That's me. I'm famous."

Several weeks later Reverend Arce, the minister at a Spanish Church called Iglesia de Dios Juan 3:16 (Church of God John 3:16) came by my apartment. Israel was there. We had been spending a lot of time together reading our Bibles and walking around praying out loud. Reverend Arce wanted us to come to his church the next night and give our testimonies. It was a Wednesday night service and he promised to come by and pick us up.

It was the first real church service I had ever been in. We sang for almost an hour. Israel and I were on the platform and the church building was packed full. Reverend Arce preached a full length sermon and then called on me to give my testimony.

After I finished speaking, I sat on the front row and listened to Israel.

It was the first time I had heard him speak in public. He stood behind the pulpit, his handsome face radiating the love of Christ. In his gentle voice he began to tell of the events which led up to his conversion. Even though we had been together daily during the past few weeks, tonight I witnessed in him a depth of feeling and expression I had never seen before. His words took me back to that night in St. Nicholas Arena when Israel had so willingly responded to the Gospel. I thought of my own attitude toward Davie. I had hated him—God knows how I hated him! How could I have been so wrong? All he wanted to do was let God love me through him—instead, I had spit on him, cursed him, wanted to kill him.

Israel's mention of David's name snapped me back to reality.

"I was still testing Wilkerson's sincerity," Israel was saying, relating his feelings after that first street meeting when he had heard Davie preach.

"One afternoon Wilkerson came by and asked me to take him to meet some of the other gang leaders. He wanted to invite them to the meetings he was having at St. Nicholas Arena.

"We went down into Brooklyn together and I pointed

out Little Jo-Jo, who was President of the Coney Island Dragons, one of the largest street gangs in the city. I just pointed him out. I didn't want him to know I set him up for Davie since they were big enemies of the Mau Maus.

"I told Davie I'd walk home. As he walked up to Little Jo-Jo, I ducked behind some apartment steps to listen. Jo-Jo looked him over real good and then spit on his shoes. This is the highest sign of contempt you can give a fellow. Jo-Jo didn't say a word, he just spit on Davie's shoes. Then he turned away and sat down on the steps.

"Jo-Jo didn't have a home. Matter of fact, he didn't have much of anything. He slept in the park in warm weather and when it rained or got cold he slept in the subway. Jo-Jo was a real bum. He stole clothes out of those big welfare boxes on the corner and wore 'em 'til they were just rags. Then he'd steal some more.

"That day he had on a pair of old sloppy canvas shoes with his toes stickin' out and some big old droopy pants like belonged to a fat man.

"I figured if Wilkerson was a phony it would show up when he met Jo-Jo. Jo-Jo could spot a phony. If Wilkerson wasn't for real, Jo-Jo would stick him with his shiv.

"He looked up at Wilkerson and said, 'Get lost, rich man. You don't belong around here. You come to New York and talk big about God changing people. You get shiny new shoes and new pants and we ain't got nothing. My old lady kicked me out 'cause there are 10 kids in our hole and no money. Man, I know your type. You down here slummin' like them rich folks who ride the bus through the Bowery. Well, you better get lost 'fore someone runs a shiv in your belly.'

"I could tell that something was getting hold of Davie's heart. Maybe he knew Jo-Jo was telling the truth. He told me later it was because he remembered something about some General Booth who had said, 'It is impossible to comfort men's hearts with the love of God when their feet are perishing with cold.' Maybe I don't quote that just right, but anyhow Davie said that's what flashed through his mind. And you know what he did? He sat down on those steps—right there on that street—and pulled his shoes off and handed them to Jo-Jo.

"Old Jo-Jo, he just looked up at Davie and said, 'What

you trying to prove preacher? That you got a heart or
something? I ain't gonna put your stinkin' shoes on.'

"But Davie talked right back to him. 'Man,' he said,
'you been griping about shoes. Now put 'em on or quit
your belly-achin'.'

"Jo-Jo said, 'I ain't never had no new shoes.'

"And Wilkerson just kept at him, 'Put 'em on,' he said.

"So Jo-Jo put on Davie's shoes. As he did Davie started
walking down the street toward his car. I kinda crouched
back in behind the steps while Jo-Jo chased Davie down
the street. Old Davie was in his socks and had to walk 2
blocks to the car with all the folks laughin' at him. That's
when I saw he was for real."

Israel paused in his testimony, choking back tears.
"Nothing Davie had said had gotten through to me. But
this guy was no phony. He lived what he preached. I knew
then I couldn't resist the kind of power that could make a
man do something like that for someone like Jo-Jo."

Following the service I made my way slowly through the
crowd still overwhelmed with the church service and the
power of the presence of God in me as I spoke. I kept
thinking that maybe God wanted me to preach. Could this
be His way of speaking to me? I didn't know, but I felt I
needed time to think about it.

The people were still milling around the vestibule and
standing out front on the sidewalk. I was still shaking
hands when I walked out the front door. Just then two
cars across the street roared to life. I heard a woman
scream. Glancing in that direction I saw gun barrels stick-
ing out the windows and recognized some of the Bishops.
They began shooting wildly in my direction as the cars
jerked away from the curb. People were falling down in
front of the church and running wildly back into the build-
ing trying to escape the fusillade of shots. I ducked behind
a door as bullets smacked into the stone beside me. The
cars sped off into the night.

As the excitement died down an old man walked up be-
side me and put his arm around my shoulder, "Son, don't
get discouraged. Jesus Himself was tempted in the wilder-
ness following his baptism. You should feel honored that
Satan has singled you out for persecution. I predict you
will do great things for God if you persevere." He patted
me on the shoulder and disappeared into the crowd.

I didn't know what "persevere" meant, but I wanted to do great things for God. I wasn't too sure that I was honored because Satan had sent the Bishops around to try to kill me, though.

Things seemed to have quieted down and I went back out to start the long walk home. Reverend Arce had driven Israel home but I wanted to walk. I needed to think. Mr. Delgado who had been working with David Wilkerson, asked me to come home and spend the night with him. He was a kind, gentle, well-dressed man. I thought he must be very wealthy. I was ashamed of my poor manners and clothes and declined his offer. He gave me a dollar bill and told me that if I ever needed money to let him know.

I thanked him and started back to the apartment. Crossing Vanderbilt Avenue, I spotted Loca standing in front of her apartment. "Hey, Nicky, where you been all this time? Someone said you dropped out of the gang. Is that right?"

I told her it was.

"Hey, baby, we miss you. Things just aren't the same without you around. How come you don't come back?"

Suddenly, someone locked their arms around me from behind. "Hey, you really do want me back, don't you?" thinking it was one of our gang. Loca's face was frozen with terror. I hoisted my head and recognized Joe, the Bishop we had kidnapped and burned.

I was struggling to get loose when I saw the knife in his right hand. He held me from behind with his left hand around my neck while he swung the blade over my shoulder toward my heart. I threw my right hand up to ward off the 8-inch blade and it stabbed me in the hand between my ring finger and little finger, going all the way through my hand and barely grazing my chest.

I spun around and he slashed at me again. "I'm gonna kill you this time," he cursed. "You think you can get away from me by hiding behind a church, then baby you're wrong. I'm gonna do the world a favor and kill a chicken who's turned square."

I shouted at Loca, "Get out of here! This guy's crazy!"

He moved toward me and jabbed the knife at my stomach. I jumped back and snatched a radio aerial off a parked car. Now the odds were even. In my hand, the aerial was as deadly as his switchblade.

I circled the boy, slashing the air with the metal rod. I

was back in my own element now. I felt confident I could kill him. I thought ahead, knowing from experience what his next move would be. When he lunged at me with his knife, I would dance back and catch him off balance. I could blind him with a back-handed swing and paralyze or kill him with the second blow.

I held the antenna in my left hand, my right hand dripping with blood, held in front of me to ward off his knife.

"Com'on, baby," I whispered. "Try it once more. Just once more. It'll be your last."

The boy's eyes were narrowed with hate. I knew I'd have to kill him because nothing else would stop him.

He started toward me and I stepped back as the knife whizzed by my stomach. Now! He was off balance. I brought the antenna back to whip it across his unprotected face.

Suddenly, it felt as though the hand of God grabbed my arm. "Turn the other cheek." The voice was so real it was audible. I looked on this Bishop not as the enemy, but as a person. I felt sorry for him standing there in the night spitting curse words with hate written on his face. I could picture myself just a few weeks before standing in the dark street trying to kill an enemy.

I prayed. For the first time, I prayed for myself. "God, help me."

The Bishop regained his balance and looked up at me. "What you say?"

I said it again, "God, help me." He stopped and stared at me.

Loca ran up thrusting the neck of a broken whiskey bottle into my hand. "Slit him open, Nicky."

The boy started to run. "Throw it at him, Nicky, throw it!"

I pulled back my arm but instead of throwing the bottle at the fleeing Bishop, I threw it against the side of the building.

Then I took my handkerchief and wrapped it around my badly bleeding hand. The blood soaked through and Loca ran up the steps to her room and brought me a bath towel to absorb the bleeding. She wanted to walk me home but I told her I could make it and started down the sidewalk.

I was afraid to go to the hospital, but I knew I needed help. I was getting weak from loss of blood. I would have to cross Washington Park from Fulton Place to get to Cumberland Hospital. I figured I'd better go before I bled to death. Standing on the corner of De Kalb by the Fire Station, I waited for the light to change. But my eyes began to roll and I knew I had to get across the street before I fainted.

I staggered out into the middle of the traffic. Just then I heard a shout and one of the Mau Maus came running out in the street to help me. It was Tarzan, a real nut who wore a huge Mexican hat.

"What you trying to do, Nicky, commit suicide?" He thought I was crazy because I had given my heart to God.

"Man, I'm hurt. Hurt bad. Help me get to Israel's apartment, will you?"

Tarzan walked with me to Israel's apartment and we climbed the 5 flights of stairs to his room. It was midnight when I rapped on the door.

Israel's mother opened the door and invited me in. She could see I was hurt. Israel came out of the other room. He looked at me and started to laugh. "Man, what happened to you?"

"I got stuck by a Bishop."

"Hey, baby, I didn't think this could ever happen to you."

Israel's mother interrupted and insisted that I go to the hospital. Israel and Tarzan both helped me down the stairs and to the emergency room at the nearby hospital. Tarzan agreed to take my wallet with the one dollar in it and tell my brother Frank what happened to me. Israel waited until the doctor examined my hand. Tendons had been cut and they were going to have to put me to sleep to operate. Israel looked serious when they wheeled me out. "Don't worry, baby, we'll get the guy who did it."

I wanted to tell him that we didn't need to get revenge any more. God would take care of that. But the door closed softly behind me.

Early the next morning Israel was in my room. I was still groggy from the anesthesia but I could tell there had been a change about him. I finally got my eyes open and saw that he had completely shaved his head.

"Hey, baldie, what's up?" I mumbled.

Israel had the old look back on his face. "Man, first they almost shoot us in front of the church and now they stab you. This Jesus business is for the birds. That guy had no right to treat you that way. I'm gonna get him for you."

I was coming to my senses and raised up in the bed. "Hey, man, you can't do that. I could've gotten him myself last night but I left it in God's hands. If you go back to the street you'll never come back. Remember what Davie said about putting your hand to the plow. . . . Man, you stick with me and leave the fighting alone."

I struggled to sit up and noticed that Lydia and Loretta had come in with Israel.

I fell back on the bed still weak from the loss of blood and the surgery. My entire arm was in a big cast from the tips of my fingers to my elbow.

Loretta was a cute black-haired Italian girl I had dated on several occasions. She spoke up. "Nicky, Israel's right. Those guys will come in the hospital and kill you if you don't come back to the gang. Let's make it like old times again, okay? You get well and come on back to the Mau Maus. We'll be waiting for you."

I turned and looked at Lydia. "Is that the way you feel too?" I asked.

She hung her head. "Nicky, there's something I've got to tell you. I'm ashamed to bring it up now when I should have done it a long time ago. I've been a Christian for two years now."

"What?" I stared at her in unbelief. "You mean to tell me you've been a Christian all this time and never did tell me. How can you be a Christian and do all the things you've done? Think about what we've done together. Don't tell me you're a Christian. Christians don't act like that. They aren't ashamed of God. I don't believe you."

Lydia bit her bottom lip and tears came to her eyes as she twisted the sheet with her hands. "I'm ashamed, Nicky. I was scared to tell you about Christ. I was afraid that if I told you I was a Christian you wouldn't want me any more."

Israel walked over to the side of the bed. "Hey, com'on, Nicky. You're just upset. You'll feel better later on. Loretta and I think you ought to come back to the gang. I don't know about Lydia. But you think about it and don't worry. I'll talk to some of the guys and we'll get that guy who did this to you."

I turned away from them. Loretta came over and kissed me on the side of the face. I felt hot tears on my cheek as Lydia bent low to kiss me. "I'm sorry, Nicky. Forgive me, please."

I said nothing and she kissed me and ran out. I heard the door close behind them.

After they left I could almost feel the presence of Satan in the room. He was speaking to me through Israel and Loretta. He was preparing me through my disappointment over Lydia. "Nicky," he whispered. "You're a fool. They are right. Go on back to the gang. Remember the good times. Remember the satisfaction of getting revenge. Remember how sweet it was to be in the arms of a beautiful girl. You've let your gang down, Nicky, but it's not too late to go back."

As he was tempting me the nurse came in with my dinner tray. I could still hear his whisper. "Last night was the first time in your life you never fought back. What a coward you are. Big brave Nicky Cruz, crying there in St. Nicholas. Running from a Bishop and letting him get away. Sissy. Square. Coward."

"Mr. Cruz?" It was the nurse speaking as she stood beside my bed. "If you'll turn over I'll fix your dinner tray."

I jerked up in bed and slapped at the tray knocking it from her hands and onto the floor. "Get the hell out of here!"

I wanted to say more but nothing else came out. All the old curse words had disappeared. I couldn't even think of them at the time. I just sat there with my mouth open and suddenly the tears flooded my eyes and ran down my face like waterfalls. "I'm sorry. I'm sorry," I sobbed out. "Please call a minister. Call Reverend Arce."

The nurse quietly picked up the dishes and patted me on the shoulder. "I'll call him now. You lie down and rest."

I lay back on my pillow and sobbed. In a short time Reverend Arce arrived and prayed with me. As he prayed I felt release from the spirit that had possessed me. He told me he was going to send Mr. Delgado up to see me in the morning and he would see I was taken care of.

That night after the nurse had helped me change my pajama top, I knelt beside the bed in the hospital room. During the afternoon they had moved someone into the other bed in the room but I thought he was asleep. I began to pray out loud, which was the only way I knew how to pray. I didn't know you could "pray to yourself." I thought you had to pray "to God" and the only way I knew how to pray was to talk to Him—out loud. So I began to pray.

I asked God to forgive the boy who had stabbed me and to protect him from harm until he could learn about Jesus. I asked God to forgive me for the way I had acted toward Lydia and for slapping the tray out of the nurse's hand. I told Him I would go anywhere and do anything He wanted me to do. I reminded Him I wasn't afraid to die but asked him to let me live long enough to one day tell Mama and Papa about Jesus.

I was on my knees for a long time before I crawled back into bed and went to sleep.

The next morning I was dressing to leave the hospital when the man in the next bed whispered and motioned for me to step closer. He was an old man with a tube in his throat. He was shaking and very pale and could barely speak above a whisper.

"I was awake last night," he whispered.

I was embarrassed and grinned foolishly.

"Thank you," he said. "Thank you for your prayer."

"But I wasn't praying for you," I confessed. "I thought you were asleep. I was praying for myself."

The old man reached over and grabbed my one good hand with his cold, clammy fingers. His grip was very weak but I could feel him squeezing. "Oh, no, you're wrong. You were praying for me. And I prayed too. For the first time in many, many years, I prayed. I, too, want to do what Jesus wants me to do. Thank you."

Big tears rolled down his drawn hollow cheeks as he spoke. I said, "God bless you, my friend," and walked out. I had never tried to minister to anyone else in all my life. I didn't know how even now. But I had a strong warm feeling that God's Spirit had ministered through me. And I was glad.

Mr. Delgado met me in the lobby. He had paid my bill and ushered me out to his car. "I called David Wilkerson last night," he said. "He's in Elmira conducting a series of meetings. He wants me to bring you and Israel up there tomorrow."

"Davie mentioned it the last time I saw him," I said. "But Israel has gone back to the gang. I don't think he'll go."

"I'll go see him tonight," Mr. Delgado said. "But today I want you to stay at my house where you'll be safe. We'll leave early in the morning and drive to Elmira."

It seemed ironic that I would be going to Elmira to be with Davie. This was where the police wanted to send me, but for a very different reason. I spent the rest of the day praying for Israel, that he wouldn't go back to the gang but would come with me to Elmira.

The next morning we got up early and drove through the city toward Brooklyn and the Ft. Greene project. Mr. Delgado said that Israel had agreed to go with us and was supposed to meet us on the corner of Myrtle and De Kalb at 7 a.m. When we got there Israel was not there. I began to feel sick at my stomach. We circled the block but didn't see him. Mr. Delgado said we were in a hurry but we'd ride by his apartment on St. Edward Street across from P.S. 67 and see if we could find him. We drove by but didn't see any trace of him. Mr. Delgado kept looking at his watch and said we would have to go on.

"Can't we circle the block just one more time," I said, "maybe we've missed him."

"Look, Nicky," he said, "I know you love Israel and you're fearful he'll go back to the gang. But he's got to learn to stand on his own two feet sometime. He said he'd meet us at 7 a.m. and he's not here. We'll circle the block one more time but it's a 6-hour drive up to Elmira and David is expecting you at 2 p.m."

We drove down the street one more time and then headed through the Bronx to pick up Jeff Morales. Jeff was a Puerto Rican boy who wanted to go into the ministry. David had asked Mr. Delgado to bring him up for the night to interpret for me when I spoke in the church.

As we pulled away from the city, I felt a sense of relief. I leaned back in the seat and sighed. The weight was lifted. But in my heart there was a deep sadness because we were leaving Israel behind and I had an ominous feeling of doom and despair about his future. I didn't know it then, but it would be 6 years before I would see him again.

That night David introduced me to the people in Elmira and I gave my testimony. David had told me to start at the beginning and tell my story just as it happened. I was hazy on the details and couldn't remember much of what had taken place. I was quickly realizing that not only had God taken many of the old desires away from me, He had wiped many of the memories out of my mind. But I told the story the best I could. Many times I would get ahead of my interpreter and Jeff would have to say, "Slow down, Nicky, give me a chance to talk." The people laughed and cried and when the invitation was given, many of them came to the altar to give their hearts to Christ. The feeling that God was calling me to a special ministry grew stronger as I saw Him at work in my life.

The next day I had a chance to talk with David for a long time. He asked me if I were serious about going into the ministry. I told him I didn't know anything about it and couldn't speak understandable English, but I felt God had His hand on my heart and was leading me in that direction. David said he would do everything possible to arrange for me to go to school.

School! I hadn't been in school for three years and then I had been kicked out. "Davie, I can't go back to school. The principal told me if I ever came back he'd turn me over to the cops."

David laughed. "Not that school, Nicky. Bible school. How would you like to go to California?"

"Where?"

"California, on the west coast."

"Is that near Manhattan?" I asked.

Wilkerson burst out laughing. "Oh, Nicky, Nicky. The Lord has got a lot of work to do in you. But I think He's just powerful enough to do it. You just wait and see. Great things are going to happen through your ministry. I believe it."

I shook my head. I'd heard the Manhattan cops were just as tough as the cops in Brooklyn. If I were going to school, I'd sure hope it'd be someplace out of the city of New York."

David wanted me to remain in Elmira while he wrote the Bible school which I later found out was in La Puente, California, outside Los Angeles. The school was a three year Bible school for boys and girls who wanted to prepare for the ministry but couldn't affort to go to college. Of course, I hadn't completed high school but David was writing an air mail letter asking them to accept me anyway. He said he was making no bones about my past career but was telling them of my dreams and ambitions and asking them to accept me on probation even though I had only been a Christian a few weeks.

But things were not so good in Elmira. Someone had spread a rumor that I was still a gang leader and was trying to form a gang up there. David was upset over the matter and knew it could mean trouble. I was staying with him at night but was afraid people would criticize David. We agreed to pray about it.

That night David talked to me about the Baptism in the Spirit. I listened intently but didn't understand what he was trying to get over to me. He read passages of scripture from the book of Acts, I Corinthians, Ephesians. He explained that after a person is saved God wants to fill him with His power. He explained about the conversion of Saul in Acts 9; that three days after Saul was converted, he received the Baptism in the Holy Spirit and was filled with new power.

"That is what you need, Nicky," David said. "God wants to fill you with power and give you special gifts."

"What kind of gifts you mean?" I asked him.

He opened his Bible to I Corinthians 12:8-10 and explained about the nine gifts of the Spirit. "These are given to those who are Baptized in the Holy Spirit. You may not receive all of them, but you will receive some of them. We Pentecostals believe that everyone who is baptized in the Spirit speaks in tongues.

"You mean I'll be able to speak in English without even studying?" I asked, amazed.

David started to say more but closed his Bible. "The Lord told the apostles to 'tarry' and they would receive power. I don't want to rush this with you, Nicky. We'll wait on the Lord and He will Baptize you when you are ready to receive it. In the meantime, we've got a problem on our hands and we've got to pray about it."

He flipped off the light and I said, "If he gives me another tongue I hope it's Italian. I know the cutest Italian girl you've ever seen and I sure would. . . ." I was interrupted by Wilkerson's pillow as it sailed across the room and smashed me in the face.

"To sleep, Nicky. Tomorrow is almost here and half the town thinks you're still a gang leader. If He gives you another tongue it had better be something these people up here can understand when you tell them you're really not a murderer."

The next morning David had a worried look on his face when he came back from the morning meeting. "Things aren't too good, Nicky. We're going to have to get you away from here before tonight and I don't know where I can send you unless it's back to New York."

"Do you think the Lord heard our prayers last night?" I asked.

David looked shocked. "Well, of course I do. That's why I pray, because I believe He hears me."

"Did you pray God would take care of me?"

"You know I did."

"Then how come you're so anxious?"

David stood and looked for a minute, "Come on, let's go get a late breakfast. I'm starved, aren't you?"

At 2 p.m. that afternoon the phone rang in the motel room. It was the pastor of the church where David was preaching. There was a woman in his office who wanted to talk to the two of us. David said we'd be right over.

We walked in and the pastor introduced us to a Mrs. Johnson who had driven 200 miles from her home in upstate New York. She was 72 years old and said that last night the Holy Spirit had spoken to her. She had read about me in the papers and said the Holy Spirit had told her I was in trouble and she was to come after me.

I looked at David and big tears were running down his face. "Your name may be Mrs. Johnson, but I think it is really Mrs. Ananias."

She looked at David with a strange look. "I don't understand."

The pastor interrupted. "He's referring to the Ananias mentioned in Acts 9 whom the Holy Spirit touched and sent to minister to Paul."

Mrs. Johnson smiled. "I only know that the Lord gave me directions to come pick up this young boy and take him home with me."

David told me to get ready to drive back with her. He told me he should have an answer back from La Puente in a few days and he would send for me as soon as he did. I didn't want to go, but after hearing what had happened the night before and seeing what was happening now, I was afraid to stay.

Two weeks later I got a call from David. He was elated. The people at the Bible Institute had written back and were so intrigued over the prospects of my coming they agreed to waive all the requirements and take me as a regular student. He told me to catch a bus back to New York. I'd leave for California the following day.

This time I didn't mind the ride back to New York. I remembered the ride with Dr. John and my depressed feeling of dropping back into the pit. But the pit was gone. This time I was on my way out of the wilderness.

I was to have a 5-hour wait in the bus station before David could meet me. I had agreed to wait in the lobby to keep out of trouble. However, trouble had a way of tracking me down. It came in the form of 10 Viceroys who formed a silent circle around me as I sat reading a magazine.

"Hey, look at pretty boy," one of them said, making reference to my suit and tie. "Hey, Dude, you're outta your territory. Don't you know this Viceroy turf?"

Suddenly, one of the boys spoke up. "Hey, you guys know who this is? This that jerk from the Mau Maus who turned preacher."

Another one walked up to me and stuck his finger against my face. "Hey, preacher, can I touch you? Maybe some your holy-roly rub off on me."

I slapped his hand away from my face. "You wanna die?" I snarled, the old Nicky breaking through. "Well, just touch me one more time and you're a dead man."

"Hey," the boy jumped back in mock surprise. "Listen to him. He looks like a preacher but he talks like a——," and he used a filthy name.

Before he could move, I sprang to my feet and sank my fist into his stomach. As he bent over from the blow, I hit him on the back of the head with my fist. He fell unconscious to the floor. The other boys were too surprised to move. The people in the bus station were scattering and hiding behind the benches. I backed out the door. "You guys try anything and I'll have everyone of you killed. I'm going after the Mau Maus. I'll be back in an hour and we'll kill every one of you Viceroys."

They knew I meant it and they knew the Mau Maus were twice as vicious and powerful as they were. They looked at each other and backed toward the other door, dragging their limp companion with them.

"I'll be back," I shouted. "You guys better be on the move because you're as good as dead right now."

I ran out the door toward a nearby subway entrance. But on the way down the block I passed a Spanish church. Something in me slowed me down and then turned me around. I walked slowly up the steps into the open building. Maybe I should pray first, I thought. Then I'll go after the Mau Maus.

But once inside the church I forgot about the Mau Maus —and the Viceroys. I began to think about Jesus. And then about my new life ahead. I knelt at the altar and the minutes passed like seconds and I finally felt a tap on the shoulder. I looked around. It was Wilkerson.

"I figured when I didn't find you in the bus station you'd be here," he said.

"Naturally," I answered. "Where did you think I'd be, back with the gang?" He laughed as we walked toward his car.

12

School Daze

The Bible Institute in La Puente, California, is small and unpretentious. It is located on a small tract of land just out of town. Most of the seventy students enrolled in the school were Spanish speaking and most of them came from modest circumstances.

Steve Morales and I arrived by plane from New York. The school was different—more different from anything I had ever experienced. The rules were very strict and the schedule very disciplined. The school was highly regimented with classes held Tuesday through Saturday. Most of the students lived in barracks type dormitories on the campus.

It took several months for me to get accustomed to the Institute. I had always had my own way, but at the Institute everything was done by a bell from the time we got up at 6:00 a.m. until lights out at 9:30 p.m. There was virtually no free time and we were required to spend more than 2 hours a day in prayer besides the 6 hours in class. My biggest problem was not being able to talk to the girls. This was strictly forbidden and the only time we could converse was a few stolen moments before and after class or while washing dishes during our regular KP duty.

However, it was the philosophy of the school to teach discipline and obedience. And even though this was very difficult for me, it was just the kind of training I needed. Anything less strict would have allowed me too much freedom.

The meals were filling but far from appetizing. Our usual breakfast was hot mush and toast, but once a week we had an egg. This type diet, however, was a definite part of our training, since most of us would be Spanish

ministers in poor sections of the nation and would be
forced to live on very meager substance.

The teachers were very patient with me. I didn't know
how to act and felt my insecurity keenly. I tried to make
up for it by acting smart and showing off.

I remember one morning during the third month of
school we were standing while the teacher led us in a
lengthy opening prayer. I had been eyeing this cute black-
haired, very pious Mexican girl in front of me for some
weeks but hadn't been able to attract her attention. In the
middle of the prayer I gently slipped the chair away from
her desk thinking she'd surely notice me now. At the
"amen" we all sat down. She noticed me all right! She
turned around from her awkward position on the floor and
looked up at me with eyes that were spitting fire. I was
overcome with laughter as I reached down to help her up.
She glared at me and scrambled to her feet unassisted. She
never said a word and somehow it wasn't funny anymore.
As she swung her chair back into position, she deliberately
jabbed the sharp leg into my shin. I don't think anything
has ever hurt as much. I could feel the blood draining from
my face and thought I was going to faint. Everyone in the
class laughed. I finally regained control of myself and
looked up at her. She glared back at me with eyes that
could burn a hole through an armored tank. I smiled weak-
ly but felt like I was going to throw up. She turned around
and sat rigidly at her desk facing the teacher.

The professor cleared his throat and said, "Now that we
have finished with the morning devotion we shall begin.
Mr. Cruz will be the first one to recite for us this morning."

I looked at him with a weak, blank look. "Mr. Cruz!" he
said, "You have prepared your recitation have you not?" I
tried to say something but my leg was hurting so badly I
couldn't talk.

"Mr. Cruz, you know the penalty for failing to have your
lesson ready. I know that you have great difficulty with the
language and that you have not disciplined your mind to
think in academic terms. We are all trying to be patient
with you but unless you cooperate I have no choice but to
give you a zero and flunk you in this course. I ask you once
more, do you have your material ready?"

I nodded and got to my feet. My mind was completely
blank. I hobbled around to the front of the room and faced

the class. I looked down at the pretty girl with the dark eyes. She smiled very sweetly and opened her notebook so I could see page after page of neatly written notes on the very material I was supposed to recite. I looked at the teacher and said faintly, "Excuse me." I ran out of the room toward the dormitory.

I had made a complete fool of myself. I thought I could act smart and everyone would laugh at me like they had in the gangs. But these people were different. They tolerated me because they felt sorry for me. I was a misfit. An outcast.

I sat down on the side of my bed and wrote David Wilkerson a long letter. I told him it was tough out here and I had made a mistake in coming. I was sorry I had let him down but was afraid I was going to embarrass him if I stayed in school. I asked him to send me a plane ticket home. I put a special delivery stamp on it and mailed it to Wilkerson's home in Pennsylvania.

His reply arrived a week later. I eagerly tore open the envelope to find a short note.

"Dear Nicky:
Glad to hear you are doing so well. Love God and flee Satan.
Sorry we have no money in the budget right now. I will write you later when we get some money. Your friend, David."

I was sick, upset, and frustrated. This time I wrote Mr. Delgado a special delivery letter. I knew he had money but was afraid to tell him I was having such a rough time at school. I told him my family in Puerto Rico needed money and I had to come home to get a job and help them. I hadn't heard from my family in a year, but this seemed the only story I could tell and get away with it.

A week later I received a special delivery letter from Delgado.

"Dear Nicky:
So glad to hear from you. I have sent money to your family so you can stay in school. God bless you."

That night I went to talk to Dean Lopez. I told him the problems I was having. I was rebelling against all authority. The day before it had been my turn to mop the auditorium and I had thrown the mop on the floor and told them I had come to California to go to school, not work like a slave. I still walked like a jitterbug. I knew I shouldn't even think like the old Nicky used to think—but I couldn't help it. When the other guys in the dorm tried to pray for me, I shook them off and told them they were too good for me. I was a crook. A gangster. They were all saints. They wanted to pray for me and put hands on me, but I refused to let them get close to me. I wept bitter tears as I sat in his little office and cried out for help.

Dean Lopez was a small, bronze-skinned man. He listened and nodded his head and finally reached for his battered Bible which was hidden under a huge stack of ungraded test papers.

"Nicky, you must get involved with the Holy Spirit. You have been saved and you want to follow Jesus, but you are never going to have any real victory in your life until you receive the Baptism in the Holy Spirit."

I sat and listened as Dean Lopez spoke to me from his open Bible of the marvelous victory that could be mine if I would receive God's Spirit.

"In Acts 1," he said, "the apostles were in your situation, Nicky. They had been saved but they had no inner power. They were depending on the physical presence of the person of Jesus Christ to give them power. As long as they could be close to Him they were filled with power. But when they were separated from him they were powerless. Only one time in the Gospels do we find record of Jesus healing anyone without being in their presence. This was in the case of the Centurion's servant. But even then, the centurion had to come to Jesus in order for his faith to be fulfilled. In Matthew it is recorded that Jesus commissioned the 12 disciples and gave them power against unclean spirits, to cast them out, and to heal all kinds of disease. But even with His commission, they still did not have the necessary power to follow through. Evidence of this is found later in the same book when a man brought his son to Jesus for healing, saying he had brought him to the disciples and they were powerless to cure him."

I listened intently as the dean's fingers flipped with ex-

pert knowledge through the pages of the well used Bible.
"In the Garden of Gethsemane Jesus withdrew from his
disciples to pray. But as soon as he was out of their sight
they became powerless. He had asked them to stay awake
and watch for the soldiers, but instead they went to sleep."

I thought to myself, "That's me. I know what He wants
me to do but I don't have the power to do it. I love Him
and want to serve Him, but am powerless."

The dean kept talking caressing his Bible with his hands
like he was touching the finger tips of a dear old friend.
His eyes glistened with moisture as he talked of his pre-
cious Lord. "Then you remember later that night when
Peter was standing outside the palace. When they took his
Lord away he lost his power. He became a spiritual cow-
ard. And that night even a servant girl called his bluff and
caused Peter to curse his Savior and deny he ever knew
Him."

Lopez caught his breath in a sharp gasp and huge tears
formed in his eyes and dropped on the yellowed pages of
the open Bible. "Oh, Nicky, that's so like all of us. How
tragic! How terribly tragic, that in His hour of need He
had to stand alone. Would to God I had been there to
stand with Him. . . . to die with Him. And yet, Nicky, I
fear I would have been just like Peter, for the Holy Spirit
had not yet come and depending on my own strength, I,
too, would have deserted him."

He had to stop talking as his voice choked up. He pulled
his handkerchief from his pocket and blew his nose loudly.

He reopened his Bible to Acts and continued. "Nicky,
do you remember what happened after the crucifixion?"

I shook my head. I knew very little about the Bible.

"The disciples all gave up. That's what happened. They
said that it was all over and they were going to go back to
their fishing boats. The only power they had was the
power that came from the physical presence of Jesus in
whom the Spirit of God lived. But after the resurrection
Jesus told the disciples to return to Jerusalem and to wait
until they received a new power . . . the promised power
of the Holy Spirit.

"The last promise Jesus gave his followers was they
would receive power. Look here in Acts 1:8." He held the
Bible across the desk so I could read it with him. "But ye
shall receive power, after that the Holy Ghost is come

upon you: and ye shall be witnesses unto me both in Jerusalem, and in all Judea, and in Samaria, and unto the uttermost part of the earth."

"You see, Nicky, this is not a command to go witness. It is a promise that you will receive power. And when the apostles received the power, they could not help but become witnesses. They received the power in the Baptism of the Holy Spirit. The Spirit had returned from Heaven in a mighty and magnificent way and had filled every one of those apostles with the same power that had filled Jesus."

I squirmed in my chair. "If He is sending His Spirit," I said, "why hasn't He sent Him to me?"

"Oh, He has," the dean answered, now back up on his feet and walking to and fro beside his little desk, "He has! You just haven't received Him yet."

"Sent Him. Received Him. What's the difference?"

"The Spirit of God is in you, Nicky. He came into your life that night in St. Nicholas Arena. 'No man can say that Jesus is the Lord, but by the Holy Ghost.' It was the Spirit who convicted you of your sin. It was the Spirit who gave you the power to accept Jesus as your lord. It is the Spirit who has opened the doors for you to be at school. But you have not let Him fill you completely."

"How do I do this?" I asked honestly. "I've tried to purify my life by getting rid of all my sins. I've fasted and prayed, but nothing has happened."

He smiled, "It's not anything you do, Nicky. You simply receive Him."

I shook my head. I was still puzzled.

Dean Lopez took his Bible once again and expertly flipped it open to the book of Acts. "Let me tell you about a man named Saul. He was going to a 'big rumble' in Damascus and was struck down by the Spirit of Christ. Three days later he was Baptized in the Spirit and began to preach. This time the power came through the laying on of hands."

"Is that the way I get it?" I asked. "Can someone lay their hands on me and I will be baptized in the Holy Spirit?"

"It could come that way," Dean Lopez answered. "Or you may receive it when you are all by yourself. But once it happens your life will never be the same."

He paused, then looking me straight in the eye said,

"The world needs your voice, Nicky. There are hundreds of thousands of young people all over America who still live where you lived—and in the same manner you lived. They are caught in the clutches of fear, hate, and sin. They need a strong prophetic voice that will rise up out of the slum and ghetto and point them to Christ who is the way out of their misery. They will not hear the eloquent pulpiteers of the day. They will not listen to the seminary and Bible school teachers. They will not hear the social workers. They will not hear the professional evangelists. They will not attend the large churches and would not be welcome even if they did. They need a prophet out of their own ranks, Nicky. And from this hour, I am praying you will be that prophet. You speak their language. You have lived where they live. You are like them. You have hated like they hate. Feared like they fear. And now God has touched your life and called you out of the gutter so you may call others to follow in the Way of the Cross."

There was a long period of sacred silence. I heard him speak again. "Nicky, do you want me to pray for you to receive the Holy Spirit?"

I thought a long time, then answered, "No, I feel this is something I must receive myself. If I am to stand alone then I must receive it alone. I believe He will fill me when He is ready. . . . for I am ready now."

Dean Lopez looked down and smiled. "You are wise, young Nicky. These words could have come only from God's Spirit. The time is fast approaching when your life shall change completely. I shall pray for you as you pray for yourself."

I glanced at the clock on the wall. I had been with him 4 hours. It was 2:00 a.m.

The next 5 nights were spent in agonizing prayer in the chapel. My days were filled with class activity but at night I'd go to the chapel to plead with God to Baptize me in His Holy Spirit. I didn't know how to pray except out loud and I got louder and louder. I would kneel at the altar and cry out to God, "Baptize me, baptize me, baptize me!" But nothing happened. It was as though the room were a box with no outlets and my prayers could not ascend to Heaven. Night after night I went to the chapel and knelt and hit the altar rail with my fists and screamed, "Baptize me,

God, please baptize me that I might have the power of Jesus." I even tried to mouth words in an unknown tongue, but nothing came out.

Friday night, after a week of fruitless praying 4 and 5 hours a night I was about to break under the strain. At midnight I left the chapel and was walking slowly across the campus when I heard a man screaming behind the class building. I dashed around the corner and ran head on into Roberto, a former junkie. "Hey, Roberto! Roberto! What's the matter?"

He threw his arms in the air and shouted, "Praise God! Praise God! Praise God!"

"What's happened? Why are you so happy?"

"I've been Baptized in the Spirit. Tonight, just a few minutes ago, I was praying and God touched my life and filled me with joy and happiness. I can't stop. I've got to tell the world. Praise God, Nicky, praise His wonderful name!" He broke away and ran across the campus, leaping in the air and shouting, "Hallelujah! Praise God!"

"Hey, wait a minute," I shouted after him. "Roberto! Roberto! Where did you receive the Baptism? Where were you when it happened?"

He turned and breathlessly pointed toward the classroom building. "In the classroom. In the big classroom. I was at the front on my knees and he filled me with fire. Hallelujah! Praise God!"

I waited to hear no more. I was off across the campus in a mad dash heading for the classroom. If He touched Roberto maybe He is still there and He will touch me too. I skidded through the door of the building and bounded down the hall to the big classroom. Screeching to a stop at the door, I peered in. It was dark and quiet.

Slowly I entered the dark empty room and felt my way through the chairs and desks to the front. I knelt beside the desk where the pretty dark-eyed girl had flopped so unceremoniously on the floor when I had pulled the chair from under her. I had no time to reconstruct the event in my mind as I put my hands together in traditional style and turned my face toward the ceiling.

Then in a loud voice I cried out, "God, it's me, Nicky! I'm here, too. Baptize me!" I waited expectantly. Nothing happened.

Maybe I'm speaking to the wrong person, I thought. I'll

try again. "Jesus," I screamed at the top of my voice. "It's me, Nicky Cruz, down here in the classroom in La Puente. I'm waiting to be baptized in your Spirit. Let me receive the Baptism." The expectancy was so strong I was almost lifted off the floor. My mouth was open ready to speak in tongues. My legs were tense under me ready to leap and run like Roberto did. But nothing happened. Nothing. Silence. The floor grew hard and my knees began to hurt and I slowly stood up and dejectedly walked back across the dark campus to my dormitory.

The smell of night blooming jasmine was in the air. The grass was wet under my feet from the early dew. In the bushes I heard the lone cry of a whippoorwill and someplace in the distance I heard the deep bellow of a night diesel pulling its cargo up from the valley. The moon slipped behind a dark cloud like a seductive lady withdrawing into her apartment and closing the door. The smell of the jasmine and gardenias wafted on the cool night air and the street lights blinked as the wind tossed the palm fronds across their shafts of light. I was alone in God's paradise.

I slipped quietly into the dorm and felt my way to my bunk. I lay back on my bed with my hands under my head and stared into the darkness. I could hear the soft breathing of the other boys. "God!" I sobbed. And I felt the hot tears come to my eyes and run down into my ears and onto the pillow. "I've been asking for a week and you've let me down. I'm no good. I know why you haven't filled me. I'm not good enough. I act like a jackass around all the other people. I don't even know how to hold my knife and fork. I can't read very well and I can't think fast enough to keep up. All I know is the gang. I'm so out of place here and I'm so dirty and sinful. I want to be good. But I can't be good without your Spirit and you won't give Him to me because I'm not good enough."

The image of my old room at 54 Ft. Greene Place flashed through my mind and I shuddered uncontrollably. "I don't want to go back, God, but I just can't make it here. All these boys and girls are so pious and holy and I'm so filthy and sinful. I know when I'm out of place. I'm going back tomorrow."

I turned over and fell into a troubled sleep.

After class the following day, I went back to my dormitory to pack my things. I had made up my mind to sneak off campus and begin the long journey home—hitchhiking. It was useless to remain here.

That evening as I sat on my bunk my thoughts were interrupted by one of the off-campus students.

"Ah, Nicky! Just the one I wanted to see."

I thought to myself, "And you're just the one I didn't want to see."

"Nicky," he continued with a joyful sound about him. "We're having a Bible study and service down at the little mission on Guava Boulevard. I want you to come with me."

I shook my head. "Not tonight, Gene. I'm tired and have a lot of studying to do. Ask one of the other boys."

"But there are no other boys around," he said as he slapped me on the back of the shoulder, "and besides, the Spirit has told me to come after you."

"Humph, the Spirit, eh? Well, the Spirit has told me to stay here and get some rest since I've been so busy talking to Him all week. Now go away and let me rest." I lay down and turned my back to him.

"I will not leave unless you come with me," he said stubbornly. And he sat down on the foot of my bed and crossed his legs.

I was exasperated. This guy was crazy. Couldn't he tell I didn't want to go?

"All right," I sighed, "I'll go with you. But don't be surprised if I fall asleep in the church service."

"Let's go," Gene said gleefully, pulling at my arm. "We're late now and I'm supposed to preach."

I had decided I'd go with him and sneak out after the service and hitchhike out of town. I stuck my toothbrush and a few other necessities in my pocket and figured I could leave the rest of the stuff here. It wasn't worth much anyway.

We arrived at the little mission about 7:30 p.m. It was brown adobe with stucco inside. The crude wooden slat benches were filled with sincere, simple Mexican people. "At least I'm among good company," I thought. "Yet even these people are better than I. At least they're here because they want to be here. I'm here because I was forced."

Gene preached about 15 minutes and then gave the altar call. I was sitting on the back row beside a grizzled man who smelled strongly of dirt and sweat. His clothes were grimy as if he had just come in from one of the farms and hadn't washed up. As Gene prayed the old man next to me began to weep. "Jesus, Jesus, Jesus," he whispered over and over. "Thank you, Jesus. Oh, thank you, Jesus."

Something moved in my soul. It was as though someone had turned on a faucet, slowly at first. Then I began to fill up. "Thank you, Jesus," the old farmer next to me prayed, "thank you."

"Oh God!" I sobbed out. "Oh Jesus, Jesus, Jesus." I was clenching my teeth and trying to hold it in but the dam had burst and I was running down the aisle toward the front, stumbling and staggering until I fell at the crudely splintered altar rail and cried uncontrollably.

I felt Gene's hand on my head. "Nicky," I could barely make out his words over my sobs. "Nicky, God was not going to let you run away tonight. His Spirit came to me an hour ago and sent me to your dormitory to get you and bring you to this meeting. I knew you were going to run away. He sent me to stop you."

How did he know? No one knew. No one but God.

"God sent me to you, Nicky. All the boys and the teachers have been praying for you at school. We feel that God has placed His hand on you in a marvelous and wonderful way. We feel He is about to move you out into a great and awesome ministry. We love you. We love you. We love you."

The tears were coming like rivers. I wanted to talk but could say nothing. I felt him step across the unpainted altar rail, put his arm around my shoulders and kneel beside me. "Can I pray for you, Nicky? Can I pray that Christ will baptize you in His Holy Spirit?"

I tried to answer but the crying grew worse. I nodded my head and made some funny sounds which he interpreted to be an affirmative answer.

I was unaware of his praying. I don't even know whether he prayed or not. Suddenly, I opened my mouth and from it came the most beautiful sounds I've ever heard. I felt a great cleansing from within, as though my body had been purged from the bottoms of my feet to the top of my head. The language I was praising God with was not English or Spanish. It was an unknown tongue. I had no idea what, I was saying but I knew it was praise to the most Holy God in words that I could never form myself.

Time had no meaning and the hardness of the unfinished two by eight that I was kneeling on seemed to make no difference. I was praising God the way I had always wanted to, and I was never going to stop.

It seemed like only moments later that I felt Gene shake my shoulder. "Nicky, it's time to go. We've got to get back to school."

"No, this is good," I heard myself say, "Let me stay here forever."

"Nicky!" he was insistent, "we've got to go. You can finish when we get back but we've got to get back to the school."

I looked up. The church was empty except for the two of us. "Hey, where is everybody?"

"Man, it's 11:00 p.m. They've been gone for over an hour."

"You mean I've been praying for two hours?" I couldn't believe it.

"Thank you, Jesus! Thank you!" I shouted as we ran for the car.

Gene let me out in front of the dorm and drove off. I ran inside and turned on the light. I was singing, "Holy, Holy, Holy, Lord God Almighty," at the top of my voice.

"Hey, what's going on? What's wrong with you?" they began shouting. "Turn that light off. What kind of a crazy nut are you anyway? Turn the light off!"

"Shut up," I shouted. "Tonight I celebrate. You don't know what has happened to me but I do and tonight I sing. . . . 'Sunshine, Sunshine in my soul today. . . .'" A barrage of pillows came at me from all over the room. "Turn the light out!" But I knew a light had been turned on in my soul that would never be turned out. It would burn forever.

That night I dreamed again, for the first time since I had been saved. In my dream I stood on the hill top near Las Piedras in Puerto Rico, where I had stood many times before in my nightmare. Looking up in the sky I saw the familiar form of a bird. I shuddered in my sleep and tried to rouse myself. O God, don't let them start again. Please!

But the bird grew nearer. Only this time it was not the legless bird or even a pigeon. It was a dove, settling gently on my head. The dream faded and I lapsed into a deep, satisfying sleep.

13

Where Angels Fear to Tread

The days that followed were filled with joy and victory. The first change I noticed was in my conduct. I wasn't a jitterbug any longer. I stood at attention during the prayers, praying with the leader. Instead of acting smart I began to show consideration to others, especially the girl who sat in front of me with the beautiful dark eyes.

I found her name was Gloria. The day I shared my testimony with the class she came up to me and shook my hand in a dignified, lady-like way, "God bless you, Nicky. I've been praying for you."

I had a feeling she probably had been praying I would "drop dead." But I knew she was genuinely happy God had touched me. It showed in her beautiful smile and deep dark eyes that twinkled like the stars at midnight.

The next week I got up enough courage to ask her to go with me to a mission service we were holding at a little church near the campus. She smiled and her dimples winked as she nodded "yes."

During the year we attended many church services together. Although we were always with a group of people, I learned a great deal about her. She was born in Arizona. Her father was Italian and her mother Mexican. They had moved to California when she was five and her parents had opened a bar in Oakland. During her senior year in high school she had been saved and decided to enter Bible School. Her pastor, Reverend Sixto Sanchez, suggested she write the Bible Institute. They accepted her and she entered school in the fall of that year.

As the school year drew to a close I sensed Gloria was going through some deep inner turmoil. The regimentation of the school was telling on her. At the close of the year

161

she told me she didn't believe she could take it another year and wouldn't be back. I was disappointed but made her promise to write me.

That first summer I remained in Los Angeles. Some friends took me in and gave me a place to stay. But I missed Gloria deeply. When school started in the fall, I was grateful to find a waiting letter. She had kept her promise.

She told me, in part, of the motivations that caused her to leave school. "My experiences were different from yours, Nicky," she wrote. "Even though Mom and Dad ran a bar, I had been raised in a good moral atmosphere. When I was saved, I went to extremes with my life. I was taught that it was sinful to copy any of the patterns of the world. I took off all my makeup, refused to wear a bathing suit, and didn't even wear jewelry. Everything about me was negative. Then when I got to school, it was even worse. I was about to crack up. I wanted to tell you but we never had any time alone. I hope you understand and will keep praying for me. But I won't be back to school. . . ."

The second year at Bible school moved fast. My grades improved and the other students were beginning to accept me. I had several opportunities to preach at street services and to give my testimony in some of the nearby churches.

In April, I got a letter from David Wilkerson. He was still living in Pennsylvania but wanted me to return to New York that summer and work with the gangs in Brooklyn. He had made plans to rent an apartment on Clinton Avenue between Fulton and Gates and had secured commitments from Thurman Faison and Luis Delgado to serve with me if I would come. Money was short but they would furnish us a place to stay and pay us each $7 a week.

That night after study hour I went to the Dean's office and called David collect. The phone rang a long time and finally a drowsy voice answered. He grunted he would accept the charges.

"Hey, Davie, it's me, Nicky. Have you finished supper?"

"Nicky, have you any idea what time it is?"

"Sure, baby, it's 10:00 p.m."

"Nicky . . . " there was just the slightest hint of exasperation in the voice, "it may be 10:00 p.m. in California, but it's 1:00 a.m. here and Gwen and I have been asleep for 2 hours. And now you've wakened the baby too."

"But Davie, I just wanted to give you the good news." I could hear the child screaming in the background.

"What can be so good that it wouldn't wait until morning, Nicky?"

"This won't wait, Davie. I'm coming to New York to work with you this summer. God has told me He wants me to come."

"That's wonderful, Nicky. It really is. I'm thrilled. So is Gwen and so is the baby. I'll be sending you a plane ticket. Good night."

I stayed awake all night making plans for my return to New York.

The trip home helped me see just how much I had changed. It was as though my whole life had been toned up—had come alive. As we began our descent to Idlewild Airport in New York, my heart tingled with memories and excitement. I spotted the silhouette of the Empire State Building on the horizon, and then the Brooklyn Bridge. I never realized how massive the city was as it sprawled out for hundreds of square miles. My heart overflowed with love and compassion for the millions of people below who were trapped in the asphalt jungle of sin and despair. My eyes blurred with tears as we circled the city. I was sad yet happy—afraid yet anxious. I was home.

David met me at the airport and we embraced and wept unashamedly. Putting his arm around my shoulder he led me to the car, bubbling over with excitement about his new dream.

I listened as he talked of his plans for the future; of his new Teen Challenge. But he could see something was troubling me and finally slowed down enough to ask what it was.

"Davie, what have you heard from Israel? Where is he? Is he okay?"

David hung his head and finally looked up at me with somber eyes. "No, Nicky, everything is not okay. I didn't say anything about it in my letters because I was afraid it would discourage you. I guess I might as well tell you now so you can begin to pray with me about it."

We sat in the hot car in the airport parking lot while David told me of Israel.

"Israel is in prison, Nicky. He was involved in a murder in December after you left for school. He's been in prison ever since."

My pulse quickened and I felt a cold sweat in the palms of my hands. I took a deep breath. "Tell me all you know, Davie, I've got to hear it."

"I didn't hear about it until it was all over and he had been shipped to prison in Elmira. I drove up to New York to see Israel's mother. She cried when she talked to me and told me there had been a big change in Israel's life after he accepted Christ, but then after the disappointment he returned to the gang."

"What disappointment?" I asked.

"Don't you know?"

"You mean about me getting stabbed? He said he was going to get the guy who did it."

"No, it was something deeper than that. His mother told me that the day you got out of the hospital Mr. Delgado came by the apartment and asked him to go with you to meet me in Elmira the next day. Israel got excited about it and said he'd go. She got him up the next morning at 4 a.m., ironed his clothes and packed his suitcase. He walked over to Flatbush Avenue and waited from 6 a.m. until 9 a.m. Somehow he missed you. He went back to the apartment, threw his suitcase on the floor and told his mother that all Christians were a bunch of fakes. That night he went back to the gang."

I could feel the tears coming to my eyes as I turned to David. "We looked for him. We looked all over for him. I wanted to stay and look some more but Mr. Delgado said we had to go. Oh, David, if only we had known. If only we had looked a little harder and a little longer maybe he would be in school with me now."

David blew his nose and continued. "After he went back to the gang, he and 4 others shot a kid from the South Street Angels in front of the Penny Arcade. He died on the spot. Israel pled guilty to murder in the 2nd degree and was sentenced to five years in the state penitentiary. He's there now."

There was a long pause and I finally asked David if he had seen or heard from him since he went to prison.

"I wrote him but found he could not write back. He

could only write his immediate family. Even his corre-
spondence courses had to be sent through the prison chap-
lain. I prayed for him all that next summer and finally
made a trip up to Elmira just to see him. They were get-
ting ready to transfer him to the work camp at Comstock
and would only let me see him for a few minutes. He was
doing all right, I guess, but he still has more than three
years to serve."

We sat in silence for a long time and I finally said, "I
think we ought to pray for Israel."

David bent over the steering wheel and began to pray
out loud. I turned around in the seat and got on my knees
on the floorboard with my elbows resting on the seat. We
spent almost 15 minutes praying there in the parking lot.
When we finished David said, "We've done all we can for
Israel right now, Nicky, but there is a city full of others
just like him that we can still salvage for Jesus Christ. Are
you ready to go to work?"

"Let's go," I said, but I knew my work would never be
finished until I was able to free Israel. David started the
car and pulled out into the heavy New York traffic. I was
on fire for the Lord. "I want to visit my old gang members
tomorrow," I said nonchalantly. "I want to tell them about
Jesus."

David cocked his head to one side as he pulled off the
highway and braked to a stop at a red light. Looking over
at me he said, "I'd go slow about that if I were you, Nicky.
A lot has happened since you've been away. You re-
member when you became a Christian? They almost killed
you. I'd be careful. There's enough to do without getting
tangled up with the Mau Maus right now. Only fools walk
in where angels fear to tread."

The stop light changed and we pulled off, swinging
wide to pass a bus. "I may be a fool, Davie, but this time
I'm a fool for Jesus' sake. He will go with me and will pro-
tect me. Angels may fear to tread in Mau Mau turf, but I
go with Jesus."

David grinned and nodded his head as he turned into
Clinton Avenue. Pulling to a stop in front of an apartment
building he said, "He's your guide, Nicky. Not me. You do
what He tells you and you'll witness nothing but victory.
Come on, I want you to meet Thurman and Luis."

The next day was the big day. I had stayed awake most of the night praying. I put on my suit and flashy tie, tucked my new leather Bible under my arm and started across town to the Ft. Greene project. I was on my way to see the Mau Maus.

The city hadn't changed much. A few of the older buildings had been condemned and boarded up, but everything else was just as I had left it two years before. But I was different. I had gained weight and cut my hair, but the big difference was inside. I was a new Nicky.

As I crossed Washington Park my heart began to beat faster, I was looking for the Mau Maus; yet, for the first time I was worried about how I would greet them—and what they would say when they saw me. How would I introduce myself? I wasn't scared, I just wanted wisdom to handle the situation for the glory of God.

As I came out of the park I spotted a gang of Mau Maus leaning up against the side of a building. David's words flashed through my mind, "only fools walk in where angels fear to tread," but I breathed a prayer out loud to the Holy Spirit to go with me, and walked up to the loitering gang.

There were about thirteen boys in the crowd. I spotted Willie Cortez and slapping him on the back I said, "Hey, Willie, baby . . ."

He turned and stared at me. "Don't tell me you Nicky?"

"Yeah, man, I'm Nicky."

"Man, you look like a saint or something."

"Cool it, baby. I've just come in from California. Things are going well for me. I'm a Christian and going to school."

He grabbed me by the shoulders and turned me around several times, looking at my clothes and my features. "Man, Nicky, I can't believe it. I can't believe it."

Then turning to the other gang members who were staring curiously he said, "Hey, you guys, take off your hats. This is Nicky. He used to be our president. He was a big jitterbug. He made history with the Mau Maus. He was the toughest of 'em all."

The boys took off their hats. Willie Cortez was the only one in the group I recognized. Most of the kids were younger, much younger. But they were impressed. They had heard of me and crowded around sticking out their hands.

I put my arm around Willie's shoulder and grinned at

him. "Hey, Willie, let's take a walk through the park. I want to talk to you."

We walked off from the group and into Washington Park. Willie was walking slowly beside me with his hands in his pockets, shuffling his shoes on the concrete. "Willie," I broke the silence, "I want to tell you what Christ has done to my life."

Willie didn't lift his head but kept on walking as I talked. I told him how I'd felt as a member of the gang two years ago and how I had given my heart to Christ. I told him of the way God had led me out of the wilderness of the concrete jungle to a place where I was now a creative human being.

Willie interrupted, and I could tell his voice was shaking. "Hey, Nicky, lay off, will ya? You make me feel bad. When you talk something happens inside my chest. Something has changed you. You're not the same old Nicky. You scare me."

"You're right, Willie, something has changed me. The blood of Christ changed me and washed me clean. I'm a different man. No longer am I afraid. No longer do I hate. Now I love. And I love you, Willie. And I want to tell you that Jesus loves you too."

We reached a bench and I motioned for Willie to sit down. He sat and looked up at me. "Nicky, tell me more about God."

For the first time in my life I realized how important it is to talk to my friends about Christ. I could see the loneliness in his face; the ignorance—the fear. He was just as I had been two years before. But now I wanted to tell him the way out.

I sat down beside him and opened my Bible to the passages I had marked in red pencil. Tediously I read the passages in the Bible concerning man's sin. As I read, "for the wages of sin is death," Willie looked up at me with fear in his face.

"What you mean, Nicky? If I'm a sinner and God is going to kill me for sinning, then what can I do? I mean, man, I've gotta do something. What can I do?" His eyes were wild with excitement as he jumped to his feet.

"Sit down, Willie, I'm not finished. Let me show you the rest of it. God loves you. He does not want you to go to hell. He loves you so much He sent His only Son to pay the price of your sin. He sent Jesus to die for you that you can have eternal life. And Willie, if you will accept Him; if you will confess Him, He will save you.".

Willie slumped back down on the bench, a look of desperation on his face. I sat looking at him, my eyes filling up with tears. I squeezed them shut and began to pray but the tears pushed through my tightly shut lids and ran down my cheeks. When I opened my eyes, Willie was crying too.

"Willie, do you know what it means to repent?"

He shook his head.

"It means to change. To turn around. Willie, if you don't mind, I want you to do something. It might hurt your pride. But I'm going to pray for you. Will you kneel down?"

I had no idea Willie would respond. People were walking up and down the sidewalk right in front of the bench where we were sitting, but Willie nodded his head and without hesitation knelt on the sidewalk. Looking up he said, "Nicky, if God can change you, He can change me too. Will you pray for me now?"

I put my hands on Willie's head and began to pray. I felt his body shaking under my hands and heard his sobbing. He began to pray. We were both praying out loud—very loud. Through my tears I cried out, "God! Touch Willie! Touch my friend Willie. Save him. Let him be a leader to lead others to You."

Willie was praying in a loud tortured voice. "Jesus. . . . Jesus. . . . Help me! Help me!" He was gulping for air as he wept and cried out, "Oh Jesus, help me!"

We remained in the park for the rest of the afternoon. At dusk Willie returned to his apartment promising to bring the rest of the gang to my place the next night. I stood and watched him walk off into the summer dusk. Even from behind you could notice the difference. Something had flowed through me to Willie Cortez. I don't think I walked back to Clinton Avenue that evening . . . I floated . . . praising God with every breath. I remembered running through the big field in front of our house in Puerto Rico, flapping my arms and trying to fly like a bird. Tonight I raised my head and breathed deep. At last, I was airborne.

I spent the rest of the summer with the gang doing street preaching and personal work. I fasted religiously, going without food, from 6:00 a.m. on Wednesday until 6:00 a.m. on Thursday. I found when I fasted and spent the time in prayer, things happened in my life. I had also been writing Gloria and just lately her letters were taking on a warm friendly tone as if she enjoyed writing me. Her plans for the coming year were still indefinite and I spent much time praying for her.

Two weeks before I was to return to school one of the Christian businessmen on David's advisory board stopped by with a check. He said the men wanted to give me something extra for the work I had done and suggested I use it for a plane ticket to Puerto Rico to visit my parents before going back to school. It was the thrill of my life.

I arrived in San Juan late Monday afternoon and caught a bus to Las Piedras.

It was almost dark when I got off the bus and started through town toward the familiar path that led up the grassy hill to the white frame house on top of the knoll. A hundred thousand memories flooded through my heart and mind. Someone shouted, "It's Nicky. It's Nicky Cruz!" and I saw a man running ahead of me up the hill to tell Mama and Papa I was home. Seconds later the door burst open and 4 of the younger boys came flying down the hill. I hadn't seen them in five years but recognized them as my brothers. Behind them, skirt flying in the wind, came my mother. I dropped my suitcase and ran up the hill to meet them. We collided in a flurry of happy screams, tears, and hugs. The boys scrambled over me, knocking me to the ground in a happy wrestling match. Mama was on her knees hugging my neck and smothering me with kisses.

Regaining my composure I saw that two of the younger boys had run after my suitcase and were lugging it up the path toward the house. I looked up toward the house and there standing straight and tall, was the powerful solitary figure of Papa looking down the path toward me. I started toward him slowly. He remained steadfast, erect, watching me. Then I began to run and he started slowly down the steps toward me until he, too, broke into a run and met me in front of the house. Grasping me in his big bearlike arms he swung me off the ground and hugged me close to his chest. "Welcome home, little bird, welcome home."

Frank had written Mama and Papa that my life had changed and I was in school in California. The word had gotten around that I had become a Christian and many of the church people in Las Piedras came to the house that night to see me. They told me that others wanted to come but were afraid to come to the "Witch's House." They believed Papa could speak to the dead and in their superstition they were afraid to come near the house. However, they wanted to have a service in the home of one of the Christians and asked me to preach and give my testimony. I told them I would conduct the service but it would be in my home. They looked at each other and the leader of the group said, "But, Nicky, many of our people are afraid of the demons. They are afraid of your Papa."

I told them I'd take care of things here and tomorrow night we would have a big Christian service in my home.

Later that evening when Papa heard what we had planned, he objected violently. "I will not have it. There will be no Christian service in this house. Those people will ruin my business. If we hold a Christian service the others will never come around . . . I will be ruined as a spiritualist. I forbid it."

Mama argued with him. "Can't you see how the Lord has changed your son? There must be something to this. The last time you saw him he was like an animal. Now he is a preacher, a Christian minister. We will have the service and you will attend."

Mama seldom argued with Papa, but when she did she always got her way. She got it this time. The next night the house was packed with people from the village as well as several preachers who had driven in from nearby towns. It was steamy hot as I stood at the front of the room and shared my testimony. I went into great detail of the devil's hold over me and how I had been loosed from his power by the power of Christ. The people were very vocal while I preached, murmuring approval and sometimes shouting and clapping in glee as I described various events in my life.

At the close of the services I asked them to bow their heads. Then, inviting those who would accept Christ as their personal Saviour to step forward and kneel, I closed my eyes and prayed silently.

There was a commotion and I could sense that some

were coming forward. I heard them weeping as they knelt in front of me. I maintained my position with my eyes closed and my face raised to heaven. I could feel the perspiration pouring off my face, down my back, and dripping off my legs. I was soaked with sweat from the heat I had generated while preaching. But I felt God was working and I continued to pray.

Then I heard a woman on the floor in front of me begin to pray. I recognized the voice and opened my eyes in joyous unbelief. There, kneeling in front of me with her face buried in her skirt, was my mother and two of my younger brothers. I fell to the floor in front of her and threw my arms around her sobbing figure.

"Oh, Nicky, my son, my son, I believe in Him too. I want Him as Master of my life. I am sick to death of demons and evil spirits and I want this Jesus to be my Saviour." Then she began to pray, and I listened to the same voice that had once sent me to my bedroom and later under the house in wild hysterics crying I hate you. . . . I now heard that voice crying out to God for salvation, and great sobs shook my body as she prayed for forgiveness. "Please, dear God, forgive me for having failed my son. Forgive me for driving him away from home. Forgive me for my own sin and for not having believed in you. I do believe. I now believe in you. Save me, oh God, save me!"

I opened my arms and encompassed my two younger brothers, one fifteen and the other sixteen, and we huddled together on the floor praying and praising God.

Eventually, I stood and looked at the crowd. Many others had come and were kneeling on the floor praying and weeping. I went from one to the other laying my hands on their heads and praying for them. Finally, I stopped and looked at the back of the room. There against the far wall stood the solitary figure of Papa, towering tall and erect above the bowed heads. Our eyes locked in a long stare and his chin quivered visibly. Tears filled his eyes—but he turned and abruptly walked out of the room.

Papa never did make an open profession of faith. But his life noticeably softened from that time on. And after that night there was never another spiritualist service held in the Cruz home. I returned to New York two days later and one of the native pastors baptized my mother and two brothers in water baptism the following week.

I had less than a week in New York before leaving for California and my last year in school. The night before I was to leave there was a big youth rally at Iglesia de Dios Juan 3:16. We made a big effort to get the Mau Maus to attend. I had become friends with Steve, their new president, and he said if I was going to be there he would make sure the gang came to the service.

I was standing in the vestibule before the service started examining the old bullet holes from 2 years back when the Mau Maus began to arrive. More than 85 of them showed up. The little church was crowded to capacity. As they came in I shouted at them. "Hey, man, this is God's turf. Take off your hats." They obeyed willingly. One fellow was standing in the far corner of the vestibule with one of the debs. He shouted, "Hey, Nicky, can I hug my girl over here."

I shouted back, "Yeah, man, go ahead but no kissing and no making out." The rest of the gang roared in laughter and went on in the auditorium.

At the close of the service, the pastor asked me to share my testimony. I turned and looked at the boys. I knew that I was leaving the next day for California and a sudden chill ran up my spine. Some of these boys would be dead or in prison when I returned. I preached. I preached as a dying man to dying men. I forgot about emotional restraints and poured my heart out. We had already been in the church 2 hours and I preached another forty-five minutes. No one moved. When I finished, the tears were streaming down my face and I pled with them to commit their lives to God. Thirteen of the boys came forward and knelt at the altar. If only Israel were here. . . .

One of the boys who came forward was my old friend, Hurricane Hector. I remembered the time I had initiated him into the gang and the time we'd had a "fair fight" and he had run when he saw I was going to kill him for stealing my alarm clock. Now, Hurricane was kneeling at the altar.

After the service I walked back toward Ft. Greene with Hurricane. He was the war councilor for the Mau Maus. Since I had been instrumental in getting him to join the Mau Maus, I felt a deep burden for him. I asked him where he lived.

"I'm staying in an abandoned apartment."

"Man, how come you're not still living with your folks?" I asked.

"They threw me out. They're ashamed of me. You remember, I was one of those guys who came forward that night at St. Nicholas Arena with you and Israel. Several weeks later I talked my folks into going to church with me and they were converted. We all got active in the church and I was working with young people. I had dropped out of the gang and everything just like you and Israel. But the church was too strict. I wanted to have parties for the young people and they didn't believe in parties. I finally got discouraged and dropped out."

It was the same old story. He had met with the Mau Maus later and they talked him into coming back to the gang, just like they tried to talk me into it. They told him that Christians were squares, punks, sissies and that the gang was the only group that had the real answers to life. They literally evangelized him back into the gang.

A series of arrests followed. His parents tried to talk to him but he was bull headed and they finally became so exasperated with him they told him he was going to have to leave unless he could abide by their rules. He chose to leave and had been living in an old condemned building.

"Sometimes I go hungry," he said, "but I would rather starve than ask my old man for anything. He's a real square. All he wants to do is go to church and read his Bible. I used to be like that but now I'm back where I belong, with the Mau Maus."

We had reached his apartment building. The windows were all boarded up and he told me he had a place behind where he could pry up a board and sneak in. He slept on a pad on the floor.

"Hurricane, how come you came down tonight?" I asked him, referring to the fact he answered the altar call.

"I came down because inside I want to be right, Nicky. I want to follow God. But I can't find the right answers. Each time I turn to Him and then turn away things get harder. I wish you were back in the gang, Nicky. Maybe I could get back to Christ if you were here."

We sat on the curb and talked into the small hours of the morning. I heard the clock in the tower chime 4 a.m., "Hurricane, I feel the Spirit of God telling me to say this to you. The clock just chimed 4 a.m. It's late. But if you will give your heart to Jesus, He'll take you back. It's late, but not too late. You feel guilty, but God will forgive you. Won't you come to Jesus now?"

Hector put his head in his hands and began to cry. But he kept shaking his head and saying, "I can't, I can't. I want to do it. But I know if I do, I'll go right back to the gang tomorrow. I can't do it. I just can't."

I told him, "Hector, you won't live another year if you don't come to Christ now. You'll be dead this time next year. They'll kill you." My heart was overflowing with words that were not mine as I prophesied to him.

Hector just shook his head. "If it happens, it happens, Nicky, and I can't do anything about it."

We were sitting on the curbstone on Lafayette Avenue. I asked him if I could pray for him. He shrugged his shoulders. "It won't do no good, Nicky, I know it."

I stood in the gutter and put my hands on his head and prayed that God would soften his hard heart so he would return to Christ. When I finished, I shook hands with him. "Hurricane, I hope to see you when I get back. But I have a strong feeling that unless you turn back to Christ, I'll never see you again."

The next afternoon I left for California. I didn't know at that time just how accurate my prophecy was.

14

Gloria!

The summer in New York transformed my life, my thinking, my point of view. I returned to California determined to preach.

But I didn't discover the greatest blessing until I returned to the campus at La Puente. Gloria had returned to school. I didn't realize just how much I had missed her until I saw her again.

But the situation at school was still impossible. Everything seemed designed to keep us apart. The regulations were just the same as they had been two years before when we faced this same frustration. Conversation at the tables was limited to "pass the salt" and hawk eyed professors watched our every move on the campus. Even though I hated KP, I began volunteering for extra duty washing dishes just to be near Gloria. The noisy kitchen was anything but private, but I found that we could carry on a semi-private conversation as long as we were both bent over the sink—I with my arms buried up to my elbows in hot soapy water and Gloria handling the rinsing and draining.

As the months flew by I realized I was falling in love with her. My grades continued to improve and I developed an appetite like a horse, due in part, I'm sure, to all the extra exercise I was getting at the dish washing sink. But I was frustrated because I couldn't express my love. Every time we had a few minutes alone someone would interrupt us. I tried to get to the classroom early, but invariably some of the other students would wander in just about the time I tried to get serious with Gloria. The frustration was driving me crazy. And even with my Spanish ancestry, I found it almost impossible to work myself into a romantic mood over a sinkful of greasy dishes in a kitchen of hymn-singing students.

One Thursday night I received permission to walk into town. I stopped at the first phone booth and called Gloria's dormitory number. When the counselor answered, I put my handkerchief over the receiver and in a low bass voice asked for Miss Steffani. There was a pause and I heard the counselor whispering to Gloria, "I think it's your father."

Gloria giggled when she heard me stammering on the other end of the phone. I was so frustrated I was desperate. "I need to be with you," I mumbled.

"Nicky, what are you trying to say?" Gloria whispered, remembering she was supposed to be talking to her father.

I stuttered and stammered but the proper words wouldn't come. All my associations with girls had been on the gang level, and I really didn't know how to talk to one as pure and sweet as Gloria. "I think if I could see you face to face I could tell you better," I said. "Maybe I better go back to my room and stop bothering you."

"Nickieeee!" I heard her scream, "don't you dare hang up on me." I could hear the other girls in the room giggling. Gloria, though, was determined to force it out of me.

"Sshhhh, they'll know it's me," I said.

"I don't care who knows it. Now tell me what you're trying to say."

I groped for words and finally said, "I'm thinking it would be nice if you'd go around with me this year at school." I had said it. It had actually come out. I stood with choked breath waiting for her reaction.

"Go around with you? What does that mean, go around with you?" Gloria was shouting again and this time I could hear the girls laughing out loud.

"Just that," I said highly embarrassed. I could feel the color rising in my cheeks even though I was standing in a phone booth a half mile away from her. "I just thought I'd ask you to go around with me."

Gloria was whispering again, "You mean you want me to be your girl?"

"Yes, that's what I mean," I said, still blushing and trying to scrooch down inside the phone booth.

I could tell she had her mouth right up against the receiver as she breathed into the phone, "Oh, yes, Nicky, that would be wonderful. I have felt God was leading us to-

gether for a purpose. I'll write you a long note and slip it
to you at breakfast tomorrow."

After I hung up I stood in the booth a long time. It was
a warm night but I was drenched with cold sweat and my
hands were shaking like leaves on a willow.

I learned later that after Gloria hung up, the counselor
looked up and with a stern frowning voice said, "Gloria
why would your father call this time of night and ask you
to go around with him?"

One of the girls spoke up between giggles and said, "Be-
cause her father's name is Nicky."

Gloria blushed through her dark complexion as the
whole room broke into gales of laughter. It's not often a
girl receives an invitation from a man of her dreams to "go
around with him" while 40 girls listen in. The counselor
was indignant and gave them 3 minutes to get ready for
bed. But Gloria spent half the night with her head under
her pillow with only the soft light from the street as illumi-
nation, writing me her first love letter. It was totally illegi-
ble, but was the most cherished letter I'd ever received.

Several weeks later I was approached by one of our
teachers, Esteben Castillo, to assist him in beginning a mis-
sion work in San Gabriel near the school. He said he had
enlisted 7 other students to work with him on the week-
ends. He had discovered a little church building that had
been closed and deserted. The students were to go on Sat-
urday and knock on every door in the surrounding neigh-
borhood to invite the people to services at the mission. The
students would help clean up the little building and teach
in a Sunday School and Professor Castillo would preach
and be the pastor.

I was honored by the invitation and especially thrilled
when he winked and told me he had also asked Gloria to
serve on the committee with me. "You are a very wise
teacher, Señor Esteben," I smiled back. "I think we can do
a great work for the Lord with this excellent committee you
have selected."

"Perhaps after you finish with the Lord's work, there
will be a little time for other important things," he grinned.

I could see that word had already gotten around that
Gloria had agreed to go around with me . . . I mean, be my
girl. I was deeply thankful for this wise and understanding

teacher who helped provide a way for our love to develop
and blossom in the natural, God-intended manner.

Every Saturday for the next month we worked at the lit-
tle mission building and went door to door inviting people
to the Sunday services. Finally, the opportunity came for
Gloria and me to spend the day together. We had seen
each other constantly but always in the presence of others.
But today, for the first time, we were going to have three
glorious uninterrupted hours alone. Gloria had packed a
picnic lunch and after a full morning of inviting people to
the services, we went into a small park to eat and talk.

We both began at once—and then giggled at each other
in our embarrassment. "You first, Nicky. Let me listen,"
Gloria said.

The minutes turned into hours as we sat and talked. I
had been so anxious to share my life with her—all the little
details. I talked on endlessly and she sat with rapt atten-
tion, her back against the trunk of a large tree. I suddenly
realized that I was doing all the talking and she was doing
all the listening.

"I'm sorry, Gloria, but there is so much on my heart and
I want you to know it all . . . all the good and all the bad. I
want to share every moment of my past with you. Forgive
me for doing all the talking. Now you talk. Tell me what's
on your heart."

She began slowly at first, but then the words came easi-
er and she poured out her heart to me. She trailed off and
grew silent. "What is it, Gloria? Go on."

"I've grown cold, Nicky. I realized it when I came back
to school and saw the change in you. You're different.
You're not silly nor insecure any more like you used to be.
You have grown, matured and you are deeply spiritual. I
see in you a life that has been yielded to the Lord. And
Nicky . . . ," and her eyes filled with tears. "I-I-I want that
for myself. I want the peace. The assurance. The confi-
dence that you have in your life. I have gone dry spiritual-
ly. Even though God healed me and led me back to school,
I am still spiritually cold. I try to pray but nothing hap-
pens. I am empty. Dead. I want what I see in you."

She dropped her head in her hands. I moved over and
put my arm awkwardly around her shoulders as we sat
under the spreading tree. She turned to me and buried
her head in my chest. Both my arms encircled her sobbing

form and I smoothed her hair with my hand. Gloria turned her tear stained face toward mine and our lips met in a long lingering kiss of love.

"I love you, Nicky." The words slipped from her moist lips into my ear. "I love you with all my heart."

We did not move from our sitting positions for a long time, but clung tightly together like two vines embracing as they reach for the heavens.

"Gloria, I want to marry you. I've known it for a long time. I want to live the rest of my life with you. I have nothing to offer. I've sinned deeply but God has forgiven me. And if you can find it in your heart to forgive me also, I want you to be my wife."

I felt her arms tighten around my waist as she buried her head deep into my shoulder. "Oh yes, my darling. Oh yes. If God will allow it, I will be yours forever."

She raised her head and our lips met in another kiss. I leaned backward pulling her down beside me. We lay on the grass, arms around each other in a deep embrace.

I felt a burning, prickling sensation in my legs. God was close but the past was still inside me. The thought flashed through my mind that this was one of God's most beautiful creatures. Was I about to contaminate her with sinful desires? The burning sensation moved up my legs. It was becoming more acute.

Suddenly, I bolted upright pushing her backward as she rolled in the grass. "Nicky!" she screamed. "What's wrong?"

"Ants!!" I hollered. "Millions of 'em! They're all over me!"

I began to run, slapping furiously at my legs and kicking my shoes off. It was hopeless. My socks were covered with thousands of little red crawling demons. I could feel them all the way up to my knees and climbing higher. No amount of slapping seemed to stop their relentless attack and forward movement. Gloria was staring at me with wild unbelief as I ran in circles slapping and scratching.

"Turn around! Turn around!" I shouted. "Look the other way! Quick!" She turned her back and looked out over the park. I frantically fumbled with my belt buckle and snatched the belt loose.

"Nicky . . . " she began and turned back around.

"Turn around! Don't look!" I screamed. She realized what I was doing and obediently turned her back.

It took a long time to brush them all off. Some of them had tried to dig in under the skin. I had to beat my pants against a tree to knock all of them off. Finally, I was able to tell Gloria it was safe to turn back around.

We walked back to the school. Or rather, she walked and I hobbled. I tried to keep from getting mad because she was laughing. But for the life of me I couldn't see a single funny thing about it.

I left her in front of the girl's dormitory and made a bee line for my dorm and the shower. Standing under the cold water and rubbing soap into the red welts that covered my legs I thanked God for Gloria—and for the protecting power of His Spirit. "God," I spoke into the cascading water that gushed out of the shower head, "I know she's for me. These ants prove it. I praise your name for showing me and pray that you won't ever have to show me again."

The next night, Sunday, I was scheduled to preach at the San Gabriel Mission. I felt the Spirit of God upon me as I shared my testimony with the small group of humble people who had come to the service. At the close of the service I gave the invitation. I saw Gloria as she slipped out of her seat at the back of the little room and walked forward. Our eyes locked in an embrace as she knelt at the altar and then bowed her head in prayer. I knelt beside her while Señor Castillo put his hands on us and prayed. I felt Gloria's hand grip my elbow as the Spirit of God filled her heart. The hand of God was upon us both.

At Christmas I went home with her to Oakland. She had arranged for me to stay with friends since her parents were still not sympathetic to her education at the Institute. Her pastor, Reverend Sanchez, lined up a speaking engagement at a small Spanish-speaking church, Mission Bethania. I spent the days with Gloria and preached at night. Nothing could have made me happier.

In the Spring of my final year I received another letter from David. He was buying a big old house on Clinton Avenue to open a center for teenagers and dope addicts. He was inviting me to return to New York after graduation and work at Teen Challenge.

I talked it over with Gloria. It seemed as though the Lord were forcing His plans upon us. We had thought we would wait another year until Gloria finished school before being married. But now doors were opening and it seemed that God wanted me to return to New York. Yet, I knew I couldn't return without her.

I wrote David and told him I would have to pray about it. I also told him that Gloria and I wanted to get married. Wilkerson wrote back saying he would wait for my answer and that Gloria would be welcome too.

We decided on a November wedding and one month later we arrived in New York to accept Wilkerson's offer and began our work at Teen Challenge.

The huge old three story mansion at 416 Clinton was in the heart of an old residential section of Brooklyn just a few blocks from the Ft. Greene project. That summer college students had come in and helped clean up the house and start the ministry. David had secured the services of a young couple to live in the big house as supervisors. They had arranged for Gloria and me to live in a tiny garage apartment at the rear of the big house.

It was very small and crude. The shower was next door in the main center and the only bed was a couch, but to us it was heaven. We had nothing and needed nothing. We had each other and we had a burning desire to serve God at any cost. When David apologized for our poor cramped accommodations, I reminded him it was no sacrifice to serve Jesus—only an honor.

Just before Christmas I made my visit back into Mau Mau turf. My heart had been burdened over Hurricane Hector and I wanted to find him and work with him personally now that I was back in Brooklyn to stay. I found a group of Mau Maus at the candy store and asked them, "Where's Hurricane?"

The fellows looked at each other and one of them said, "Talk to Steve, our president, he'll tell you what's happened."

I was afraid of the truth but went to Steve's apartment. "What happened to Hector?" I asked him after we exchanged greetings.

Steve shook his head and stared at the wall. "Let's go

downstairs and I'll tell you. I don't want my old lady to hear."

We walked down the stairs and stood just inside the door to escape the cold wind while Steve told me the story.

"After he talked to you that night before you went back to California, he became very restless. He was impatient. I've never seen him that way. We had a big rumble with the Bishops and he was like a wild man, trying to kill everyone who got in his way, even the Mau Maus. Then, three months later, he got it."

"How did it happen?" I asked, the depression bubbling up into my heart and lungs and causing my breath to come in shallow gasps. "Who did it?"

"Hurricane, Gilbert, two other guys and me went to kill a Bishop. He lived by himself on the 5th floor of an apartment. We found out later we had the wrong guy. But Hurricane was determined to kill this guy and we went with him to help. Hurricane had a revolver. We knocked on this guy's door. It was dark. But this guy was smart. Cracking the door he peeked out and saw Hurricane with his revolver. He jumped out into the hall and swung at the light bulb with a two foot bayonet. It was one of them bulbs that hang down from the ceiling and he smashed it. We couldn't see nothing. He was like a crazy man, swinging and jabbing with that bayonet. Hurricane shot his gun three times and then we heard a big scream, "He kill me! He kill me!" We didn't know who it was and thought Hurricane had killed the Bishop. We all beat it down the steps—five flights of 'em, and out into the street."

Steve turned and looked back up the steps of his own apartment to see if anyone was trying to listen. "When we got to the street we saw Hurricane wasn't with us. Gilbert ran back up the steps and found Hurricane standing up against the wall with that bayonet stuck all the way through him. Gilbert said it was poking out his back. The Bishop had run back in his room and locked the door. Hector was scared and was crying. He was leaning up against the wall with that big knife poked all the way through his gut begging Gilbert to keep him from dying. He said he was scared to die. He cried something about the clock striking and then he fell down in the hallway on top of the knife and died."

My throat was dry and my tongue felt like it had cotton stuck on it. I stuttered, "Why did you leave him there?"

"Because we were all scared. We panicked. We'd never seen death like that. All the guys scattered and ran. The cops came but there was no proof and they let the Bishop go. It shook us up pretty good."

I turned to leave when Steve asked me, "Nicky, what do you think he meant about the clock striking?"

I shook my head. "I dunno. I'll see you later."

I was in a daze as I walked back toward Clinton Avenue. With each step I could hear the clock on the tower at Flatbush Avenue chime and could hear my voice saying to Hurricane Hector, "It's late, Hector, but not too late. But if you don't give your heart to Christ I'll never see you again."

"Dear God," I whispered, "please don't let me ever walk away from another of my friends without trying a little harder."

My beginning salary was $10 a week plus room and board. Since the little garage apartment had no kitchen facilities, we ate all our meals over at the big house. Gloria and I both loved hot Spanish food. But at the center they had to eat very stable foods, so we squandered most of our $10 each week on Spanish food. This was our one extra pleasure in life.

We began our work in the streets. Wilkerson had written a little tract which we called the "Chicken Tract." It had a message to teenagers challenging them to accept Christ and not be "chicken." We passed these things out by the thousands on the streets of Brooklyn and Harlem.

It was immediately evident that our major work was going to be with the dope addicts. Many of the gang members who before had been satisfied to smoke marijuana and drink wine had graduated to heroin.

Our method was a brazen one. We'd walk up to groups of kids standing on the street corners and start conversation.

"Hey, baby, you want to kick your habit?"

Almost invariably they would answer, "Yeah man, but how?"

"Come to Teen Challenge over on Clinton. We'll pray for you. We believe God answers prayer. You can kick the habit through the power of God." We'd give them a copy of the chicken tract.

"Yeah, man, is that so? Well, maybe I'll call you or come by someday." It was slow to begin with. Most of my time was spent just standing around on the street corners talking. The addicts don't work. They get their money by stealing, robbing, mugging and purse snatching. They break into apartments and steal the furniture and sell it. They pick pockets. They steal clothes off the lines, milk off the doorsteps, anything to pick up enough money to feed their habit. All through Williamsburg there are little gangs of 8 to 10 persons standing on the corners planning robberies or trying to figure out how to get rid of stolen property.

By Christmas I had my first convert at the Center.

His name was Pedro and he was a Mau Mau. He was a big tall colored boy who had been living with a married woman. One day the woman's husband confronted him in a bar and Pedro slashed him with a knife. The husband was a member of the Scorpions, an across-town gang, and Pedro heard the gang was coming after him. I found him one night and listened to his story and offered him refuge at Teen Challenge. He willingly accepted. Three days after moving into the Center he accepted Christ and gave his heart to the Lord.

For the next three months we lived, breathed, and ate Pedro. Gloria and I spent our first Christmas as husband and wife in our small two room apartment with Pedro as our guest. He ate every meal with us. He went with us every place we went. On weekends we'd ride the subway to various churches to attend services. Pedro always went with us.

One night in March I came to bed late as usual. Gloria had already crawled into our sofa-bed in the front room. I thought she was asleep and undressed quietly to keep from waking her. Slipping into bed I gently put my arm around her shoulders when I realized she was crying. I could feel her body shaking and sobbing under my arm.

"Hey, baby, what's the matter?"

That was all it took and the tears came in huge sobs. I lay beside her rubbing her back and comforting her until she calmed down enough to talk. "What is it, Gloria? Don't you feel good or something?"

"It's not that, Nicky. You don't understand and you never will."

"Understand what?" I was confused by her hostile attitude.

"That leech!" Gloria spit out the word. "That leech, Pedro! Can't he understand I want to spend some time with you alone. We've only been married 4 months and he has to go with us every place we go. He'd probably take a bath with us except there's only room for one in the bathroom."

"Hey, com'on," I soothed, "this doesn't sound like my Gloria. You oughta feel proud. He's our first convert. You oughta be praising the Lord."

"But, Nicky, I don't want to share you all the time. I married you and you're my husband and at least I ought to be able to spend some time with you without that grinning Pedro hanging around all the time saying, 'Praise the Lord.'"

"You're not serious about that are you, Gloria?"

"I've never been more serious about anything. One of us has to go. Either you're married to me or you can go sleep with Pedro. I mean it. But you can't have us both."

"Aw, listen, darling. If we send him back on the street, he'll go right back to the gang or the Scorpions will kill him. We've got to keep him here."

"Well, if he goes back to the gang then there's something wrong with your God. What kind of God did Pedro give himself to, anyway? A God who will turn loose of him the first time he gets into trouble? I don't believe that. I believe that if a man has had a conversion experience, God is big enough to keep him forever. And if we're going to play nursemaid to every one of these fellows you're inviting in here then I'm getting out." Gloria's voice reached a fever pitch as she talked.

"But, Gloria, he's my first convert."

"Maybe that's what's wrong with you and him too. He's *your* convert. Maybe if he was the Lord's convert you wouldn't have to be so worried about him going back to the gang."

"Well, maybe you're right. But we still have to give him a place to stay. And remember, Gloria, the Lord has called me to this work and you agreed to go with me."

"But, Nicky, I just don't want to have to share you all the time."

I cuddled her close to me. "You don't have to share me now. And tomorrow I'll talk to Pedro and see if he can't find something to do instead of hanging around us all the time. Okay?"

"Okay," she mumbled as she put her head against my shoulder and snuggled close.

Sonny arrived the last day of April—along with a prediction of a May snow. He was the first addict I worked with.

I walked into the chapel that night and noticed a pale faced boy sitting in the far corner. I could tell he was an addict and went to him and sat down beside him. Putting my arm around his shoulders I began to talk frankly to him. He kept his head bowed and his eyes staring at the floor while I spoke. "I know you're an addict . . . a junkie. I can tell you've been hooked many years and that you can't break the habit. You think no one cares. You think no one can help you. Let me tell you God cares. He can help you."

The boy raised his head and gave me a blank stare. Finally, he told me his name was Sonny. I found out later he had been raised in a religious home, but had run away and been in jail countless times for addiction and theft. He'd had to kick the habit "cold turkey" in jail several times, but he was hopelessly hooked.

Sonny was a compulsive addict, who had a unique way of getting money to feed his habit. His buddy would run down the street and snatch a woman's purse and when she began to scream, Sonny would run up saying, "Don't scream, lady. I know that thief. I'll get your purse back. Just wait here and I'll be back in a minute." The woman would stop screaming for the police and stand waiting while Sonny darted off down the street to join his friend and divide the spoils.

Kneeling beside him in the chapel, I said, "I want to pray for you. You need Jesus in your life." I felt a surge of compassion race through my heart and began to cry as I prayed. "God, help this man. He's dying. You're the only one who can help him. He needs hope, love. Please help him."

When I finished Sonny said, "I have to go home."

"I'll take you home."

"No," he said with a look of panic on his face. "You can't do that."

I knew he was scheming so he could get out and get a shot. "Then we'll keep you here," I said.

"No," he said again. "I have to go to court in the morning. They're going to sentence me to jail. I don't even know why I'm here."

"You're here because God sent you," I said. "God is using me to help you. Stay with us here at the center tonight and I'll go to court with you in the morning." He insisted on going home and I promised I'd pick him up at 8:00 a.m.

Early the next morning I went with him to court. On our way up the courthouse steps I told him, "Sonny, I'm going to pray God will cause the judge to postpone your trial for two months so you can break the habit and find Christ. After that, he might let you off altogether."

Sonny sneered, "Fat chance. That stinkin' judge never postpones anything. He'll have me in jail before noon. Just you wait and see."

I paused on the steps of the courthouse and began to pray out loud, "God, I ask you in Jesus' name to send your Holy Spirit to touch that judge and have him postpone Sonny's case so Sonny can become a Christian. I thank you for answering my prayer. Amen."

Sonny looked at me like I was crazy. I tugged at his arm, "Com'on, let's go hear the judge say he's going to postpone your case."

We entered the courtroom and Sonny reported to the bailiff at the front of the room. He then took his seat with the other defendants while I sat in the back.

The judge heard three cases and sentenced the boys to long jail terms. The third boy to be tried began to scream when the judge passed sentence on him. He scrambled up on the table and tried to get to the judge, screaming he was going to kill him. Everyone in the courtroom jumped to their feet while the police knocked the boy down and handcuffed him. As they dragged him out the side door screaming and kicking, the judge mopped his brow saying, "Next case." Sonny stood nervously while the judge thumbed through his file. Glancing up over his glasses he said, "For some reason your pre-trial investigation is not complete. I want you to report back in 60 days."

Sonny turned and looked at me with eyes full of disbelief. I smiled and motioned him to come with me. We had a difficult task ahead and needed to get started.

Coming off heroin "cold turkey" is one of the most agonizing experiences imaginable. I prepared a room for Sonny on the 3rd floor of the center. I knew it would take constant supervision so I warned Gloria that I was going to spend the next three days with Sonny. I set up a phonograph with religious records and determined to sit beside him in that room until he had screamed it out.

The first day he was restless, pacing the floor and talking rapidly. That night he began to shake. I sat with him through the night as he had hideous sieges of chills, shaking until his teeth clattered and the whole room vibrated. At times he'd break loose from me and run for the door, but I had it locked and he couldn't break through.

At dawn the second day his shaking subsided and I managed to get him downstairs for a little breakfast. I suggested we take a walk around the block and he no sooner got outside until he began to throw up. He bent low over the sidewalk, holding his stomach and retching. I pulled him upright but he broke away and staggered into the street where he collapsed. I dragged him back to the gutter and held his head in my lap until the seizures passed and he regained his strength. Then we returned to our room on the third floor to wait and pray.

As the night approached he screamed out, "Nicky, I can't make it. I'm too far gone. I've got to have a shot."

"No, Sonny, we're going to come through this together. God will give you the strength to make it."

"I don't want the strength to make it. I want a shot. I've got to have it. Please, please, please, Nicky. Don't keep me here. For God's sake let me go. Let me go."

"No, Sonny, for God's sake I will not let you go. You are precious to Him. He wants to use you but He cannot do it as long as this demon has possession of you. For God's sake, I'll keep you here until you're whole again."

I sat with him through the long night as he broke into cold sweats and heaved until I thought his stomach would turn inside out. I bathed his head with wet towels, turned the phonograph up loud, and sang to him with Bev Shea and the Statesmen Quartet.

The next day I was dead on my feet. Once again I tried to get food down him but it came right back up. I sat beside his bed and prayed until sundown.

He fell into a fitful sleep, moaning and twitching. Twice he bolted up in bed and tried to get to the door. The last time I had to tackle him and drag him back to bed.

About midnight, sitting in the chair beside his bed, I felt the black cloud of sleep dscending on me. I tried to fight it off but I had been 42 hours without sleep. I knew if I went to sleep now he might sneak out and never come back. We were close to victory, but I couldn't fight it any longer and felt my chin touch my chest. "Maybe if I close my eyes for a moment . . . "

I awoke with a start. The eerie glow from the street lights reflected in the large bare room on the third floor of the building. I didn't think I had been asleep more than a few seconds but something inside warned me I had slept far longer. I glanced at Sonny's bed. It was empty. The covers were ruffled and thrown back. He was gone!

My heart leaped into my throat. I jumped to my feet and started for the door when I spotted him kneeling on the floor beside the window. A wave of relief swept over me as I walked slowly to the window and knelt on the bare hardwood floor beside him. A light spring snow was falling and reflecting in the street lights on the sidewalk. The street and sidewalk were blended together in a pure white carpet and the tree branches outside the window with their tiny delicate buds just beginning to peep out, were sparkling with the soft white snow. Each tender flake glistened individually as it floated by the street light, reminding me of a scene that might appear on the front of a Christmas card.

Sonny said, "It's beautiful. It's indescribable. I have never seen anything so beautiful, have you?"

I was staring at him. His eyes were clear and his voice steady. There was a radiance about his face; his tongue was no longer thick nor his speech slurred.

He smiled at me, "God is good, Nicky. He is wonderful. Tonight He has delivered me from a fate worse than hell itself. He has released me from bondage."

I looked out the window at the delicate picture of pure beauty before me and whispered, "Thank you, Lord, thank you." And I heard Sonny murmur, "Thank you."

For the first time I left Sonny alone and walked through the new snow back to the apartment. I was bareheaded and the frosty snow that fell so gently stuck in my hair and puffed softly under my feet as I walked up the outside wooden steps.

I knocked softly and Gloria unlatched the door. "What time is it?" she said drowsily.

"About 3:00 a.m.," I answered. We stood in the door and I held her close to me while we watched the soft gentle snow drift silently to earth covering the dark and ugly with a beautiful blanket of pure innocence.

"Sonny has come to Christ," I said. "A new life has been born into the Kingdom."

"Thank you, Jesus," Gloria said softly. There was a long pause as we stood just inside the door and watched the panorama of beauty before us. Then I felt Gloria's arm tighten around my waist. "Sonny is not the only new life that has come into existence. I haven't had time to tell you, you've been so busy these last three days, but there is a new life in me, too, Nicky. We're going to have a baby."

I caught her up and crushed her against my chest in love and joy. "Oh, Gloria, I love you! I love you so much!" Very gently I bent over and slipped my arm under the back of her knees and slowly lifted her into my arms. I kicked the door and it clicked shut, plunging the room into total darkness. I carried her to the sofa and tenderly lowered her onto the bed. Sitting down beside her I gently laid my head against her soft tummy, cuddling as close as possible to the new life inside. She took both her hands and stroked my face and head. The exhaustion took over and I fell into a deep peaceful sleep.

Following his conversion, Sonny introduced us to the dark underworld of the big city and showed us the world of the addicts, the prostitutes, and hardened criminals.

Gloria and I spent many hours on the streets handing out tracts and our numbers increased at the Center. We had very few teenagers however. Most were adults. We opened the third floor to house the women. Gloria helped with the girls and I worked with the men, although as the director, I was in charge of both groups.

David had moved to a home on Staten Island and was coming in each day when he was in town to supervise the work at the center. We purchased a small 9-passenger bus and Gloria and one of the boys went out twice a week to pick up gang members and bring them to the center for services.

Pedro left to take an apartment in Jersey but Sonny stayed until September when he left for La Puente and the Bible Institute. That same summer the apartment on the 2nd floor of the center became vacant and Gloria and I moved into 416 Clinton. The men's dormitory room was at the rear of the 2nd floor. Downstairs we had our office, kitchen, and dining hall, and a big room we used for a chapel. I hoped that since we had relocated to the big building it would help ease Gloria's tension. Yet, having to live in the same house with 40 narcotic addicts does not lend itself to a life of calm and ease.

The tension continued. Gloria and I had very few private moments since I was spending every waking hour with the addicts. In the fall of 1962 I had to make an emergency trip home to Puerto Rico. Mama had sent a cablegram to Frank. Papa was dead. Frank, Gene and I took our wives and flew to Puerto Rico where I conducted my father's funeral service. I had returned as a Christian minister and even though Papa never openly accepted Christ as God's Son, I buried him with the assurance that there had been a change in his life and that God, in his loving mercy, would be able to judge him according to his heart. The "Great One" was dead—but the memories of a Papa I had learned to love lived on in my heart.

Alicia Ann was born in January 1963. She helped fill a void in Gloria's lonely life since she now had someone with whom to share her love during the long days. I yearned to spend time with them, but my driving desire to minister to the junkies kept me away from dawn 'til midnight. I warned her not to let anyone else hold the baby, for even though I loved the addicts I knew that minds severely damaged by drugs were capable of anything.

But I never knew how many nights Gloria cried herself

to sleep in the loneliness of our apartment. She must have been God's choice for my life. No other woman would have been able to stand the strain.

15

Excursion into Hell

I had been out of town for a couple of days and when I returned, Gloria told me about Maria. Twenty-eight years old, she had come in off the street half frozen, suffering acute withdrawal symptoms from heroin, and at the edge of death. Gloria asked me to remember her especially that night as I preached in the little chapel.

After the services, Gloria brought Maria into my office. She stammered out the words as we talked, still suffering from her withdrawal.

"Tonight," she said, "I had the strangest feeling that I wanted to turn loose of my worthless life. As you preached I had this feeling that I really wanted to die to this wretched life of mine. And yet, for the first time in all my life, I want to live. I can't understand it."

I explained to her that she was experiencing what the Bible calls "repentance." "Maria, you cannot receive the love of God until you are willing to die to yourself. Tell me, do you want to die to the old way of life? Do you want the life of drugs and prostitution to be put to death, buried, and forever forgotten?"

"Oh yes, yes, yes," she sobbed. "I'm willing to do anything to escape it."

"Are you willing to die to self?" I probed.

"Yes," she answered, choking back the tears, "even that."

"Then let me tell you about a love so wonderful, so beautiful, so magnificent that it can take even a person like you and make them clean and pure. Let me tell you about Jesus." And for the next 10 minutes I talked to her about God's perfect love that was poured out to us in Jesus Christ.

She buried her face in her hands and sobbed. I walked over to her and put my hand on her shoulder. "Maria, let's kneel here and pray. . . ." and before I could finish my sentence, Maria was on the floor on her knees. I could feel the dam burst. Maria had been born again to a new life in Jesus Christ.

A month later Maria stopped by my office. The drug urge was tearing her apart and she wanted to leave the Center. Her boy friend, Johnny, had already given in to the call of the drug, and had left the Center some days before in the middle of the night.

I got up and closed the door behind her. "Maria," I said, "nothing else in all my life is as important as your future. Let's talk about what has happened in your life."

She was ready. She went back to the time she was 19 and had graduated from high school. I let her talk.

"It was Johnny who taught me how to smoke marijuana. My girl friends had told me about their experiences with marijuana. They said it was okay as long as you didn't go on to something stronger. Johnny always seemed to have a supply of reefers and I thought it was a lot of fun."

Maria paused as if remembering those first days as she began her descent into hell, and I thought how typical she was of the dozens of addicts who were coming to the Center. Ninety percent of them started with a stick of pot and then graduated to dope. I knew what was coming but felt she needed to express it. "Tell me about it, Maria, what was the effect?" She relaxed in her chair, her eyes half closed, as she told me her story.

"I felt my troubles would just float away," she answered. "One time I felt myself floating miles and miles above the earth. Then I began to come apart. My fingers left my hands and floated off into space. My hands left my wrists. My arms and legs left my body. I came into a million pieces and floated off on a soft breeze."

She paused again, recollecting. "But the pot wasn't enough. All it did was whet my desire for something stronger. I was mentally hooked.

Johnny gave me my first "fix." He had been talking about it for several weeks. One afternoon I had been crying all day. Nothing had gone right and Johnny came in with the needle and spoon. I knew what he was going to do, but he seemed so confident that it would help me, I let him go ahead. I didn't know about drug addiction then. But he assured me I'd be all right.

He pulled the belt tight around my arm above my elbow until the vein stood out like a big mound under my skin. He emptied the white, sugar-like contents of the little envelope into a spoon. Adding water with an eye dropper, he held a match under the spoon until the liquid boiled. Once again he used the eye dropper and sucked the now dissolved heroin back into the dropper. Then, with expert knowledge, he jabbed the vein with the end of the hypodermic needle. Then, carefully with the eye dropper, he squeezed the potent liquid into the open end of the hypodermic. Laying the dropper aside he worked the needle up and down in my arm until the liquid disappeared in the vein. I felt nothing as he withdrew the needle. I didn't know it then, but I had just become a "mainliner."

"Johnny, I'm getting sick," I said.

"Naw, you're all right baby," he said, "just take it easy and pretty soon you'll be floating. Johnny promises and I don't ever go back on my promises, do I?"

But I couldn't hear him. I began to heave and before I could move I had vomited on the floor. I fell back across the bed and began to shake and perspire. Johnny sat there beside me and held my hand. Soon I relaxed and a warm, fluid feeling swept over me. I thought I was rising up toward the ceiling and above me I could see Johnny's smiling face. He bent over me and whispered, "How's it doing, baby?"

"Swell," I whispered, "Man, that's getting good." I had begun my excursion to hell.

I didn't have another fix for about a week. This time when Johnny suggested it I was ready. The next one came three days later. After that, Johnny didn't have to suggest it to me, I was asking for it. I didn't know it at the time, but I was addicted . . . hooked.

The following week Johnny came home and I was beginning to shake. I asked him for a fix.

"Now listen, baby, I love you and all that, but this stuff costs money, you know."

"I know it, Johnny, but I need a fix."

Johnny smiled, "I can't do it, baby. Man, you're beginning to cost me."

"Please Johnny," I pleaded with him, "don't tease me. Can't you see I need a fix?"

Johnny started toward the door. "Not today. Just sweat it out. I ain't got the time or the money."

"Johnny!" I was screaming. "Don't leave me. For God's sake don't leave." But he was gone and I heard the key turn in the lock.

I tried to get hold of myself but I couldn't do anything. I walked to the window and saw Johnny down at the end of the block talking to a couple of the girls. I knew who they were. They worked for Johnny. He referred to them as part of his 'stable.' They were prostitutes who bought his stuff on the money they made at their trade. Johnny always kept them supplied and they would pass the stuff along to their customers for a commission.

I stood there at the window and watched him as he reached into his coat pocket and slipped one of the girls a small white envelope. I knew it was the stuff. I watched Johnny give away the precious heroin and could hardly stand it. Why should he give it to her and not let me have it? God, I needed it.

Suddenly, I heard myself screaming, "Johnny! Johnny!" I was screaming out the window at the top of my voice. He looked up and then started back toward the apartment. When he came in, I was across the bed sobbing and shaking. I had lost all control of myself.

He closed the door behind him. I sat up on the bed and tried to talk, but before I could say anything he came to me and I felt the back of his hand as it smashed across my mouth.

"What the hell are you trying to do?" he screamed. "You trying to get me picked up or something?"

"Johnny, please. Help me. I need a fix. I saw you give the stuff to those girls. Why don't you give it to me? Please?" I had reached a stage of complete desperation. I was shaking and sobbing at the same time. I could taste the blood as it ran down the side of my mouth but I didn't care. All I wanted was that needle.

Johnny grinned. "Now listen, baby, you're different from those sluts down there on the street. You got class. But this stuff ain't free. It costs—plenty. Those girls down there work for theirs. What're you doing for yours? Huh?"

"I'll work, Johnny. I'll do anything. Anything. Just give me that needle."

"I don't know," said Johnny. "You got too much class to be working out there on the street."

"Johnny, I'll do anything. Just tell me." I could feel the floor coming up toward me as I sank to his feet and put my arms around his knees and legs to keep from falling on my face.

"You mean you're willing to hustle for me on the street?" He paused and then continued with enthusiasm. "You can do it, baby, I know you can if you want to. Man, you can out-do those other chicks ten to one. The guys would come flocking to you and between us we could make a real killing. How about it? I'd be making money and could buy you as much H as you wanted—you'd never have to go through this again. What about it? Is that what you want?"

"Yes, Johnny, yes, yes, yes. Just give me a shot."

Johnny walked over to the stove and turned on the burner. He pulled out his spoon and sprinkled a little bit of the white powder into the bottom and held it over the flame. Filling the needle, he walked over to where I was crouched on the floor.

"Man, baby, this is the beginning of heaven for both of us. With you on my side we can reach the moon." I felt the needle penetrate the vein. The shaking stopped almost immediately—within seconds. Johnny helped me up and onto the bed where I sank into a deep sleep. But Johnny was wrong. It wasn't the beginning of heaven. It was the beginning of a long, horrible nightmare that would last for eight terrifying years. Not heaven—But hell.

Hell is a bottomless pit, where you keep on falling, going down, down, never reaching bottom. In the fall into drug addiction there is no place to stop and catch on. There is no way to arrest the descent. I was on my way down.

Johnny couldn't use me unless I was addicted. But when I became a slave to drugs, I also became his slave. I had to do what he wanted . . . and he wanted me to prostitute for him to bring in the money. He kept me supplied, but I could see that things weren't quite the heaven he said they would be.

For one thing, I soon learned Johnny also had another

woman. I knew he didn't want to marry me, but never thought he was keeping another woman. I found out about it the hard way.

Things had been a little slow the night before and I had gotten up and gone down the street the next afternoon to do a little shopping. I liked to get out and forget what I was and pretend I was just like all the other people. I was standing at the corner of Hicks and Atlantic waiting for the light to change when I felt a hand on my shoulder that spun me completely around.

"You're Maria, ain't you?" She was a dark woman with long black hair that flowed down across her shoulders. Her eyes were spitting fire. Before I could answer her she said, "Yeah, you're the one. I've seen you before. You're the one messing with my man. I'll teach you, you cheap whore."

I tried to back away from her but she slapped me in the face. The light had changed and people were milling all around but I wasn't going to be pushed around by anyone, not like this. I reached out and snatched her hair and pushed her backwards at the same time.

She screamed like a wild woman. "You dirty slut. Sleeping with my man. I'm gonna kill you." She was crazy. She swung at me with her purse and I ducked. I pushed my body against her and she fell backward against the rail around the entrance to the subway. I heard her gasp for air as her backbone slammed into the hard iron pipe.

I took her head in my hands and pushed her backwards over the pipe and down toward the black steps that led to the subway below. I was trying to get my fingernails into her eyes where I knew I could hurt her. Suddenly, she sunk her teeth into the side of my hand. I could feel the flesh tear as I ripped my hand out of her mouth screaming with pain.

As I backed up someone grabbed me from behind and the crowd moved in between us. The man who grabbed me whirled me around and pushed me out into the street where I stumbled and fell. The crowd was still milling around the other woman and I darted across the street and down the sidewalk on the other side.

I never looked back, but ran to the apartment, soaked my hand and got the girl across the hall to bandage it. That night I was back on the street. . . . I never saw her again.

I didn't feel any more obligations to Johnny, though. I knew I could get a fix from one of a dozen guys, all who would be glad to have me working for them. So it became a long nightmare. I lived with one man after another. All were drug addicts. I sold my body and they went out and stole.

I learned to work in partnership with some of the other girls. We'd rent a room for the night. Then we'd go out on the street and wait. Some of the men were regular customers. Most were complete strangers. Niggers, wops, Orientals, Puerto Ricans, whites . . . their money was all the same color.

Some nights I'd draw a complete blank. Others, I'd get as many as 9 or 10 during the evening. That was a good night. But by then, it was costing me almost $40 a day just to keep in fixes, and that meant I had to get at least 5 customers a night to keep going.

It was sheer hell. When I could sleep during the day I'd wake up screaming from horrible dreams. I was imprisoned in my own body and I was my own jailer. There was no escape from that fear, dirtiness, and ugliness of sin.

I was afraid of drunks. Some were perverts and sadists. Several of the girls had been tortured into unnatural acts. One girl got in with a guy one night who got his kicks out of beating a girl with a belt. He was half drunk and by the time they got to the room, he was almost crazy with excitement. He made her undress and then took her bra and tied her hands to the doorknob and beat her across the stomach and breasts with his belt until she passed out from screaming.

I preferred to use the room I'd rented. On some occasions the man might want me to go to his apartment or to a hotel room. Some of them were businessmen in town for trips or conventions. But I was afraid to go to a man's room. Terrible things happened and some of the girls never came back.

Some of the men were afraid to go to my room, afraid they'd get rolled. They'd want me to go with them in their car.

After a couple of bad experiences, I put a stop to this.

One man let me out clear over on the other side of town, and it took me all night to get back home on the subway. The other man took me out on a lonely road. He was drunk and demanded his money back. When I refused he put a pistol to my head and pulled the trigger. The gun misfired and I ran, but it was my last time to go in someone's car.

The guys on the street weren't the only ones to give me trouble. I was in constant trouble with the police, too. I was in jail 11 times over the 8 years of my addiction. The longest sentence was 6 months. I was picked up for everything. Shop lifting. Drug addiction. Petty theft. Vagrancy. And yes, prostitution.

I hated the jails. My first time in jail I cried and cried. I promised myself I'd never do anything to get picked up again. But 4 months later, I was back. Ten times I was back.

The police were constantly bugging me. One cop would come around every couple of days while I was on the street and try to get me to go with him. But I knew there wasn't any money in it, so I never did.

But the heroin was tearing me apart. I remember my first overdose. I was still working and had moved back in with mother. I had left Johnny. Mother was working in a factory and I was in an office. I told mother I needed some new clothes for my job and begged her into getting a loan at the bank.

I came home from work early one afternoon and got the money out of the bureau. Going down into Harlem where the pusher lived, I bought the stuff and put it inside my bra. Then I went down a couple of blocks to a basement where some junkies I knew lived. I was desperate. Shaky. I loaded the needle from a bottle cap and shot myself in the vein. I knew at the time something was wrong. I got dizzy and fainted. I can remember someone playing around with me, trying to get me to my feet. I think they got scared when I didn't respond. Someone ripped my bra off, got the rest of the H, and then pulled me out of the basement leaving me crumpled on the sidewalk.

When I woke up I was in Bellevue. The police had found me and taken me to the hospital. Someone had rolled me. All my money was gone. There were three cops standing around my bed, all of them asking me questions at the same time. I told them I had been drinking and someone had put something in my liquor. But they knew.

And they had the doctor mark an "OD" on my record for "overdose." That was the first of three.

The last one almost killed me.

I had been drinking in my room. The combination of cheap wine and the overdose of heroin knocked me out.

I fell asleep on the bed and my cigarette fell in my hair. I can remember the strange feeling. I dreamed that the hand of God reached down and shook me . . . and kept shaking me. I can remember saying, "Damn it, God, leave me alone. Stop that shaking." But the shaking didn't stop. And I woke up.

I knew something was wrong, but felt nothing. I could smell something putrid—the smell of burned meat. I tried to get up but fell on the floor. Crawling to the mirror I pulled myself up and looked. The face I saw wasn't mine. I was bald. All my hair had burned off. My face was a mass of blisters and charred flesh. Both ears were almost completely burned off. The smoke, like smoke from burned toast, curled up from both my ears. Both hands were burned and blistered where subconsciously I had tried to beat out the fire.

I began to scream. A man across the hall heard my hysterical screaming and knowing I was a junkie came and pounded on the door.

I stumbled to the door and grasped the knob trying to open it, but the flesh on my palms stuck to the metal when I turned the knob. The flesh slipped off my hands and I couldn't twist the knob.

Somehow, he got the door open from the other side. He wanted to take me to the hospital but I refused. I collapsed back on the bed and asked him to take me to my friend Inez's apartment. He did. I spent the night there.

But the burns were 2nd and 3rd degree and the pain became unbearable. I was scared of the hospital. I had been there before. Knowing I was hooked, I realized if I went to the hospital, I'd have to kick the habit and come off cold turkey. I didn't think I could stand it. I would die. And I was afraid of dying.

But the next day, Inez forced me to go to the hospital. She didn't have to force much. I knew I was going to die unless I did. I was there a month and a half while the burns healed.

After I was released, I went back to the street. I took

my first shot 45 minutes after walking out the door of the hospital and that night I was back on the beat. Only it was harder now because of the scars and burns. No one wanted me. My clothes were covered with cigarette burns and coffee stains. My flesh was dirty and smelled. Sometimes I would walk down the street gagging. And the addiction was driving me insane.

A Spanish fellow named Rene used to talk to me on the streets. He had been a pusher but had gotten tangled up with Teen Challenge and had kicked the habit. He had become a Christian and for the last several months had been after me to come here and kick it also.

One cold night in March, I was desperately craving a fix. I stumbled down the block and around the corner to 416 Clinton and collapsed on the stairway next to the desk.

Mario was at the desk that night. He called Gloria. She gently picked me up and I leaned on her as we walked through the side door in front of the desk and into the chapel.

"Kneel down, Maria," she said. "Kneel down and pray." I was in a stupor and thought I was dying. But if it took this to stay alive, I'd do it. I knelt on the floor behind one of the benches but before I could get my head down, I began to vomit. I vomited all down the front of my blouse and on the floor. I began to cry and shake and collapsed in a heap on the floor, with both hands in front of me in my own vomit.

I looked up and the other girls in the room had come around me. I recognized some of them that I had seen in jail, but they were different. They all looked like angels, floating on air across the chairs and tables coming slowly toward me. They were smiling. There was a shine on their faces. Their eyes sparkled, not from pot or H, but from an inward light that shone down on me.

I was in a daze and it seemed like my head was spinning round and round.

Gloria was there beside me and I was aware that she was kneeling in my vomit. I turned my head to try to cry but could only heave.

The girls gathered around me and I could hear them praying. Gloria stood to her feet and I could feel her hands on my head. A power, an electric, spiritual power came flooding through my body, almost picking me up off the floor as it flowed through her delicate hands into my burned out body.

I heard music. Some of the girls were singing. I shuddered and threw up again.

"Please, can't I go to bed?" I stammered.

I felt strong arms under my armpits as one of the girls picked me up and almost carried me up the stairs. I heard water running and could feel them pulling at my clothes. I was too sick to care. I thought they were going to drown me. I thought maybe they were all a bunch of queers and were going to kill me. I didn't care.

They gently put me under the shower and washed me off. It was the first time in months I had been clean all over and it helped. They helped me dry off and put a clean slip on me and led me to a bunk bed in a large room that was filled with other bunks.

"Can I have a smoke?" I asked one of the girls. Gloria said, "Sorry, Maria, we don't smoke here. But here's some candy. Try it. I think it will help."

I collapsed across the bed and began to shake. They took turns rubbing my back. Every time I'd ask for a smoke Gloria would pop another piece of candy in my mouth.

They sat with me for two days and two nights. During the night, I'd wake up trembling and see Gloria there beside my bed, reading her Bible or praying out loud. I was never alone.

It was on the third night that Gloria said, "Maria, I want you to come downstairs to the chapel service." I was weak. So weak. But I came down to the chapel and sat in the back of the room.

That was the night you were speaking. And it was that night that I came into this office and knelt here and cried out my heart to the Lord."

Maria stopped talking. Her head was bowed forward, her eyes staring at the Bible resting on top of my desk.

"Maria," I whispered gently, "didn't the Lord hear that cry?"

She looked up, "Oh yes, Nicky. I've never doubted that. But when the pull of the drugs gets so strong, I want to give in." A tear ran down her cheek. "Just keep praying for me. With God's help I'll make it now."

16

With Christ in Harlem

David was on the road most of the time, recruiting summer workers and raising money for the center. As time went on, he had less and less personal contact with the addicts themselves and found himself in the role of an administrator—a role which I felt he did not want to assume but which was thrust on him by circumstances.

The majority of our field work was done in the street meetings and in personal street corner encounters. Almost every afternoon we set up our platform and loudspeaker in some ghetto section of the city.

One afternoon Mario and I took a small group in our passenger bus into the heart of Spanish Harlem. We were handing out tracts, trying to round up a crowd for a street service, but meeting with little success.

Mario said to me, "I'm gonna get us a crowd."

"Not this afternoon," I said. "No one cares. We might as well pack up and go home."

"No," Mario said. "We're gonna get a crowd. You and the others start putting up the speakers. In less than an hour we're gonna have the biggest street meeting we've ever had."

"Man, how do you think you're gonna have a meeting without any people? They're just not interested today."

"Never mind. Just let me handle it," Mario said. Smiling shyly he hurried down the street and around the corner.

We started putting up the equipment. It was strictly a faith venture. I felt like Noah building his ark on the top of a dry mountain. But we hammered away, trusting God to provide the showers.

He did. Fifteen minutes later we had finished and I was back on the corner handing out tracts when I saw a huge mob of boys running down the street toward me. They were waving sticks and baseball bats and yelling at the top of their voices. I turned and started back to the platform when I saw another mob of kids coming from the other direction, shouting and waving sticks. "I gotta get out of here," I thought. "These kids are going to rumble." But it was too late! I was surrounded by the screaming, elbowing gangs. I kept waiting for them to start slugging.

Suddenly I saw Mario running down an alley in the middle of the block shouting up the fire escapes: "Hey, everybody, the leader of the vicious Mau Mau gang from Brooklyn is going to speak in 15 minutes. Come hear him. Come hear the great Nicky Cruz, the most dangerous man in Brooklyn. Come prepared. He's a killer and still dangerous."

The kids were pouring from the apartments, down the fire escapes, and running toward me. They were flocking by me shouting, "Where's Nicky? I want to see him. Where's the leader of the Mau Maus?"

Mario came up, grinning from ear to ear. "See, I told you I'd get a crowd."

We looked around. He'd gotten a crowd all right. There must have been 300 kids milling around in the middle of the street.

I shook my head. "I just hope you don't get us all killed. Man, these kids are mean."

Mario was still grinning and puffing from running. "Come on, Preacher. Your congregation's waiting."

With perspiration running down his face, he crawled up to the mike and held out his hands for silence. The kids listened as he spoke, much like a carnival barker getting an audience keyed up for the sideshow.

"Ladies and gentlemen. Today is the big day. The leader of the vicious and famous Mau Maus is going to speak to you . . . the most dangerous man in New York. He's feared by young and old alike. Only he's not the leader any more. He's the ex-leader. And this afternoon he's gonna tell you why he's no longer with the gang and why he's running with Jesus. I now give you the one and only, NICKY CRUZ, ex-leader of the Mau Maus."

He was shouting when he finished and I jumped to the platform behind the mike. The kids in the crowd began to shout and clap. I stood there on the platform grinning and

waving my hand while they applauded. Many of them rec-
ognized me or had read about me in the paper. About
two hundred adults had gathered at the back of the crowd.
Two police cars pulled up, one on each side of the mob.

I held out my arms and the shouting, whistling and ap-
plauding grew quieter. In a moment the crowd was silent.

I felt strongly anointed by the Holy Spirit as I began to
preach. The words came freely and without strain. "I used
to be the leader of the Mau Maus. I can see you've heard
of my reputation." Once more the crowd broke into spon-
taneous applause. I held out my arms and they quieted
down.

"This afternoon I want to tell you why I'm the *ex*-leader
of the Mau Maus. I'm the *ex*-leader because Jesus changed
my heart! One day, in a street meeting just like this, I lis-
tened to a preacher tell me of someone who could change
my life. He told me Jesus loves me. I didn't even know
who Jesus was. And I knew *no*body loved me. But Davie
Wilkerson told me Jesus loves me. And my life is now
changed. I gave myself to God and He gave me new life. I
used to be just like you. I was running in the streets. Sleep-
ing on rooftops. I had been kicked out of school for fight-
ing. The police were looking for me and I'd been arrested
many times and put in jail. I was afraid. But then Jesus
changed my life. He gave me something to live for. He
gave me hope. He gave me new purpose in life. No longer
am I smoking pot and fighting and killing. No longer do I
lie awake at night afraid. No longer do I have nightmares.
Now people speak to me when I pass by. The police re-
spect me. I'm married and have a little baby. But most of
all, I'm happy and am no longer running."

The crowd was hushed and attentive. I finished my mes-
sage and gave an altar call.

Twenty-two responded to the invitation and knelt down
at the front of the crowd while I prayed.

I finished praying and looked up. The policemen had
left their cars and were standing with their hats in their
hands and their heads bowed. I turned my face toward the
sky. The sun was shining in Harlem.

Spanish Harlem became a favorite place for us to hold
street meetings. We seemed to be able to draw bigger
crowds and the need for the Gospel was more apparent

than any other place we preached. I kept reminding our team that "where sin abounded, grace did much more abound."

Gloria had a hard time accepting Spanish Harlem. She couldn't get used to the smell. She tried not to act snobbish, but some of the open markets were almost more than she could stomach. It was even hard for me to get used to the flies that swarmed over the meats, fruits and vegetables.

And then, added to this, was the odor of the addicts. They seem to ooze a foul odor. And when grouped together, especially during the heat of the summer, the smell is almost repulsive.

We learned much during those first months of street preaching. We learned that the ones who had the most success were the ones who had come off the streets and could present a first-hand testimony of the changing, transforming power of Jesus Christ. I was not as successful in preaching to dope addicts as some of the addicts themselves. We found they made our best preachers. Their honest, sincere bumbling testimonies made a terrific impact on other addicts. More and more we began to carry them with us into the streets to do our preaching. However, this too raised problems.

Many times at the street preaching services the addicts on the street would try to tempt and tease our men and women. They'd light up a pot stick in front of them and deliberately blow the smoke in their faces. I've even seen a man pull out a needle and package of heroin and wave it in the face of one of our addicts saying, "Hey, Baby, don't you miss this? Man, this is living. You gotta try it." The temptation was almost overpowering, but these lives were protected by a shield of God's strength.

I found Maria, in particular, to be unashamed to stand before a crowd of her former associates, prostitutes and junkies, and testify to the grace of God. Her simple testimony often moved the crowds to tears as she told of a God who is a close personal friend. Who, in the form of his Son Jesus Christ, walks the hard streets of the city touching people in their sin and making them whole. Most of them had never been exposed to a God like this. The God they had heard of, if they had heard of one at all, was a God of judgment who curses sin and whips people into line like a policeman. Or perhaps they identify God with the cold, formal, mumbojumbo churches they had seen.

One day a former gang member, a young negro boy who had been on heroin, was testifying concerning his childhood. He told of having to leave home at the age of 13 because the apartment was too crowded. He spoke of different men who lived with his mother. He told of sleeping on the rooftops and in the subways. He testified of having to scrounge food for himself, begging and stealing. He had no home at all and would use the rooftops or the alleys for a latrine. He was living like a wild animal in the streets.

As he talked, an old woman in the back of the crowd began to weep. She became almost hysterical in her weeping and I went around behind the crowd to minister to her. After her weeping subsided, she told me this boy could have been her son. She had five boys to leave home and live just like that in the streets of the city. Her guilt was more than she could bear. We gathered around her and prayed for her. She threw her head back and looked toward the Heavens, crying out for God to forgive her and protect her sons, wherever they were. She found her peace with God that afternoon, but the damage to her boys had already been done. And in thousands of other cases the damage was still being done. We felt like we were trying to dry up the ocean by dipping at the surf with a teaspoon. However, we knew that God did not expect us to win the world—just to testify and be faithful. And that was our goal.

Late one Thursday evening we set up a street meeting in the corner of a school yard in Spanish Harlem. It was a hot summer night and a large crowd had gathered to listen to the peppy Spanish choruses and fast Gospel music that blared from our loudspeakers.

The crowd was restless and jumpy. As the music moved into a faster tempo some of our girls and boys stood in front of the mike and began to sing, clapping their hands to the fast songs. To one side, though, I noticed a disturbance. A group of "little people" were dancing to the music. There were about five or six of them jitterbugging in the street, wiggling their hips and kicking their feet. Some of the audience was distracted and had begun to urge them on, laughing and clapping with them. I left my position and walked around to them.

"Hey, you kids. How come you're dancing here? This is Jesus' turf."

One of them said, "That man over there paid us to dance. See, he gave us a dime." They pointed to a slim young man, about 28 years old, who was standing on the edge of the crowd. I walked over to talk to him. He saw me coming and began to jitterbug to the music himself.

I tried to talk to him. He kept dancing up and down, kicking his feet and shaking his hips saying, "Man, that's tough music, cha-cha-cha."

He spun around in the street and slapped his hands against his thighs. Shaking his hips and throwing his head back like a wild man he chanted, "Be-bop, cha-cha-cha. . . . dum-de-dum-dum . . . swingin', man, swingin'."

I finally broke through to him, "Hey man, I want to ask you something."

He kept right on dancing to the time of the music, "Yeah, Daddio, whatcha want? . . . whatcha want? . . . be-bop, de-dum-dum . . . whatcha want?"

I said, "Did you give those kids money to make them dance and break up our meeting?" My patience was beginning to wear a little thin.

Whirling around he said, "That's right, man, you got the right daddy this time. I'm your man . . . da-da-de-da" . . . . He was smacking his lips and kicking his feet high in front of his face as he whirled.

I thought he was crazy. "Why?" I shouted at him. "Man, what's wrong with you anyway?"

"Because we don't like you. We don't like Christians. No. No. No. We don't like Christians. Da-da-dum-de-dum."

I was exasperated. "Well, man," I said, balling up my fists and starting toward him, "We're gonna finish this service and you're gonna shut up or I'll bust you against that building and shut you up for good."

He could see I was serious, but he couldn't shut off his mischief quite that fast. He clapped his hand over his mouth in an obvious move and then stared back over his hand in mock terror. But he stopped dancing and he shut up.

I went back to the microphone and preached that evening about my experiences growing up in New York. I testified about the dirt, poverty, shame and sin that had been in my life. Then I preached about the sin of parents who allow their children to grow up in such sin. I begged them to set a good example for their children.

People began to take off their hats as I spoke. This is one of the best signs of reverence and respect. I noticed tears in the eyes of many of the people and the appearance of scattered handkerchiefs. I knew that the power of Christ was moving in a special way, but didn't realize the impact that He was to have in the moments to follow.

As I spoke I noticed an old man, an obvious wino, standing in the middle of all those people weeping. A young girl close to the front buried her head in her hands and knelt in the street, her bare knees against the hard, dirty pavement. One of our girl workers left the group and knelt beside her, praying with her. I continued to preach.

It was obvious that the power of God's Spirit was at this meeting. As I finished preaching and gave the altar call I noticed an addict on the edge of the crowd in great agony of spirit. He reached into his shirt pocket and pulled out several "bags" and threw them into the street at his feet. He began to scream, stomping on the little white envelopes. "I curse you, you filthy powder. You've ruined my life. You've driven my wife away. You've killed my children. You've sent my soul to hell. I curse you! I curse you!"

He collapsed to the pavement on his knees, weeping and rocking back and forth with his face in his hands. One of our male staff members hurried to his side. Two other of our addicts gathered around him, one with his hand on his head and the other kneeling, all of them praying out loud as he cried out for forgiveness.

Eight or nine addicts came to the front of the crowd and knelt in the street in front of the microphone. I went from one to the other, laying my hands on their heads and praying for them, completely oblivious to the sound of the heavy traffic and the stares of curious onlookers.

After the service we counseled with those who had come and told them about the Center. We invited them to come and live with us while they kicked the habit. There were always some who would come with us right then. Others would be hesitant and refuse. Some would come around a week or so later and ask to be admitted.

As the crowd departed, we gathered up our equipment and started to load it in the bus. One of the little kids who had been dancing in the street began pulling on my coat sleeve. I asked him what he wanted and he said that the "dancing man" wanted to talk to me. I asked him where the man was and he pointed across the street to a dark alley.

It was already night and I had no desire to walk into a dark alley where a crazy man was hiding. I told the kid to tell the man I would be glad to talk to him—out here under the street lights.

The kid went back and in a few minutes he returned. We had almost finished disassembling our equipment. He shook his head and said the man needed to see me but he was too embarrassed to come out in the light.

I started to tell the kid, "no dice." But suddenly I remembered David Wilkerson coming to me in the basement room where I had gone to hide after that first street service. I remember how he walked in unafraid and said, "Nicky, Jesus loves you." It was this fearlessness and compassion that led me to accept Christ as my Saviour.

So, looking into the black sky I told the Lord that if He wanted me to talk to this wild "dancing man", I would go. But I was going in His Spirit and not in my own might and power and I was expecting Him to go before me—especially into that dark alley.

I made my way across the street and stopped at the entrance to the alley. It was like the entrance to a tomb. I whispered a prayer, "Lord, I sure hope you've gotten here ahead of me," and in I went. I felt my way down the masonry walls into the darkness.

Then, I heard the muffled sound of a man sobbing. I moved forward and in the dim light could see him crouched on his haunches in the midst of a group of stinking garbage cans. His head was between his legs and his body was racked with convulsive sobs. I moved forward and knelt beside him. The rank odor from the garbage cans was overpowering. But here was human need, and the desire to help was even stronger than the stench from the alley.

"Help me. Please help me." He sobbed out. "I read about you in the papers. I heard that you had been converted and had been to Bible school. Please help me."

I couldn't believe that this was the same man who only minutes before had been dancing and singing in the street, trying to break up our meeting.

"Will God forgive me? Tell me, have I slipped too far? Will He forgive me? Please help me."

I told him God would forgive. I knew. He had forgiven me. I asked him about himself. He poured out his story as I knelt there in the filth of the alley beside him.

He had once felt that God was calling him into the ministry. He had given up his job and attended a Bible School to study for the ministry. Returning to New York, however, he met a woman who seduced him away from his wife. His wife and two children begged him not to leave them. They reminded him of his vows to God and his marriage vows. But he was a man possessed with a demon and left his wife and moved in with the other woman. Then two months later she left him, telling him she was tired of him and he wasn't any fun any more. He had gone to pieces and was now smoking pot and taking pills. I asked him what kind of pills and he said he was taking Bombitas (Desoxyn), Nembies, Tuinal, and Seconal (barbiturates). He felt he was losing his mind.

"I was trying to drive you away," he moaned. "That's why I acted like I did out on the street and in the school yard. I was afraid. I was afraid of God and afraid to face Him. I want to come back to God. I want to go back to my wife and children but don't know how. Will you pray for me?" He raised his head and I saw eyes full of pathos and guilt, pleading for help.

I helped him to his feet and we walked out of the alley and across the street to the bus. Six of us got in the bus. He sat in one of the middle seats with his head bent over on the back of the seat in front of him. We began to pray with him, all of us praying audibly. He was praying also. Suddenly I was aware that he was quoting Scripture. From out of his memory and his training at Bible School poured forth the words of the 51st Psalm—the Psalm that King David prayed after he committed adultery with Bathsheba and sent her husband into battle to be killed. Never have I felt the power of God so close as I did when this former minister, who had become a servant of Satan, received the Spirit of Christ and cried out his prayer of confession and request for forgiveness in the words of the Holy Scripture.

> Have mercy upon me, O God, according to thy loving-kindness: according unto the multitude of thy tender mercies blot out my transgressions.
>
> Wash me thoroughly from mine iniquity, and cleanse me from my sin.
>
> For I acknowledge my transgressions: and my sin is ever before me.
>
> Against thee, and thee only have I sinned, and done this evil in thy sight: that thou mightest be justified when thou speakest, and be clear when thou judgest.
>
> Behold, I was shapen in iniquity, and in sin did my mother conceive me.
>
> Behold, thou desirest truth in the inward parts, and in the hidden part thou shalt make me to know wisdom.
>
> Purge me with hyssop, and I shall be clean! wash me, and I shall be whiter than snow.
>
> Make me to hear joy and gladness; that the bones which thou hast broken may rejoice.
>
> Hide thy face from my sins, and blot out all mine iniquities.
>
> Create in me a clean heart, O God, and renew a right spirit within me.
>
> Cast me not away from thy presence; and take not thy Holy Spirit from me.
>
> Restore unto me the joy of thy salvation; and uphold me with thy free spirit.
>
> Then will I teach transgressors thy ways; and sinners shall be converted unto thee.
>
> Deliver me from blood guiltiness, O God, thou God of my salvation; and my tongue shall sing aloud of thy righteousness.

He finished praying. The bus was quiet. Then Gloria spoke up in a soft, beautiful voice, finishing the words of the Psalm. "The sacrifices of God are a broken spirit: a broken and contrite heart, O God, thou wilt not despise."

We all arose from our knees. He was wiping his face with his handkerchief and blowing his nose. The rest of us were blowing and sniffing too.

He turned to me. "I gave my last dime to those crazy kids to dance in the street. Could you give me a quarter to call my wife and catch a subway. I'm going home."

I've made it a practice never to give junkies or winos

money. I know that almost without exception it will go for dope or booze. But this was the exception. I reached in my pocket and pulled out my last dollar bill. He took it and hugged me around the neck, his face still wet from tears. Then he went to the others and hugged each of them too.

"You'll be hearing from me," he said. "I'll be back."

He was back. Two days later he brought his wife and two children by the center to introduce them. There was a radiance in his face that could never be produced by drugs or pills. It was the light of God.

17

Through the Valley
of the Shadow

It is almost impossible to put 40 drug addicts under one roof without having problems—especially when they're supervised by green inexperienced personnel. The only thing that kept the organization of Teen Challenge from exploding was the Holy Spirit. We were sitting on a powder keg and anyone of us could light the fuse on some psychopathic mind and blow us all into oblivion. Our only hope was to stay as close to God as possible.

It was difficult to tell those who were genuine from those who were counterfeit, for most of these men and women were professional con artists. They made their living telling lies. But we trusted them as far as we could.

I was a stickler for discipline and soon learned most of them didn't resent it if it were just and reasonable. In fact, they relished it because it gave them a firm base of operation—a solid sense of belonging. However, I knew all of them didn't feel this way.

David agreed with my philosophy. But the distasteful responsibility of having to constantly reprimand the offenders began to weigh heavily upon me. Many times I had to get out of bed in the middle of the night to quell a disturbance and sometimes even dismiss someone for an infraction of the rules.

Most of the major decisions were left up to me and we had to add additional staff members, most of them just out of college. I became keenly aware of my lack of formal training and sensed my own insecurity. I knew little or nothing about administrative procedures and even less about the psychological aspects of interpersonal relations necessary to maintain communication and rapport with my fellow staff members. I could sense jealousy on the part of some of those working under me and became aware of a gradual breakdown in relationships.

When David would stop by the center, I'd try to explain that I had problems too big to handle, but he'd always come back at me with, "You can handle it, Nicky. I have great confidence in your ability."

But the problems continued to stack up like dark clouds on the horizon before a storm.

In the fall I flew with Davie to Pittsburgh to speak in Kathryn Kuhlman's city-wide crusade. Miss Kuhlman has one of the world's greatest Spirit-filled ministries. Her work through the Kathryn Kuhlman Foundation reaches all parts of the globe. She had visited Teen Challenge and had taken a personal interest in my work. I had shown her around the city and taken her into the ghetto. "I thank God for lifting you out of these slums," she had said to me. "If you ever have a problem too big to handle, call me."

I thought I might try to talk to her while I was in Pittsburgh because the burden on my heart was becoming heavier. However, I got caught up in the bigness of her program. That night, speaking through my friend Jeff Morales who had come along to interpret, I shared my testimony with several thousand people in the great auditorium. After the service we had dinner in a small restaurant but I never had the opportunity to speak to Miss Kuhlman alone. So I left Pittsburgh even more frustrated over my inability to handle my own personal problems.

By January 1964, we had grown too large to keep the women on the third floor at 416 Clinton. We made arrangements to secure a house across the street for the women's quarters. I was aware of conspiracies behind my back with some of the junkies I had been forced to discipline. Besides this, we had taken several Lesbians into the Center who were giving us considerable trouble. I was constantly afraid one of them might try to seduce some of the inexperienced college girls who had been brought in to work as counselors.

Handling addicts was like trying to beat out a forest fire with a wet towel. Every time I got one little situation under control another would break out. I found myself getting personally involved and when a junkie returned to the world, I began to take it personally.

Gloria warned me about trying to bear all the burden alone, but the responsibility fell heavy on my shoulders.

Then Quetta came to the center. She was a "male" Lesbian and at one time had been "married" to another girl. She wore men's clothes, pants, jacket, even men's shoes and underwear. She was in her early 30's with very fair skin and pitch black hair cut like a man. She was a thin, willowy, attractive girl with an outgoing personality.

Quetta was one of the biggest narcotic pushers in the city. For years she had run a "shooting gallery" in her apartment. Men and women had come not only to buy heroin, but to participate in sexual immorality. She supplied all that was needed—needles, cookers, heroin, pills, and for those with unnatural desires—men and women. It was a messy situation.

When the police raided Quetta's apartment they picked up 12 persons including some professional prostitutes and uncovered 10 "outfits" (spoon, needle, and eyedropper). They literally demolished the apartment, ripping out the walls and tearing up the floor until they discovered her cache of drugs worth thousands of dollars.

Quetta came to the center while on probation. I explained the rules to her and told her she was to dress in women's clothing and let her hair grow. Furthermore, she was never to be alone with one of the other junkies unless a woman staff member was present. She was too sick to disagree and seemed thankful to be out of jail. In less than a week she made a profession of faith and gave every outward evidence of being converted.

I soon realized, however, that even conversions can be counterfeit. Even though we used Quetta to testify in many of the street meetings, I felt there was something false about her.

Two weeks later one of the girl counselors came to me early one morning. She was white as a sheet and shaking like a leaf. "What's wrong, Diane? Come in and sit down."

Diane was our newest staff member, a country girl from Nebraska who had just recently graduated from Bible College. "I don't know how to tell you, Nicky," she said. "It's Quetta and Lilly."

Lilly was one of the junkies who had come into the center just a week before. She had been attending the services but hadn't made any commitment to the Lord. I felt my mouth go dry. "What about them?" I said.

Diane blushed and hung her head. "They were in the kitchen together last night about midnight. I walked in on them, and Nicky, they were . . . were . . . ," Her voice trailed off in shame and embarrassment. "I haven't been able to sleep all night. What can we do?"

I got up from my chair and paced back and forth around the desk. "Go back to the building and tell them I want to see them in my office immediately," I choked out. "This place is dedicated to the Lord. We can't have any of this type thing going on."

Diane left and I sat at my desk with my head in my hands, praying desperately for wisdom. Where had I failed? We had let Quetta testify for the center. The newspapers had carried her story and given much publicity. She had even spoken in churches about the change in her life.

I waited more than an hour and then started out the door to see what was keeping them. Diane met me on the steps. "They left. Both of them. They got scared and said they were leaving. We couldn't stop them."

I turned and walked slowly back to the center. I took the defeat personally—and hard. For three days Gloria prayed with me and talked to me as I sulked over my seeming inability to reach these addicts with the true message.

"Nicky, even Jesus had failures among his followers," she said. "Remember all those who have been faithful and successful. Remember Sonny who is in Bible school studying to be a minister. Think of Maria and the wonderful change in her life. Remember what God had done for you. Have you forgotten your own salvation experience? How can you doubt God and grow discouraged over these isolated failures?"

Gloria was right, but I was unable to pull myself out of my despondency. As the summer wore on the burden of guilt grew greater. I felt I was a total failure. Communications had broken down between me and most of the other staff members. David still believed in me, but I was acutely and painfully aware of the constant failures in the center. The tension grew greater. Gloria kept trying to pull me out of my defeated attitude, but I was entirely negative in everything I did.

The only bright spot was the arrival of Jimmy Baez. Jimmy had been hooked on narcotics for 8 years. He wandered into the center asking for medicine, thinking it was a hospital.

"We have no medicine here but Jesus," I told him.

He thought I was crazy. "Man, I thought this was a clinic. You're a bunch of kooks." He looked wildly around trying to get out of my office.

"Sit down, Jimmy. I want to talk to you. Christ can change you."

"No one can change me," Jimmy mumbled. "I've tried and can't leave it alone."

I got up from my desk and walked over to him. Placing my hands on his head I began to pray. I felt him shudder and he fell to his knees calling out to God. From that night on he never wanted another shot of heroin.

"See," Gloria said, when I told her about Jimmy's conversion, "God is showing you He can still use you. How can you continue to doubt Him? Why not be positive? It's been several months since you went out for the street services at night. Get to work for God and you'll feel the leadership of the Holy Spirit like you used to."

I took her advice and agreed to lead the street services the last week in August. The first night out we set up our platform in Brooklyn and I began to preach. It was a hot sultry night but the crowd was large and attentive. I preached hard and felt good about my message. As I neared the end of my sermon I gave the altar call.

Suddenly, I glanced up and on the far back edge of the crowd I saw him. His face was unmistakable. It was Israel. All these years. I had been praying, searching, inquiring . . . and suddenly there he was, a face in the crowd.

My heart leaped. Perhaps God has sent him back. I felt the old fire pour into my heart as I gave the invitation. He seemed to be listening intently, stretching his neck to hear my words. The portable organ began to play and the girl's trio broke into song. I saw Israel turn and start to walk away.

Jumping down from the platform I elbowed my way furiously through the crowd, trying to reach him before he disappeared in the mob of people.

"Israel! Israel!" I shouted after him. "Wait! Wait!"

He paused and turned around. It had been six years since I'd seen him. He was heavier and more mature. But his handsome face was like chiseled marble and his eyes were deep and sad.

I threw my arms around him and tried to pull him back toward the crowd. He resisted and stood unmovable. "Israel," I screamed bubbling with joy. "Is it really you?" I jumped back and held his shoulders at arm's length looking him over. "Where have you been? Where are you living? What are you doing? Tell me everything. Why haven't you called me? I've looked all over New York for you. This is the greatest day of my life."

His eyes were distant and cold, his manner strange and withdrawn.

"I've got to go, Nicky. It's been good to see you again."

"Got to go? I haven't seen you in six years. You've been in my daily prayers. You're coming home with me." I began to tug at his arm but he shook his head and pulled his arm away from me. I could feel the strong muscles rippling under his skin.

"Someday, Nicky. Not now." He shrugged me off and started to walk away.

"Hey, wait a minute. What's wrong with you? You're my best friend. You can't just walk away."

He turned and froze me in one spot with a chilly stare from those steel gray unflinching eyes. "Later, Nicky!" he spat out. He turned sharply and walked down the sidewalk into the darkness.

I stood and called out to him in despair. But he never turned around. He just kept walking into the darkness from whence he came.

I returned to the center a broken man. I dejectedly made my way up the narrow stairs to the third floor and shut the door behind me in one of the attic rooms. "God," I cried out in an agonized voice, "what have I done? Israel's lost and it's my fault. Forgive me." I dropped to the floor and fell into a period of uncontrollable crying. I beat my hands against the wall in utter despair. But I received no answer. For two hours I remained in the hot attic room, exhausting myself physically, emotionally, and spiritually.

I knew I was going to leave the center. I felt my ministry was finished. I was a failure in everything I tried to do. Everyone I touched went bad. Quetta. Lilly. Now Israel. It was hopeless for me to stay on and fight the mounting battles that I couldn't overcome. It was hopeless for me even to remain in the ministry. I was finished. Whipped. Beaten. I pulled myself to my feet and stood looking out the small attic window at the dark sky. "God, I'm beat. I've been wrong. I've been trusting in myself and not in you. If this is the reason you've let this thing come to pass, I am willing to confess my terrible sin. Humble me. Kill me if you must. But, dear God, don't throw me on the scrap heap."

The sobs came again and shook my body. I stood in the door looking back. The room was silent. I didn't know whether He heard me or not. But at that moment it made little difference. I had done all I knew to do.

I went back down the steps to my apartment. Gloria had put the baby to bed and was clearing the remnants of her late supper from the table. I closed the door and walked toward the chair. Before I could sit she was in front of me. Her arms encircled my waist as she drew me close. She knew nothing of what had taken place in the street or the upper room, but because we were one flesh, she could sense I had been wounded. And she was beside me to hold my failing spirit and give strength in time of need.

I crushed her to me and buried my face in her shoulder as the tears began again. For a long time we stood there, pressed tightly against each other, my body racked with sobs. At last the crying passed and I pulled her face up with my hands and looked deep into her eyes. They were filled with tears, like deep fountains with water springing up from the pure earth beneath. But she was not crying. She was smiling, ever so faintly. And the love that flowed from her heart overflowed in her eyes as the tears spilled out over the edges and ran in little rivulets down her light bronze cheeks.

I held her face tightly in my hands. She was beautiful. More beautiful than ever before. She smiled and then her lips parted as she reached for me in a soft lingering kiss. I could taste the salt from my own tears and the moist warmth of her mouth against mine.

"It's over, Gloria. I'm finished. I'm going to leave. Maybe I've grown proud. Maybe I've sinned. I don't know, but I know the spirit has departed from me. I'm like Samson going out to fight the Philistines without the power of God. I'm a failure. I ruin everything I touch."

"What is it, Nicky?" her voice was soft and gentle. "What has happened?"

"Tonight I saw Israel. For the first time in six years I saw my dearest friend. He turned his back on me. It's my fault he's like he is. Had I not left him alone in the city six years ago, he would be working beside me today. Instead, he spent five years in prison and tonight is lost. God doesn't care any more."

"Nicky, that is almost blasphemy," Gloria said, her voice still soft. "You cannot blame yourself for what happened to Israel. You were just a scared kid that morning you drove out of town. It wasn't your fault you missed Israel. It's wrong to blame yourself. And how can you dare say God doesn't care any more? He does care. He cared enough to save you."

"You don't understand," I said, shaking my head. "Ever since Davie told me Israel went back to the gang I have blamed myself. I have carried the burden of guilt on my heart. Tonight I saw him, and he turned his back on me. He wouldn't even speak to me. If only you could have seen the cold hardness in his face."

"But, Nicky, you can't give up now, just when God is beginning to work . . ."

"Tomorrow I'm going to resign," I interrupted. "I don't belong here. I don't belong in the ministry. I'm not good enough. If I stay, the whole Teen Challenge will be destroyed. I'm like Jonah. Maybe I'm still running from God and don't know it. They need to throw me overboard so a fish can eat me up. If they don't get rid of me the whole ship will sink."

"Nicky, that's crazy talk. Satan is causing you to say that," Gloria said, on the verge of tears.

I pulled away. "Satan is in me all right. But I'm still going to resign."

"Nicky, the least you can do is talk to Davie first."

"I've tried, a hundred times. But he's always too busy. He thinks I can handle things. Well, I can't take it any more. I'm a misfit and it's time for me to admit it to myself. I'm a failure . . . a failure."

After we went to bed Gloria slipped her arm around my head and rubbed the back of my neck. "Nicky, before you resign will you promise me one thing? Will you call Kathryn Kuhlman and talk to her?"

I nodded my head in agreement. My pillow was wet with tears as I heard Gloria whisper, "Nicky, God will take care of us."

I buried my head in my pillow, praying that God would never let the sun come up on another day in my life.

In those days of darkness and indecision a single bright star appeared in the form of this tall dignified lady who seemed to exude the very presence of the Holy Spirit. Just talking with Miss Kuhlman on the phone the next morning seemed to help. She insisted I come to Pittsburgh at her expense before making my final decision.

The next afternoon I flew to Pittsburgh. I was surprised she didn't try to talk me into staying at Teen Challenge. Instead, she said, "Perhaps God is leading you into a different ministry, Nicky. Perhaps He is leading you through the valley of the shadow in order to bring you out into the sunshine on the other side. Just keep your eyes on Jesus. Don't become bitter or discouraged. God has placed His hand on you, He will not desert you. Remember, Nicky, when we go through the valley, He goes with us."

We prayed together and she prayed if it were God's will for me to leave Teen Challenge that He keep the cloud of discouragement close around me. If He wanted me to stay, that He lift the cloud so I could feel free to remain in New York.

I flew back to the city the next morning, thankful for the friendship and confidence of this gracious and dynamic Christian.

That night, after the baby was in bed, I sat at the kitchen table and talked again to Gloria. I just wanted out. We would start all over, maybe in California. Gloria said she would follow me wherever I went. Her great love and confidence gave me a new strength. Before I went to bed I took a piece of paper and a stub of a pencil and wrote out my resignation.

It was a miserable weekend. Monday morning when

David arrived at the center, I handed him the resignation and waited while he read it.

He hung his head. "Am I the one who has failed you, Nicky?" he asked softly. "Have I been in such a hurry I haven't been here to help you when you needed me? Come into the office and talk to me."

I silently followed him down the hall and into the office. He closed the door behind us and looked at me with a deeply grieved face. "Nicky, I don't know what's behind this. But I know I'm to blame for much of it. I have been chastizing myself daily for not spending more time with you. But I've been on the go so much raising money for the center. I haven't even been able to spend time with my family. The burden has rested heavy on my shoulders. So before we talk I want to ask you to forgive me for having failed you. Will you forgive me, Nicky?"

I hung my head and nodded it silently. David sighed deeply and collapsed into a chair. "Talk to me, Nicky."

"It's too late to talk, Davie. I've been trying to talk to you. I feel this is what I have to do."

"But why, Nicky, why? What has caused this sudden decision?"

"It's not sudden, Davie. It's been coming for a long time." And then I poured my heart out to him.

"Nicky," David said, his piercing eyes looking straight at me. "All of us go through these periods of depression. I have let people down and have been let down by people. I have wanted to throw in the towel many times. Often I have found myself with Elijah under the juniper bush crying, 'It is enough, O Lord, take away my life.' But, Nicky, you have walked where angels fear to tread. I just can't see you running from these little defeats."

"They aren't little to me, Davie. My mind is already made up. I'm sorry."

The next day I put Gloria and Alicia on a plane for Oakland and two days later I flew to Houston to keep my last scheduled speaking engagement. It was August 1964. I had been at Teen Challenge two years and nine months.

In Houston I was ashamed to tell the people that I had resigned from Teen Challenge. But my preaching was cold and ineffectual. I was anxious to get on to California and be with Gloria.

Flying across the nation I slowly became aware that I was no longer flying on an expense account. We had saved very little money and the plane tickets and moving expenses would just about drain us. I was scared. Insecure. Frightened.

I remembered the times people had tried to press cash into my hand when I was speaking in rallies and conferences. I would thank them and ask them to write out a check to Teen Challenge. I wanted nothing for myself. My whole life had been wrapped up in the center. It seemed ironic that even in Houston I had continued to tell the people to make out the checks to Teen Challenge, knowing I barely had enough money to live on for the next few days.

Gloria met me at the airport. She had rented a small apartment. We were broke and depressed. I had given God almost six years of my life and I felt He had turned His back on me. I'd quit, leave the ministry, and start from the bottom in some other field. The sun sank into the Pacific Ocean and my whole world plunged into blackness.

I had no idea which way to turn. I found myself withdrawing from everything. I didn't even want to go to church with Gloria, preferring to just sit around the house staring at the walls. Gloria tried to pray with me but I felt hopeless and shrugged her off, telling her she could pray but I was empty.

Within weeks word got around I was back in California. Invitations to speak in churches began to pour in. I soon got tired of telling them "no" and trying to make up some kind of excuse. I finally told Gloria not to take anymore long distance calls and not to answer the letters that came in the daily mail.

But we were getting desperate financially. We had used up all our savings and Gloria had been unable to get a job.

As a last resort I accepted an invitation to preach in a youth crusade. I was spiritually cold. For the first time in my life I went into the pulpit without praying. Sitting on the platform I was amazed at how hard and cold I was. I was shocked at my mercenary attitude. Yet I was desperate. If God had let me down like I felt He had in New York, then I felt no obligation to seek His blessing in preaching. If they'd pay me. I'd take it. It was as simple as that.

But it was not quite that simple with God. Obviously, He had far bigger plans than for me just to draw a paycheck for preaching. Preaching to Him is sacred business —and He has promised, "My word. . . . shall not return to me empty."

When I gave the invitation something happened. First, a young teenage boy stepped out from the crowd and came forward, kneeling at the altar. Then another came from the far side of the auditorium. Then more streamed forward until the aisles were full of young people coming to the altar rail and kneeling to commit their lives to Jesus Christ. The crowd was so great at the front of the church that many had to stand behind those kneeling at the crowded rail. In the back of the church I saw people falling to their knees and crying out to God. Still they came. I had never been in a service when the Spirit of God swept through a congregation with such power.

God was trying to say something to me, not in whispers, but in thundering tones. He was telling me He was still on His throne. He was reminding me that even though I had let Him down, He was not going to let me down. He was telling me in unmistakable terms He was not through with my life . . . that He still had use for me, even when I was unwilling to be used.

I felt my knees shaking and tried to hold on to the back of the pulpit. Suddenly, my eyes were full of tears as I, the preacher of the night, stumbled forward and knelt at the back side of the altar rail. There, with heart overflowing with repentance, I poured out my soul to God in recommitment.

Following the service Gloria and I sat in the car in the church parking lot. We had planned to go out and eat and then take a drive. Instead, we agreed to go home.

As we entered the door, I fell to my knees. Gloria was beside me and we both wept and cried out to God. And I knew. I knew there was more. I knew that all things do work together for good to them that love God. I looked up through the tears and suddenly realized He was beside me. I could feel His presence. I could almost hear Him say, "Yea, though I walk through the valley of the shadow of death I will fear no evil, for thou art with me. Thy rod and thy staff they comfort me. . . ."

We had been through the valley of the shadow. But His

grace had brought us through and now the sunlight of to-morrow glistened on the distant mountain peaks signifying the dawning of a new day.

18

Walkin' in Jesus' Turf

The big break came just before Christmas when I received an invitation from a layman's group known as the "Full Gospel Business Men's Fellowship International." It was through this group of dedicated businessmen that speaking invitations from high schools and colleges began to pour in. During 1965 I traveled to most of the major cities across the nation. My crusade rallies, many of them sponsored by churches of all denominations, were having wonderful success and I spoke to crowds up to ten thousand.

I thanked God daily for His goodness. But I was still restless and had a deep yearning in my heart. I couldn't seem to put my finger on the problem but I was becoming more restless every day.

Then I met Dan Malachuk, a tall, extroverted businessman from New Jersey who unknowingly brought my problem to the surface. He casually mentioned one night that he understood my original desire was to work with the "little people." I didn't respond to his question but neither could I get it out of my mind.

I remembered my own childhood. If only someone had cared enough to lead me to Christ as a child then maybe——

I talked it over with Gloria. God was using my testimony in large crusades, but every time I saw an article in the newspaper about children arrested for sniffing glue or smoking marijuana, my heart ached. We kept praying that God would provide a way for us to reach these children.

A few months later Dan helped arrange a 4-day crusade in Seattle. All this time I had been speaking through my interpreter, Jeff Morales. Jeff had moved to California in order to travel with me to the large rallies where the audiences had trouble with my accent. But just a half hour before I was to leave for the airport Jeff called.

"Nickey, I'm in bed with pneumonia. The doctor refuses to let me go. You're going to have to be on your own."

Standing on the platform before a battery of microphones and TV cameras I surveyed the huge crowd. Could they understand me with my Puerto Rican accent? Would they laugh at my poor grammar? Nervously I cleared my throat and opened my mouth to speak. No words—only a garbled mumble. I cleared my throat and something came out that sounded like uuuggghhhllkfg."

The crowd fidgeted nervously but politely. It was hopeless. I was too used to having Jeff stand beside me. I bowed my head and asked for power. "Dear Lord, if you can give me an unknown tongue to praise your name, then I'm trusting you to give me a known tongue to tell these kids about you."

I raised my head and started to speak. The words were perfect and flowed from my mouth with supernatural power. Jeff had been replaced by Jesus and from that moment on I knew as long as I was speaking for Him I would never need an interpreter.

After the final service Dan stopped by my hotel room.

"Nicky, God is blessing in a marvelous way. They took a love offering of $3,000 for you to use in your ministry."

"Dan, I can't take that money."

"Nicky," Dan said as he made himself at home sprawling on the couch and kicking off his shoes, "the money is not for you. It's for God's work through you."

"And I can use it any way I feel God wants?" I asked.

"That's right," Dan said.

"Then I'll use it for the little people. I want to start a Center to minister to them."

"Wonderful," Dan exploded, straightening up on the sofa, "call it Outreach for Youth."

Outreach for Youth it was. I returned to California with the $3,000 determined to open a center where I could take the little people off the street and win them to Christ.

We set up our Center in Fresno at 221 N. Broadway. We applied for our official California charter and I hung out a sign on the front porch, "Outreach for Youth, Nicky Cruz, Director."

Right away I started combing the streets. My first day out I found an 11-year-old boy sitting in a doorway. I sat down beside him and asked his name.

He looked at me out of the corner of his eyes and finally said, "Ruben, whatcha wanna know fer?"

"I dunno," I slurred back, "you just looked kinda lonesome and I thought I'd talk to you."

He willingly told me his father was a junkie. He'd been sniffing glue just the day before. He was a 6th grade dropout at school. I listened and then told him I was opening a Center for kids like him and asked if he'd like to come live with me.

"You mean you want me to come?"

"Sure," I said, "but we'll have to talk to your daddy first."

"Hell," the 11-year-old boy answered, "my old man'll be glad to get rid of me. The one you gotta clear it with is my probation officer."

The probation officer was delighted and that night Ruben moved in with us.

Within the next several weeks we picked up two more kids. We enrolled them all in school and held daily Bible studies at the Center. Ruben gave us a great deal of trouble at first, but at the end of the second week he made a profession of faith during one of the Bible studies. The next afternoon when he came from school he went straight to his room and began to study. Gloria winked at me. "What more evidence could you want that his conversion was sincere?" she said. I needed none. Deep inside I felt good. The restlessness was disappearing.

As the days went by we began getting calls from distraught mothers who said their children were completely out of hand and begging us to take them in. In a matter of weeks we were full and still getting calls. Gloria and I spent much time in prayer asking God to direct us.

Early one morning, after only a couple of hours of sleep, the phone rang. I fumbled for the receiver. It was Dan Smith, an active member of the Full Gospel Business Men's chapter in Fresno.

"Nicky, God is leading in a mysterious way. Several of us have been praying about the work you are doing. God has laid it on my heart to help you form a Board of Directors. I have talked with Earl Draper, an accountant, with

Reverend Paul Evans, and H. J. Keener, manager of a local TV station. We are willing to work with you if you want us."

It was another answer to prayer as this small group of business and professional people rallied behind the Center to help give direction.

Later that same month Dave Carter joined our staff to work with the boys. I had known Dave, a tall, quiet Negro, when he was a gang leader in New York. He had gone to Bible School after his conversion and since he had no family connections was able to spend many hours counseling individually with the love-starved boys. We also had two young Mexican girls, Frances Ramirez and Angie Sedillos, join us to add the woman's touch and help with the secretarial work.

The final member of the staff was someone very special to me. It was Jimmy Baez. Jimmy had just graduated from Bible School and married a quiet, soft spoken girl. He was coming to work as our Supervisor, but to me he was more than that. He was walking proof of the changing, transforming power of Jesus Christ. It was difficult to imagine this scholarly looking young man with handsome face and dark rimmed glasses was the same frail, emaciated lad who had crawled into Teen Challenge shaking from withdrawal of heroin and begging for drugs.

With our hearts filled with faith in God and our hands busy with the "little people" we moved forward. God was blessing and I didn't think I could hold any more of His marvelous surprises. But for those who love God there is no limit to the surprises of tomorrow.

That Fall, Dan Malachuk arranged for me to return to New York for a series of speaking engagements. After meeting me at the airport we drove back into town past mile after mile of slum apartments. I sat slumped in the front seat of Dan's car and watched the ghetto flash by. Something kept tugging at my heart. I was no longer a part of the ghetto but it was still a part of me. I began to wonder about old friends and gang members—especially Israel. "Jesus," I prayed, "please give me one more chance to witness to him."

After the meeting that night Dan followed to my hotel room. The phone was ringing when we entered.

I answered and there was a long silence on the other end before I heard a weak but familiar voice say, "Nicky, it's me. Israel."

"Israel!" I shouted. "Praise God! My prayer is answered. Where are you?"

"I'm home, Nicky, in the Bronx. I just read in the paper you were in town and called your brother, Frank. He said I could catch you at the hotel."

I started to say something else but he interrupted me. "Nicky, I-I-I was wondering if I might be able to see you while you're in town. Just to talk over old times."

I could hardly believe my ears. I turned to Dan. "It's Israel. He wants to see me."

"Ask him to meet us at the hotel tomorrow night for dinner," Dan said. The long awaited reunion was set for 6:00 p.m. the next evening.

I prayed for him all that night asking God to give me the right words to touch his heart for Christ.

Dan and I paced the hotel lobby from 5:30 until 7:00 p.m. He hadn't shown up. My heart was in my throat as I remembered that early morning nine years before when we had missed him the first time.

Suddenly I saw him. His handsome features, deep set eyes, wavy hair. Nothing had changed. I couldn't speak as the tears came to my eyes. "Nicky," he choked out as he grasped my hand, "I can't believe it." Suddenly we were laughing and talking at the same time, completely oblivious to the human traffic all around us.

Long moments later he pulled away and said, "Nicky, I want you to meet my wife, Rosa."

Beside him was a short, sweet little Puerto Rican girl with a grin that spread all the way across her beautiful face. I reached down to take her hand but she grabbed me around the neck and kissed me solidly on the cheek.

"It like I know you," she winked and said with broken English. "I been living with you all this time. Israel talk about you much these three years."

We started downstairs to the Hay Market Room for dinner. Israel and Rosa hung back and I could sense something was bothering them. "Hey, Israel, what's the matter, baby? Dan is paying for it. Come on."

Israel gave me an embarrassed look and finally pulled me to one side. "Nicky, I don't belong in such a fancy place. I've never been to a swanky joint like this. I don't know what to do."

I put my arm around his shoulder. "I don't know what to do either," I said. "Just order the most expensive thing and let the 'Jolly Green Giant' pay for it," I grinned, pointing at Dan.

After dinner we took the elevator to my room on the fourteenth floor. Israel was relaxed and seemed his old self as he told us of his home in the ghetto.

"It isn't the most pleasant place to live," he said. "We have to keep our dishes in the refrigerator to keep the roaches off. But it could be worse. Downstairs the rats come in out of the alley and bite the kids while they sleep."

Israel paused and reflected. "It's like you're chained down there," he said. "You can't get away. It's a bad place to raise the kids. Last week three little girls in my building, all around nine years old, were raped in the back alley. We don't dare let the children out on the street and I'm sick of it. I want out. But——."

His voice trailed off and he got up from his chair and walked to the window looking out toward the glimmering tower on the Empire State Building. "But you gotta live someplace, and any place else the rent's too high. But maybe next year . . . maybe next year we can move to a nicer place. I haven't done too badly. I started out as a dishwasher and have worked my way up to a clerk on Wall Street."

"But after you make it, what then?" I interrupted.

Israel turned and looked at me with a puzzled stare. "What did you say?" he asked.

I knew the time had come to dig deeper into the past. "Israel, tell me what went wrong."

He walked back to the couch where Rosa was sitting and sat nervously beside her. "I don't mind talking about it. I guess I need to. I've never even told Rosa. You remember that morning after you got out of the hospital when you and that man were going to meet me?"

I nodded. The memory was painful.

"I waited out there for three hours. I felt like a fool. I was sick of Christians and that night I went back to the gang."

I interrupted. "Israel, I'm sorry. We looked for you. . . ."

He shook his head. "Who cares? It was a long time ago. Maybe things would have been different had I gone with you. Who knows?"

He paused and then began again. "After that we got in this trouble with the South Street Angels. This guy came in our turf and we told him we didn't want no jigs around. He got smart and we hit him. He ran and five of us chased him into South Street turf and caught him at the Penny Arcade. We dragged him outside and started fighting with him. The next thing I know one of our guys had this gun in his hand and was shooting. Paco started holding his belly and mocking saying, "Oh, I'm shot! I'm shot! All our guys were laughing."

"Then the jig fell to the ground. He really was shot. He was a dead man. I could see the hole in his head."

Israel paused. The only sound was the muffled roar of the traffic on the street far below.

"We ran. Four of us got caught. The other guy got away. The guy who pulled the trigger got twenty years. The rest of us got five to twenty."

He stopped talking and hung his head. "It was five years of hell."

Regaining his composure he continued. "I had to get a 'fix' to get out of prison."

"What do you mean a 'fix'?" Dan interrupted.

"My Parole Board said I would be released when I could prove to them I had a job waiting for me. They said I'd have to go back to my old home. I didn't want to go back to Brooklyn. I wanted to start out all over again but they said I had to go back home. So I got a 'fix' through this junkie who was in there with me. He knew a man who had a dress factory in Brooklyn and this man told my mother if she'd pay him $50 he'd promise me a job. She gave him the money and he wrote a letter saying I had a job when I got out of prison. It was the only way I could get a job. Man, who wants an ex-con working for him?"

"But did you get the job?" Dan asked.

"Naw," Israel said. "I told you it was a 'fix.' There wasn't any job. This was just a way to get out of jail."

"So I came out and went to the employment agency and lied to them about my past. You think they'd have hired me if I told them I just got out of prison the day before? I got a job as a dishwasher and then a dozen other jobs. I've been lying ever since. You've got to lie to get a job. If my boss now knew I was an ex-con he'd fire me, even though I've been out of prison 4 years and done a good job. So, I lie. Everyone does."

"Didn't your parole officer help you?" Dan asked.

"Yeah, that was one guy who really tried. But what could he do? He had a hundred other guys to help too. No, it was up to me and I've made it this far on my own."

The room grew quiet. Rosa had been sitting quietly beside Israel all this time. She had never heard him speak of this part of his life.

I said, "Israel, do you remember that time we went looking for the Phantom Lords and ran into an ambush?"

Israel nodded, "I remember."

"You saved my life that night, Israel. Tonight I want to return that favor. Tonight I want to tell you something that will save your life."

Rosa reached over and ran her arm through his. They both turned and looked at me expectantly.

"Israel, you're my dearest friend. You can tell there's been a change in my life. The old Nicky is dead. The person you see tonight is not really Nicky at all. It's Jesus Christ living in me. Do you remember that night at St. Nicholas Arena when we gave our hearts to the Lord?"

Israel nodded, his eyes dropping toward the floor.

"God came into your heart that night, Israel. I know it. God made a bargain with you. And He is still keeping His end of that bargain. He has not turned loose of you, Israel. You've been running all these years, but He still has hold of you."

I reached for my Bible. "In the Old Testament there's a story of a man called Jacob. He, too, was running from God. Then one night, just like tonight, he had a rumble with an angel. The angel won and Jacob surrendered to God. And that night God changed his name. No Jacob any more—but Israel. And Israel means 'one who walks with God.'"

I closed my Bible and paused before continuing. Israel's eyes were wet with tears and Rosa was clutching his arm. "I have laid awake at night for years praying for you—thinking how wonderful it would be to have you working beside me—not like we used to do—but in God's work. Israel, tonight I want you to become one who walks with

God. I want you to step out and start walkin' in Jesus' turf."

Israel looked up, his eyes full of tears. He turned and looked at Rosa. She was puzzled and spoke to him in Spanish. I had been talking in English and realized Rosa had not understood all I said. She asked him what I wanted. Israel told her I wanted them to give their hearts to Christ. He talked rapidly in Spanish, telling her his desire to return to God—like Jacob of old to go back. He asked her if she would come with him.

She smiled and her eyes sparkled as she nodded.

"Praise God!" I shouted. "Kneel down beside this sofa while I pray."

Israel and Rosa knelt beside the sofa. Dan slipped from his chair and knelt on the other side of the room. I put my hands on their heads and began to pray, first in English, and then in Spanish, slipping back and forth between the two languages. I felt the Spirit of God flowing through my heart and down my arms and fingertips into their lives. I prayed, asking God to forgive them and bless them and receive them into the fullness of His Kingdom.

It was a lengthy prayer. When I finished I heard Israel begin to pray. Slowly at first, then with intensity as he cried out, "Lord, forgive me. Forgive me. Forgive me." Then his prayer changed and I could feel the new strength shudder through his body as he began saying, "Lord, I thank you."

Rosa joined in, "Thank you, God, thank you."

Dan put Israel and Rosa in a cab and paid their fare back to their apartment in the Bronx. "Nicky," he said, wiping his eyes as they drove away, "this has been the greatest night of my life and I feel God is going to send Israel to California to work with you."

I nodded. Maybe so. God always had a way of taking care of things.

Epilogue

It was a late Spring afternoon as Nicky and Gloria lounged on the front steps of the Center at 221 N. Broadway watching Ralphie and Karl cutting the grass in the deepening twilight. It was almost time for the street meeting in the ghetto. In the backyard you could hear the happy sounds of Dave Carter and Jimmy Baez laughing at Allen, Joey, and Kirk playing croquet. Supper was over and inside Francie and Angie supervised the other boys in the nightly clean-up. Alicia and little Laura, now 16 months old, played happily in the fresh mown grass.

Gloria sat on a lower step gazing affectionately and thoughtfully at her dark skinned husband as he leaned against the post, eyes half closed as if lost in a dream world. She reached up and placed her hand on his knee.

"Honey, what's wrong? What are you thinking?"

"What do you mean?" he asked drowsily, reluctant to turn loose of his thoughts.

"I mean, what are you dreaming about now? Are you still running? We have the Center for the little people. Israel and Rosa are living in Fresno and serving the Lord. Sonny is pastoring a big church in L.A. Jimmy is working with you and Maria is serving God in New York. Next week you fly to Sweden and Denmark to preach. Why are you still dreaming? What more could you ask from God?"

Nicky straightened up and looked deep into the inquiring eyes of his companion. His voice had a faraway sound as he said, "It's not what I ask of God, Sweetheart, but what He's asking of me. We are only scratching the surface with our ministry."

There was a long pause. Only the sounds of the happy activity echoed around the house. "But Nicky," Gloria

237

said, still gazing intently at him, "it's not just your task. It's the task of all Christians—everywhere."

"I know that," he said. "I keep thinking about all those big churches in the inner city that are sitting empty during the week. Wouldn't it be wonderful if those unused classrooms could be turned into dormitories filled with hundreds of unloved children and teenagers from the slums? Each church could become its own Center manned by volunteers. . . ."

"Nicky," Gloria interrupted, squeezing his knee, "you're too much of a dreamer. Do you think those church people are going to turn their beautiful buildings into dormitories for lost and homeless kids? These church people want to help, but they want someone else to do it for them. They fuss now if a drunk interrupts a worship service. Think what they would say if they came to church some Sunday morning and found their sacred temples desecrated with beds and cots and a bunch of former junkies and glue sniffers in the spic and span halls. No, Nicky, you're a dreamer. These people don't want to get their hands dirty. They rebel against having their carpets stained with dirt from bare feet."

Nicky shook his head. "You're right, of course. I keep wondering what Jesus would do. Would He get His hands dirty?"

He paused and looked past her toward the distant mountains, reflecting. "You remember last year when we drove out to Point Loma on the bay in San Diego? Remember that huge lighthouse? For years it's guided ships into the harbor. But now times have changed. I read just last week that there is too much smog and they've had to build a new lighthouse down near the water so the light can shine under the smog."

Gloria listened intently.

"This is what's happened today. The church still stands with its light shining high. But few can see it because times have changed and there is much smog. A new light is needed to shine near the ground—down where the people are. It is not enough for me to be a keeper of the lighthouse, I must be a bearer of the light as well. No, I'm not running any more. I just want to be where the action is."

"I know," Gloria said, her voice reflecting her deep pride and understanding. "And that's what I want for you.

But you may have to go it alone. You know that, don't you?"

"Not alone," Nicky said, reaching down and placing his hand over hers. "I'll be walking in Jesus' turf."

The sound of the boys laughing in the back yard grew louder as they finished their game and headed inside. Karl and Ralphie had picked up their Bibles and were sitting on the curb in front of the house.

Nicky lowered his head and glanced at Gloria out of the top of his eyes. "I got a call this afternoon from a mother in Pasadena." He paused for an expected reaction. Gloria just waited for him to continue. "Her twelve-year-old boy has been picked up by the police for peddling marijuana. Her husband wants to put him in prison." Nicky stopped talking and his voice trailed off. "But we don't have any room and we're out of money."

They sat in silence. Nicky watched a small sparrow hopping up and down in the grass. His eyes filled with tears as he thought of the unknown child . . . so typical of thousands of others . . . hungry for love . . . willing to risk jail just to get some attention . . . looking for something real . . . looking for Jesus Christ and not knowing it.

Gloria interrupted his thoughts. "Nicky," she said softly, her fingers entwining with his, "What are you going to do?"

Nicky grinned and looked her in the face saying, "I'm going to do what Jesus would have me do. I'm going to get involved."

"Oh Nicky, Nicky," Gloria said as she threw her arms around his legs. "I love you! There's always room for one more. And God *will* provide."

Jimmy backed the bus out of the driveway. The boys scrambled aboard for the street service in the ghetto. Nicky pulled Gloria to her feet, " 'Vamanos!' Let's run. It's time to do Jesus' work."